T0301255

The Shape of the Division of Labour

Cournot Centre for Economic Studies

Series Editor: Robert M. Solow, *Institute Professor Emeritus of Economics, Massachusetts Institute of Technology; President of the Cournot Centre for Economic Studies, Paris, France*

Conference Editor: Jean-Philippe Touffut, *Director of the Cournot Centre for Economic Studies, Paris, France*

The Shape of the Division of Labour

Nations, Industries and Households

Edited by

Robert M. Solow

Institute Professor Emeritus of Economics, Massachusetts Institute of Technology; President of the Cournot Centre for Economic Studies, Paris, France

Jean-Philippe Touffut

Director of the Cournot Centre for Economic Studies, Paris, France

THE COURNOT CENTRE FOR ECONOMIC STUDIES SERIES

Edward Elgar

Cheltenham, UK • Northampton, MA, USA

Published by
Edward Elgar Publishing Limited
The Lypiatts
15 Lansdown Road
Cheltenham
Glos GL50 2JA
UK

Edward Elgar Publishing, Inc.
William Pratt House
9 Dewey Court
Northampton
Massachusetts 01060
USA

A catalogue record for this book
is available from the British Library

Library of Congress Control Number: 2010927670

ISBN 978 1 84980 496 7 (cased)
ISBN 978 1 84980 510 0 (paperback)

Typeset by Servis Filmsetting Ltd, Stockport, Cheshire

Printed and bound by MPG Books Group, UK

Contents

List of figures and tables	vi
List of contributors	viii
Preface	xi
Acknowledgements	xii
About the series: Professor Robert M. Solow	xiii
Introduction: the moving lines of the division of labour *Robert M. Solow and Jean-Philippe Touffut*	1
1. The changing global economic landscape: the factors that matter *Jan Fagerberg*	6
2. How global is foreign direct investment and what can policymakers do about it? Stylized facts, knowledge gaps, and selected policy instruments *Peter Nunnenkamp*	32
3. Labour market frictions as a source of comparative advantage: implications for unemployment and inequality *Elhanan Helpman*	56
4. Exports of knowledge-intensive services and manufactures: the role of ICTs and intersectoral linkages *Valentina Meliciani*	75
5. How integrated are Chinese and Indian labour into the world economy? *Richard N. Cooper*	101
6. The changing sexual division of labour *Shelly Lundberg*	122
7. Round table discussion: how do nations adapt to changes in the division of labour? *Bina Agarwal, Martin Baily, Jean-Louis Beffa and Robert M. Solow*	149
Index	191

Figures and tables

FIGURES

1.1	Convergence versus divergence in GDP per capita, 1960–2000	7
1.2	Measuring capabilities	14
1.3	GDP per capita and innovation system (2002–04)	17
1.4	Openness to ideas (75 countries, 2002–04)	23
1.5	Openness to business (75 countries, 2002–04)	24
1.6	Openness to people (75 countries, 2002–04)	25
2.1	Changes in national FDI policies (number of 'more favourable' minus 'less favourable'), 2000–06	33
2.2	Composition of worldwide FDI stocks, 1980–2008	34
2.3	Number of BITs concluded, 1969–2005	40
2.4	Gender disparity in schooling, 1980 and 2000/2005 in low-, middle- and high-income countries	48
3.1	Optimal strategies for firms with different productivity levels	61
3.2	Average unemployment across wage quantiles	71
6.1	Female total work minus male total work compared to real GDP per capita, 27 countries	124
6.2	Women's labour force participation rate and per capita income, 2005	126
7.1	Hourly wage of workers and gas/fuel prices	157
7.2	Foreign trade balance: United States	161
7.3	Foreign trade balance: France	161
7.4	Foreign trade balance: United Kingdom	162
7.5	Foreign trade balance: Germany	162
7.6	Foreign trade balance: Japan	163
7.7	Foreign trade balance: China	163
7.8	Foreign trade balance: Russia	164
7.9	Foreign trade balance: Brazil	165
7.10	Foreign trade balance: India	165
7.11	Rice production, exports and imports (% of world total)	167
7.12	Wheat production, exports and imports (% of world total)	168
7.13	Maize production, exports and imports (% of world total)	168
7.14	Cereals production, exports and imports (% of world total)	169
7.15	Total labour force in agriculture (%)	170

7.16 GDP from agriculture (%) 171
7.17 Females in total agricultural labour force (%) 171
7.18 Climate change and rice production 173
7.19 Climate change and wheat production 173
7.20 Climate change and maize production 174
7.21 Climate change and daily calories per capita 175
7.22 World cereal stocks, 2000–07 (million tonnes) 178

TABLES

1.1 Capabilities and GDP per capita 19
2.1 Share of selected groups of developing countries in worldwide FDI stocks (%), 1980–2007 35
2.2 Fixed-effects OLS estimation results on the effects of BITs on bilateral FDI flows 42
2.3 GMM estimation results on the effects of labour rights on bilateral FDI flows 46
2.4 Tobit estimation results on the effects of gender disparity in education on bilateral FDI flows 49
4.1 Share of knowledge-intensive services in total industry output 85
4.2 Descriptive statistics 88
4.3 Correlation coefficients in knowledge-intensive manufacturing industries 89
4.4 Correlation coefficients in knowledge-intensive service industries 90
4.5 Regression results for knowledge-intensive (KI) manufacturing industries 91
4.6 Regression results for knowledge-intensive (KI) service industries 93
5.1 Total and working-age population, China and India (in millions) 103
7.1 Climate change effect on 2050 production relative to no climate change effect (% change) 172

Contributors

Bina Agarwal is Director and Professor of Economics at the Institute of Economic Growth, Delhi University. She is the first woman President-elect of the International Society for Ecological Economics. She is also a member of the UN Committee for Development Policy, and serves on the editorial boards of several international academic journals. Agarwal has been Vice President of the International Economic Association, President of the International Association for Feminist Economics, and a member of the Board of the Global Development Network from its inception until 2006, and is a founding member of the Indian Society for Ecological Economics. Her research focuses on the environment and development; land and livelihoods; the political economy of gender; poverty and inequality; and agriculture and technological change. In 2010, she was awarded the Leontief Prize by Tufts University, given for work that advances the frontiers of economic thought.

Martin Baily, former Senior Fellow (2001–07) at the Peterson Institute for International Economics, is a Senior Fellow at the Brookings Institution, where he held the same position from 1979 to 1989. He was chairman of the Council of Economic Advisers during the Clinton administration (1999–2001) and one of three members of the council from 1994 to 1996. He is an academic adviser to the Congressional Budget Office. He was a research associate at the National Bureau of Economic Research and he co-founded the microeconomics issues of the Brookings Papers on Economic Activity. His research focuses on labour markets, employment, monetary and fiscal policy, and capital markets.

Jean-Louis Beffa is Honorary Chairman of the Board of Directors of the Compagnie de Saint-Gobain and Co-President of the Cournot Centre for Economic Studies.

Richard N. Cooper has been the Maurits C. Boas Professor of International Economics at Harvard University since 1981. He was previously Chairman at the National Intelligence Council (1995–97), Chairman at the Federal Reserve Bank of Boston (1990–1992) and Under-Secretary of State for Economic Affairs (1977–81). His research interests include management of the international economic system; global energy use, policies, and environmental issues; US–European, US–Japanese economics; as well as China and the world economy.

Jan Fagerberg is Professor of Economics at the University of Oslo, where he is affiliated with the Centre for Technology, Innovation and Culture (TIK). He has worked for the Norwegian Ministry of Finance, the Norwegian Institute for Foreign Affairs (NUPI), and the University of Aalborg. Fagerberg is an advisory editor of *Research Policy* and a member of the editorial boards of the *Journal of Evolutionary Economics*, *Industry and Innovation* and *Technology Analysis & Strategic Management*. He has been a consultant to the European Commission, the OECD and the United Nations. Fagerberg's research focuses on the impact of technology on trade, competitiveness and growth.

Elhanan Helpman is the Galen L. Stone Professor of International Trade at Harvard University and a Fellow at the Canadian Institute for Advanced Research. He was a member of the Advisory Board of the Bank of Israel, the Council for National Planning, and the National Council for Research and Development. Helpman served as co-editor of the *Journal of International Economics* and the *European Economic Review* and he is a co-editor of the *Quarterly Journal of Economics*. He is a Fellow of the Econometric Society and was its President, and he is a member of the Israel Academy of Sciences and Humanities and a Foreign Honorary Member of the American Academy of Arts and Sciences. Helpman's research focuses on international trade, economic growth and political economy. He is a co-founder of the 'new trade theory' and the 'new growth theory', emphasizing the roles of economies of scale and imperfect competition.

Shelly Lundberg is Castor Professor of Economics and Director of the Center for Studies in Demography and Ecology at the University of Washington. She is also Professor of Economics at the University of Bergen and a Research Fellow at the Institute for the Study of Labor in Bonn. She is a member of the editorial boards of the *American Economic Review* and the *Review of Economics of the Household*, and is an associate editor of the *Journal of Population Economics*, and deputy editor of *Demography*. In 2008, she was elected Fellow of the Society of Labor Economics, and currently serves as first Vice President of the society. Her research focuses on labour and demographic economics and the economics of the family.

Valentina Meliciani is Professor at the Faculty of Political Science of the University of Teramo. She was a Visiting Fellow at SPRU (Sussex University). She has led EU-funded research projects on the social and economic changes created by the new information-based economy. Her research focuses on the impact of technology on international competitiveness and economic growth.

Peter Nunnenkamp is a Senior Economist at the Kiel Institute for the World Economy. He joined the Development Economics Department of the Kiel Institute about 30 years ago and has headed several research divisions, including 'International Capital Flows' until 2005, and 'Global Division of Labour' until 2009, of which he remains a member. He has also joined the research area 'Poverty Reduction, Equity, and Development'. His major interests are the determinants and effects of foreign direct investment (FDI) in (developing and developed) host countries, possible repercussions of FDI in the home countries, and the allocation and effectiveness of official as well as private aid.

Robert M. Solow is Institute Professor Emeritus at the Massachusetts Institute of Technology. In 1987, he received the Bank of Sweden Prize in Economic Sciences in Memory of Alfred Nobel for his contributions to economic growth theory. He is the Robert K. Merton Scholar at the Russell Sage Foundation, where he is a member of the advisory committee for the Foundation's project on the incidence and quality of low-wage employment in Europe and the USA. Professor Solow is President of the Cournot Centre for Economic Studies.

Jean-Philippe Touffut is Co-Founder and Director of the Cournot Centre for Economic Studies. His research interests include probabilistic epistemology and the exploration of evolutionary games from neurological and economic perspectives.

Preface

This volume is one of a series arising from the conferences organized by the Cournot Centre for Economic Studies, Paris. These conferences explore contemporary issues in economics, with particular focus on Europe. Speakers, along with other participants and members of the audience, are drawn from backgrounds in academia, business, finance, labour unions, the media and national or multinational governmental and non-governmental agencies.

The first versions of these revised and edited texts were delivered at the twelfth conference of the Cournot Centre for Economic Studies held on 12 and 13 November 2009.

Acknowledgements

Our heartfelt thanks go to Therrese Goodlett and Lucia Scharpf. From the organization of the conference to the preparation of the manuscript, they have enabled this work to see the light of day under the best possible conditions. A very special thanks also goes to Janice Murray, Richard Crabtree and Bernard Gazier for the English edition. A film of the whole conference is available on the Cournot Centre's website: www.centre-cournot.org.

About the series

Professor Robert M. Solow

The Cournot Centre for Economic Studies is an independent French-based research institute. It takes its name from the pioneering economist, mathematician and philosopher Antoine Augustin Cournot (1801–77).

Neither a think-tank nor a research bureau, the Centre enjoys the special independence of a catalyst. My old student dictionary (dated 1936) says that catalysis is the 'acceleration of a reaction produced by a substance, called the *catalyst*, which may be recovered practically unchanged at the end of the reaction'. The reaction we have in mind results from bringing together (a) an issue of economic policy that is currently being discussed and debated in Europe and (b) the relevant theoretical and empirical findings of serious economic research in universities, think-tanks and research bureaux. Acceleration is desirable because it is better that reaction occurs before minds are made up and decisions taken, not after. We hope that the Cournot Centre can be recovered practically unchanged and used again and again.

Notice that 'policy debate' is not exactly what we are trying to promote. To have a policy debate, you need not only knowledge and understanding, but also preferences, desires, values and goals. The trouble is that, in practice, the debaters often have only those things, and they invent or adopt only those 'findings' that are convenient. The Cournot Centre hopes to inject the findings of serious research at an early stage.

It is important to realize that this is not easy or straightforward. The analytical issues that underlie economic policy choices are usually complex. Economics is not an experimental science. The available data are scarce, and may not be exactly the relevant ones. Interpretations are therefore uncertain. Different studies, by uncommitted economists, may give different results. When those controversies exist, it is our hope that the Centre's conferences will discuss them. Live debate at that fundamental level is exactly what we are after.

There is also a problem of timing. Conferences have to be planned well in advance, so that authors can prepare careful and up-to-date texts. Then a publication lag is inevitable. The implication is that the Cournot Centre's conferences cannot take up very short-term issues of policy. Instead, a balancing act is required: we need issues that are short-term enough so that they are directly concerned with current policy, but long-term enough so that they remain directly relevant for a few years.

I used the words 'serious research' a moment ago. That sort of phrase is sometimes used to exclude unwelcome ideas, especially unfashionable ones. The Cournot Centre does not intend to impose narrow requirements of orthodoxy, but it does hope to impose high standards of attention to logic and respect for facts. It is because those standards are not always observed in debates about policy that an institution like the Cournot Centre has a role to play.

OTHER BOOKS IN THE COURNOT CENTRE SERIES

2009. *Changing Climate, Changing Economy*
Edited by Jean-Philippe Touffut
Contributors: Michel Armatte, Jean-Pierre Dupuy, Olivier Godard, Inge Kaul, Thomas Schelling, Robert M. Solow, Nicholas Stern, Thomas Sterner, Martin Weitzman

2009. *Does Company Ownership Matter?*
Edited by Jean-Philippe Touffut
Contributors: Jean-Louis Beffa, Margaret Blair, Wendy Carlin, Christophe Clerc, Simon Deakin, Jean-Paul Fitoussi, Donatella Gatti, Gregory Jackson, Xavier Ragot, Antoine Rebérioux, Lorenzo Sacconi, Robert M. Solow

2008. *Central Banks as Economic Institutions*
Edited by Jean-Philippe Touffut
Contributors: Patrick Artus, Alan Blinder, Willem Buiter, Barry Eichengreen, Benjamin Friedman, Carl-Ludwig Holtfrerich, Gerhard Illing, Otmar Issing, Takatoshi Ito, Stephen Morris, André Orléan, Nouriel Roubini, Robert M. Solow

2007. *Augustin Cournot: Modelling Economics*
Edited by Jean-Philippe Touffut
Contributors: Robert J. Aumann, Alain Desrosières, Jean Magnan de Bornier, Thierry Martin, Glenn Shafer, Robert M. Solow, Bernard Walliser

2006. *Advancing Public Goods*
Edited by Jean-Philippe Touffut
Contributors: Patrick Artus, Avner Ben-Ner, Bernard Gazier, Xavier Greffe, Claude Henry, Philippe Herzog, Inge Kaul, Joseph E. Stiglitz

2005. *Corporate Governance Adrift: A Critique of Shareholder Value*
Michel Aglietta and Antoine Rebérioux

2004. *The Future of Economic Growth: As New Becomes Old*
Robert Boyer

2003. *Institutions, Innovation and Growth: Selected Economic Papers*
Edited by Jean-Philippe Touffut
Contributors: Philippe Aghion, Bruno Amable, with Pascal Petit, Timothy Bresnahan, Paul A. David, David Marsden, AnnaLee Saxenian, Günther Schmid, Robert M. Solow, Wolfgang Streeck, Jean-Philippe Touffut

Introduction: the moving lines of the division of labour

Robert M. Solow and Jean-Philippe Touffut

How is labour allocated between men and women, between North and South, on the farm and in the plant? Traditional analyses in terms of market or factor endowments have been enhanced by studies on demography, trade and technological change, but the questions remain of how and where countries specialize. The answers may depend on the dividing lines, on the increase in the variety of tasks or on their growth in numbers, but then further questions arise about the asymmetries that the division of labour creates. When economists study the dynamics of the feminization of the labour market, deindustrialization or foreign direct investment and its impact on growth, can they use the same concept of the division of labour?

In this book, the contributions move in two complementary directions: the first weighs and updates the relative importance of the different determining factors; the second deepens the analysis by adding further determinants and by making productive entities understandable through the study of their interactions. The impact of the division of labour must be perceived through the light of its 'demographic, territorial, and thus political, effects', as Augustin Cournot put it.[1] Through the authors' different approaches, the classical opposition fades between the central role of the market in determining the degree of the division of labour among productive units, as suggested by Adam Smith, and the factor endowments and international trade developed by David Ricardo.

The concept of the division of labour followed a trajectory of decline and rehabilitation in the twentieth century. The marginalist equilibrium analysis found it difficult to deal with the association between the division of labour and increasing returns, and the resulting possibility of falling supply and cost curves.[2] In general, the analysis of the division of labour between countries worked through the traditional mechanisms of specialization and trade. The aim was to identify how they influence productivity. At the international level, comparative advantage was understood as a combination of specific and transferable competitive advantages particular to organizations, to regions and to institutional contexts. The process, however, was studied mainly at the sectoral level, even after analyses of trade had shown that exchanges took place foremost within each industry and that the division could be made at any level.

One can divide labour into such categories as gender, assets, sectors, industries and nations. To what extent do economists write of the same process when they describe the division between men and women or between China and Japan? The division affects these categories at a high level of abstraction in the same way. It is as if the economy were a densely woven fabric in which the thickest areas are treated as distinct entities, provided they display sufficient structural or functional unity. The interactions between these abstractions matter more than the abstractions themselves. Depending on the stages of reasoning, these subsets take on different meanings; they are merged or broken up according to methodological or technological developments that contribute to differentiating between objects usually considered homogeneous. The transactional nature of the division of labour then becomes the object of study, rather than its delimitations.

In the opening text, Jan Fagerberg (Chapter 1) studies the division of labour between countries. At comparable size and distance, frontiers still matter: agents in two different nations still exchange less when they are separated by a frontier. It is also true that the statistics for gross domestic product (GDP) or productivity show that the gaps between countries have rarely been narrowed since 1960. To understand this phenomenon, Fagerberg presents a very extensive multifactor analysis developed to highlight the virtues of the countries that are catching up with the others. The databases on which Fagerberg's work is based reach beyond the context of the technological and legal specificity of economies, taking into account the openness of each country in terms of investment, trade, migration and respect for minorities. He examines the heterogeneous factors that shape the global economic landscape, and especially those that have changed the position of some countries, while reinforcing the specialization of others. A study of the change in GDP as a function of initial GDP brings to light two main categories: countries that remain mired in poverty and countries that continue to pull ahead. Countries that are catching up or losing ground are not common. Fagerberg summarizes the explanations proposed by economists: whether the problem resides in the accumulation of capital, technological development, legal framework, the complementarity or contradiction between institutions, the differences between countries persist. This persistence testifies to the failure of the development strategies promoted by international financial institutions (the 'Washington Consensus'): it is impossible to correlate the improvement in a country's specialization with its propensity to trade, to imitate Western political institutions or even to open up to foreign investment. The only robust criterion appears finally to be linked to the permissive nature of a society.

Peter Nunnenkamp's analysis (Chapter 2) confirms that there is no surefire recipe for improving one's place in the division of labour. It also shows that the most diligent pupils are not always those who have enjoyed the highest growth. The statistics on foreign direct investments (FDIs) appear to be good indicators of the dynamics of trade from the a priori favourable perspective of access to technologies and capital. His first conclusion concerns the extension of zones of investment. Whether or not they are successful, investments cause structural changes within countries that compete for FDI. The ranking of countries that attract foreign capital has hardly changed since 1990. The number of countries competing for foreign investment has increased, of course, but their success is not related to whether their institutions are brought into line with international standards, in terms of lifting restrictions on rights to ownership, access to economic sectors or the nature of tax incentives. These are the results presented in the literature, which deals almost exclusively with the winners, not with those who have failed to attract investors. The recommendations are nonetheless aimed primarily at this second category. The greater the number of criteria taken into account in the studies of direct investment, the harder it is to formulate conclusions in terms of economic recommendations. Saying that the size and growth of a country are the only aspects that always matter hardly suits governments seeking to influence more seizable aspects. The most thorough studies conclude that reforming education, social security or taxation has ambiguous effects in terms of attracting foreign investment, especially from the big transnational groups. The win–win situation of less gender discrimination and more FDI is confined to developing countries with high per capita incomes.

Narrowing the sexual division of labour is precisely the subject of Shelly Lundberg's study (Chapter 6): economics has long treated this division as the result of interactions between domestic production and market structures and the biological differences between men and women. Technological change has steadily increased the relative wages of women and the benefits of their being active on the labour market rather than in the home. Demographic changes, the marketization of domestic work and growing investment in human capital all favour the economic convergence of the two sexes, but how and to what extent? The increasing control of women over household income is probably already perceptible in the allocation of resources in the economy as a whole. Lundberg presents a robust study of the impact of convergence on growth.

From the company perspective, only some firms operating within a given sector export their products. Elhanan Helpman (Chapter 3) takes this observation as his point of departure to take up the recent analysis of the heterogeneity of industries and of the institutional factors that organize labour markets: this analysis has enriched our understanding of the origins of comparative advantages. He takes the analysis further, opening up a very promising field of investigation. Using some of the results to which he has largely contributed over the last 30 years, he explores three subjects in greater detail: the impact of a country's labour market frictions on its trade partners, the consequences of lifting trade barriers as a function of a country's market frictions, and the effects of trade on inequalities and unemployment. When an economy opens up to international trade, unemployment rises all the more when wages are low.

The specificities of industries and services in the information and communications technology (ICT) sector is the subject of investigation in Valentina Meliciani's contribution (Chapter 4). If technological factors are at least as important as price in determining national specializations, this is because they accentuate the fall in frontier effects, as the long-term data show. Exchange rate volatility, consumer preferences or the maintenance of networks within a country are of secondary importance. Meliciani's econometric studies start by confirming the standard results: ICT indirectly influences a country's competitiveness by affecting productivity and prices and directly influences the production of a wider variety and higher quality of products. ICTs have a positive impact on export capacities for production and services in this sector. The role of ICT in the catching-up process of developing countries is no longer considered an inexplicable remainder. The literature on growth has highlighted how a country's growth rate is dependent on its national technology, compared to the rest of the world. Growth rates in developing countries are, in part, explained by a 'catch-up' process in the level of technology. In a typical model of technology diffusion, the rate of economic growth of a developing country depends on the extent of adoption and implementation of new technologies that are already in use in leading countries. Does this phenomenon follow the same process from one developing country to another?

Industrial sectors like ICT are not the only field where India and China differ. Richard Cooper, in his contribution (Chapter 5), opposes the cases of India and China, analysing the evolution of employment in the two countries. What information does this provide about the integration of these two countries into the international division of labour? One revealing indicator of integration is changes in wage levels, especially for unskilled work. It is hard to measure this indicator in fast-growing economies, but the engagement of the Chinese labour force is much greater than that of

India. In India, it seems that only the ICT sector is involved in this process of integration. India is having trouble creating unskilled jobs outside farming, and appears to be in a worse position than China, where national geographical and professional mobility remains very high.

The round table discussion that concludes this work (Chapter 7) returns to the relation between technological change and employment as a matrix of the division of labour. Martin Baily and Jean-Louis Beffa note that the changes that have affected industry in the developed countries, particularly job losses, are primarily linked to technology, although international trade and exchange rates are essential factors. In any event, employment in the industrialized countries is very sensitive to productivity. There remains the question of whether it is up to companies or the State to frame the international positioning of the country. Beffa emphasizes the importance of their coordination to master specialization. How do policies and specialization coincide? Their correspondence varies a lot from country to country for the industrial sectors. Policies can also, however, go against specialization, such as in the case of agriculture. Bina Agarwal shows that policies are often organized far from where they are applied. The correspondence between policy and specialization is decisive not only in the balance of power in a sector, but also in the internal division of labour in the producing countries. It remains to be seen how a new global order or a set of international agreements could best influence the allocation process.

NOTES

1. Cournot, A. (1860), 'Du libre échange', *Principes de la théorie des richesses*, Tome IX des oeuvres complètes, Vrin [1981], pp. 299–320.
2. Groenewegen, Peter (1987), 'Division of labour', in John Eatwell, Murray Milgate and Peter Newman (eds), *The New Palgrave: A Dictionary of Economics, 1 (A–D)*, London and Basingstoke: Macmillan, pp. 901–5.

1. The changing global economic landscape: the factors that matter[1]

Jan Fagerberg

INTRODUCTION

The global economic landscape is changing. Asian countries – starting with Japan in the early post-Second-World-War period, followed by the 'Asian Tigers' a few decades later, and China, India and several others more recently – are becoming more economically and politically important, while the roles of other parts of the globe diminish.

Are these developments examples of a more general long-run trend towards eliminating the large differences in income and productivity that continue to exist between countries, what in economic jargon is called 'convergence'? Unfortunately not. As an illustration of the long-run evidence on the matter, consider Figure 1.1, which covers more than 90 countries for a period of four decades (starting in 1960). The figure plots annual average growth of gross domestic product (GDP) per capita over the period (horizontal axis) against its initial level (vertical axis). Dashed lines represent sample averages (of growth and level of GDP per capita, respectively). In this way four quadrants emerge. The countries in the top left quadrant have a high initial GDP per capita level, but grow relatively slowly (hence, they 'lose momentum'). In contrast, the countries in the top right quadrant continue to grow fast despite being relatively wealthy at the outset. These countries are 'moving ahead'. The bottom right quadrant contains countries that were relatively poor to begin with, but that have been growing faster than the average. These are the countries that succeed in 'catching up'. The least fortunate countries are to be found in the bottom left quadrant, representing initially poor countries that are growing slowly. Arguably, these countries risk 'falling behind' in the global economy.[2]

It is clear from the figure that there is a lot of diversity in how countries perform. By closer inspection, however, it becomes evident that there is a higher tendency for countries to cluster in the bottom left and top right than in the two other quadrants. Thus, if there is a general tendency, it

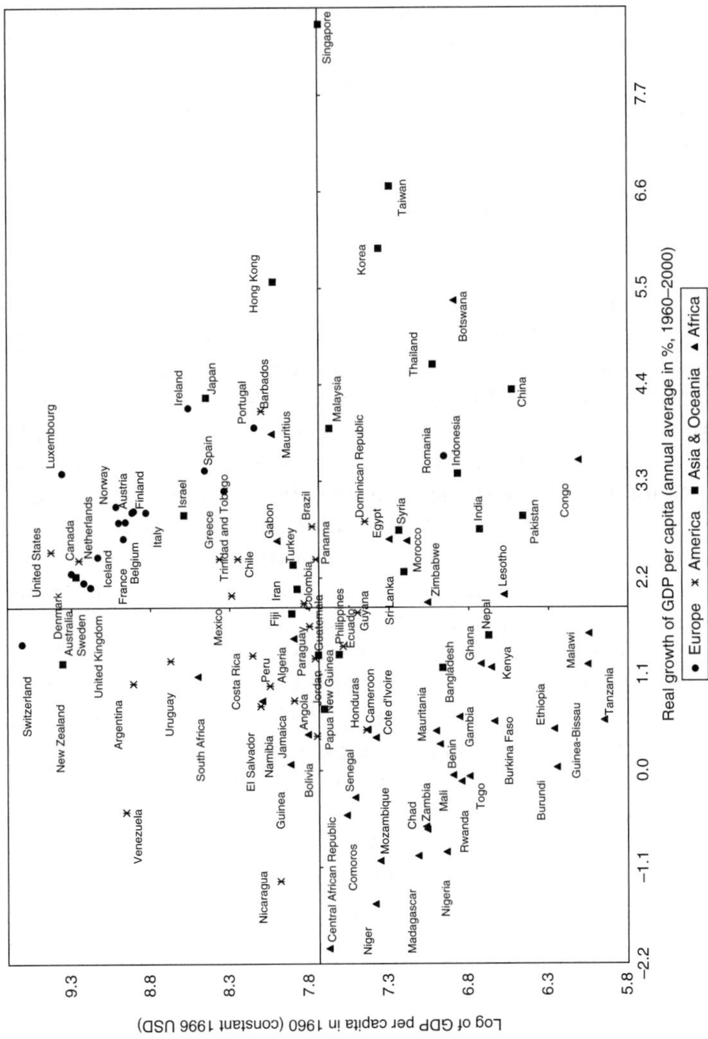

Source: Fagerberg and Srholec (2005) based on *Penn World Table Version 6.1* (Heston et al., 2002).

Figure 1.1 Convergence versus divergence in GDP per capita, 1960–2000

points more in the direction of divergence than convergence in GDP per capita across countries.[3] The countries that fall behind are overwhelmingly African in origin while those that move ahead are mostly from the Western hemisphere (for example, OECD countries). Those that succeed in catching up are mostly of Asian origin, including well-known cases such as Korea, Taiwan, Singapore and China.

The failure of most poor countries to improve their position in the global economy puzzles economists, and has done so for a long time. In fact, the classical political economists, from Adam Smith onward, were already concerned with this issue. Since they believed that capital accumulation was the source of economic growth, they tended to put the blame for such failures on impediments to capital accumulation, particularly regulatory hurdles. Such arguments are still central of course. Nevertheless, since at least the 1960s, when Robert Solow presented his neoclassical theory of economic growth (Solow, 1956), economists have known that the source of long-run growth in productivity and income is not capital accumulation, but improvements in our ability to produce goods and services and the knowledge (technology) that underpins it.[4] Solow, at that time, was not concerned with how such improvements came about, but the standard view became that the development of such knowledge mainly occurred in advanced economies (and particularly in the USA) from which it gradually spread to the rest of the world. Since economists generally assumed that knowledge had strong public goods properties, diffusion was often seen as a relatively easy affair, providing poor countries with ample opportunities for catching up technologically and economically if they 'kept their house in order' – that is, emulate Western (or US) political and legal systems, allow markets to work (with minimal interference), promote free trade, and have a liberal policy stance with respect to foreign direct investments (FDI). This policy package became the cornerstone of, among others, the International Monetary Fund (IMF) and the World Bank's policies towards developing countries. In the 1990s this approach came to be known as the 'Washington Consensus'.[5]

Today, however, this once very popular approach, at least among the Consensus promoters, is generally seen as discredited. The world simply does not seem to work that way. In fact, several countries that have succeeded in catching up during the last 50 years clearly did not adopt these policies. FDI, for example, played virtually no role in the spectacular catch-up by Japan and Korea, while governmental interference in the economy was very frequent (Johnson, 1982; Amsden, 1989; Wade, 1990). Moreover, it is difficult to deny the fact that several poor countries that have managed to get out of the low growth trap (and started to catch up) have political systems that are far removed from Western democracies.

China is, of course, the most obvious example, but there are several others. On the other hand, many poor countries, particularly in Africa, that have tried their best to adopt the policies described by the 'Washington Consensus' have failed to reap the growth bonus that was assumed to follow (Fagerberg and Srholec, 2005). Furthermore, research into the assumed positive 'spillovers' from FDI in the developing part of the world has generally failed to document their existence (Görg and Greenaway, 2004). Similarly, the evidence on the assumed beneficial effects of openness to trade for developing country performance is mixed at best (Rodrik et al., 2004; Fagerberg and Srholec, 2008).[6]

All this suggests that there may be something wrong with our understanding (or theory) of what fosters growth in the developing part of the world. In the next section, I discuss what I see as perhaps the most important mistake in the approach outlined above. I argue that the whole approach rests on a fundamental misunderstanding of the role that knowledge plays in growth and development. This flaw affects our analysis of developed countries as well, but has had particularly damaging effects on our ability to understand the challenges facing developing countries. It is argued that we need to broaden our approach to include not only knowledge creation but also the factors influencing its absorption and exploitation. This is, of course, not an entirely new idea. It is, for example, widely accepted in management and is also adopted by historians and other social scientists.[7] Building on some of this work, I discuss ways to conceptualize and measure the factors influencing the ability of developing countries (and to some extent other countries as well) to exploit knowledge to their advantage. Drawing on recent research by Martin Srholec and myself (Fagerberg and Srholec, 2008, 2009), I show how such an approach may be implemented empirically in an analysis of why some countries make it (while others fail). In light of this research, I return in the final part of the chapter to the seemingly paradoxical finding in the literature that 'openness' does not seem to matter much for development.

KNOWLEDGE AND DEVELOPMENT

There is no lack of sophisticated analyses of knowledge in economics.[8] For some reason, however, these insights seem to have failed to have a large impact on the literature on growth and development. Instead, a rather simplistic view has been dominant for a long time now, in which knowledge is portrayed as a so-called public good, that is, something people all over the world can use freely as much as they like, and which will benefit everybody, independent of where they live. The following remark by

Edward Denison – perhaps the most prominent analyst of international growth differences in the early post-Second-World-War period – is typical in this respect, 'Because knowledge is an international commodity, I should expect the contribution of advances of knowledge [. . .] to be of about the same size in all the countries' (Denison, 1967, p. 282). Add to this the now commonly shared view that knowledge is the most important source of growth and development, and one ends up with a paradox: if knowledge is so fluid, why isn't the whole world developed?

To be able to consider this question in a proper manner, it is necessary to take one step back to what one knows about knowledge and its role in the economy. First, there is no such thing as a worldwide stock of homogeneous knowledge that flows across the globe at the speed of light. Rather, there are many different types of knowledge and knowledge holders. Not all knowledge is scientific, as the Nobel laureate Friedrich von Hayek pointed out long ago (Hayek, 1945). Much knowledge is practical and context specific (which does not make it less useful economically of course). Knowledge is widely distributed across actors and contexts. As Hayek repeatedly emphasized, it is totally impossible for any actor, be it a person or a firm (or even a government), to know 'everything' that may be relevant for the solution of an economic problem (what is often called 'perfect knowledge'). In fact, even to identify what the relevant areas of knowledge are (and how these can usefully be approached) may be challenging. That is one of the main reasons why large, knowledge-intensive firms all over the world regularly devote substantial resources to such search activities.

Even when the relevant knowledge can be identified, is codified and easily accessible, there is no guarantee that the knowledge will be successfully transferred. The knowledge may, for example, be difficult to understand and absorb. Higher education – even a doctorate or a whole group of people with such qualifications – may be required. Hence, it is not sufficient to have access to knowledge; one must also have the necessary capabilities to understand, absorb and exploit it. Building such capabilities may be demanding, costly and time-consuming.

Moreover, humans do not reproduce themselves by consuming knowledge. What they consume are goods and services produced with the help of, among other things, knowledge. Producers of these goods and services cannot rely on only one type of knowledge. They need to be able to access, absorb, combine and use many different types related to, for example, finance, logistics, products, markets, production, and so on. Access to necessary resources, such as information and communication technologies (ICTs), transport, skilled labour, and knowledge about how to access, keep and exploit such things, is also crucial. Arguably, it is of little help to be aware of the knowledge if you cannot get hold of the resources necessary to reap the potential benefits from exploiting it.

The knowledge about how to produce goods and services is normally called 'technology', and a commonly used term for the ability of a firm to acquire, hold and use such knowledge is 'technological capability'. The term was coined by the Korean development economist Linsu Kim (1980, 1997). His analyses were based on lessons of how Korean electronics firms, such as Samsung, gradually upgraded from a passive role of implementing foreign technology to a more active role, before finally arriving at the forefront of innovation-based competition in the industry. Kim defined technological capability as 'the ability to make effective use of technological knowledge in efforts to assimilate, use, adapt and change existing technologies. It also enables one to create new technologies and to develop new products and processes' (Kim, 1997, p. 4). It has become common (see Romijn, 1999, for an overview) to consider three aspects of technological capability: production capability, investment capability and innovation capability. Production capability is the ability to produce efficiently and reliably. Investment capability is needed to establish and finance new production facilities. Finally, innovation capability is required to create new technology, for example, to develop new products or services that better meet the specific requirements of the market. Kim expected the requirements to become more stringent, in particular with respect to innovation capabilities, as countries climb up the development ladder. Thus, following this view, for a firm or country in the process of catching up, the appropriate level of technological capability is a moving target (Bell and Pavitt, 1993).

A related concept that has become popular in the literature on growth and development is 'absorptive capacity'. In development economics, the term has been used for a long time, as referring to the ability of a developing country to absorb new investments in a productive way (Adler, 1965; Eckaus, 1973). As the role of knowledge for growth and development has become more widely recognized, however, the expression has come to be associated with the ability to absorb knowledge. Wesley Cohen and Daniel Levinthal, in an influential contribution (Cohen and Levinthal, 1990) defined it as 'the ability of a firm to recognize the value of new, external information, assimilate it and apply it to commercial ends' (p. 128). This definition is close to Kim's definition of 'technological capability', and Kim (1997) uses the two concepts interchangeably.

Firms are not isolated islands. Their performances depend to a crucial extent on the characteristics of the environment in which they operate. Thus, a firm's technological capabilities do not only depend on its own activities, but also on the capabilities of its customers, suppliers and other firms and organizations with which the firm is in regular contact (Lundvall, 1992). Hence, although initially developed for analysis of firms, the technology capability concept may also be applied to networks (of firms and organizations), industries or countries. Sanjaya Lall, in a survey (Lall, 1992), emphasizes three aspects of 'national technological capability' as he phrases it: (1) the ability to muster the necessary (financial) resources and use them efficiently; (2) skills, including not only general education, but also specialized managerial and technical competence; and (3) what he calls 'national technological effort', which he associates with measures such as research and development (R&D), patents and technical personnel. He also makes a distinction between technological capabilities proper and their economic effects. These effects, he notes, also depend on the incentives that economic agents face, whether resulting from political decision making (for example, governance) or whether they are embedded in more long-lasting institutions (legal frameworks, for instance).

That the social, institutional and political characteristics of the environment in which a firm operates have a strong impact on its capabilities and performance is not a new insight. Already in the 1960s, Irma Adelman and Cynthia Morris pointed out, on the basis of an in-depth study of a number of indicators on development for a large number of countries, that 'the purely economic performance of a community is strongly conditioned by the social and political setting in which economic activity takes place' (Adelman and Morris, 1965, p. 578).[9] This point was also emphasized by the economic historian Moses Abramovitz, who used the term 'social capability' to describe this aspect (Abramovitz, 1986). He defined it as:

> countries levels of general education and technical competence, the commercial, industrial and financial institutions that bear on the abilities to finance and operate modern, large-scale business, and the political and social characteristics that influence the risks, the incentives and the personal rewards of economic activity. (Abramovitz, 1994, p. 25)

By 'social characteristics', Abramovitz is referring (among other things) to the spread of honesty and trust in the population, which he holds to be important for the ability to exploit technological opportunities. In fact, it is widely accepted that such factors may matter for economic development. Kenneth Arrow, for example, pointed out more than three decades ago that 'It can plausibly be argued that much of the economic backwardness in the world can be explained by lack of mutual confidence' (Arrow, 1972, p. 357). More recently, the importance of these matters has been brought to the fore by Robert Putnam and other writers on 'social capital' (as they phrase it).[10] This has contributed to a rapidly increasing body of research on the role of social capital in development (Woolcock and Narayan, 2000). A central theme in the policy relevant literature on the subject has thus become what governments can do to support the creation of trust and strengthen constructive collaboration across different (social, political, religious, ethnic, and so on) groups.

Thus, the lessons from this are (1) that the generation of (firm-level) technological capabilities is a must for countries that wish to catch up, and (2) that the degree of success in this aim depends to a large extent on wider social, institutional and political factors (or framework conditions). While many would agree with these propositions, they might perhaps have doubts about the possibility to test these empirically in a rigorous manner. In fact, Abramovitz, who pioneered much of this work, was pessimistic in this regard. The next section will show, however, that the availability of indicators has improved a lot in recent years – not the least for 'non-economic' aspects of development – and recent research has made progress in dealing with these issues.

MEASURING CAPABILITIES AND THEIR IMPACTS

How can technological and social capabilities be measured (if at all)? Figure 1.2 lists the main dimensions of reality pointed to by these two concepts, along with possible empirical indicators.

As discussed above, the concept of technological capability refers to the ability to develop, search for, absorb and exploit knowledge commercially. An important element of this is what Kim (1997) termed 'innovation capability'. There are several data sources that capture different aspects of this. For example, the quality of a country's science base, on which invention and innovation activities to some extent depend, may be reflected in articles published in scientific and technical journals. R&D expenditures measure some (but not all) resources that are used for developing new products or processes, while patents count (patentable) inventions coming out of that process. R&D data are not available for many developing countries, however. Patent data, on the contrary, are available for all countries. Nevertheless, many, if not most, innovations are never patented, thus, as for many other indicators, patenting gives only a partial view of what one wishes to measure.[11]

Another important aspect of technological capability mentioned by Kim (1997) is 'production capability'. A possible indicator of this might be the adoption of quality standards (ISO 9000). Although ISO certification is mainly procedural in nature, it is increasingly seen as a requirement for firms supplying high-quality markets, and is therefore likely to reflect a

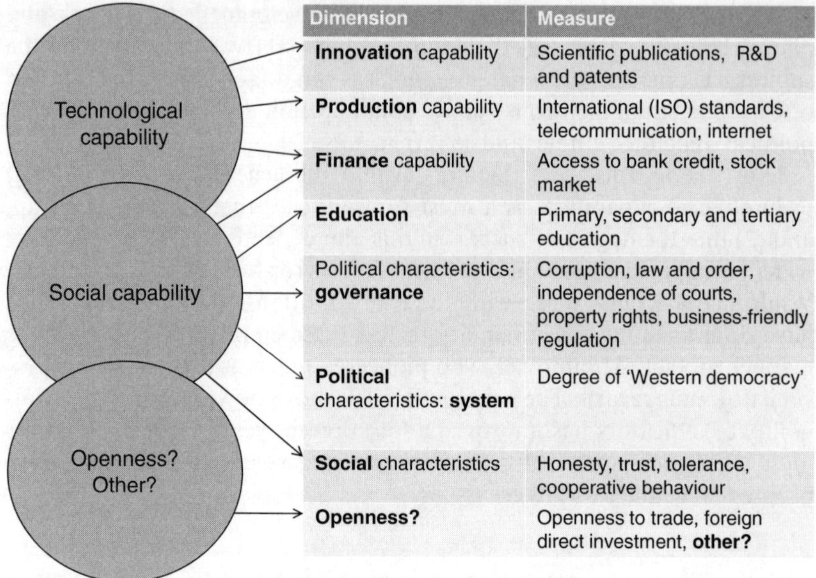

Figure 1.2 Measuring capabilities

strong emphasis on quality in production. Moreover, although earlier studies such as Lall (1992) did not place much emphasis on capabilities in ICT, nowadays a well-developed ICT infrastructure must be regarded as a critical factor for a country that wishes to catch up. Arguably, this holds not only for production capability but also for the ability to innovate. Possible indicators reflecting ICT use may be number of personal computers, internet users, and fixed/mobile phone subscribers. These indicators are available for most countries.

The important role that a country's financial system may play in mobilizing resources for catching up was pointed out already by Abramovitz, who included this as one aspect of social capability, and Kim, who saw it as an element of technological capability (so-called 'investment capability'). Both attached a qualitative dimension to this that is difficult to measure with the available data. What can be measured is the (quantitative) development of the financial sector of a country, for example, as reflected in the amount of credit (to the private sector) or by capitalization of companies listed in domestic capital markets.

A different set of factors, emphasized, for example, by Abramovitz and Lall, relates to education and skills.[12] Abramovitz and Lall were especially concerned about specialized managerial and technical skills. This is again, however, an example of a type of information that is hard to get, particularly for a broad sample of countries at different levels of development. For most countries, more basic education statistics are available, such as the literacy rate, the teacher–pupil ratio in primary schools, and the rates of enrolment in secondary and tertiary education.

With respect to political characteristics, governance and institutions – furnishing economic agents with incentives for creation and diffusion of knowledge – are generally acknowledged as being of high importance for development. Although such factors often defy 'hard' measurement, especially in a broad cross-country comparison, there exist some survey-based measures, often collected by international organizations, which may throw some light on these issues. For example, there now exist survey data reflecting how widespread corruption is conceived to be, the extent to which law and order prevails, the independence of the courts, whether (intellectual) property rights are enforced, how easy it is to set up and operate a business, and so on.[13] All these aspects are potentially important for innovation and may, to some extent at least, be achieved within different political systems.[14]

Nevertheless, the impact of government's actions on innovation activities and development outcomes may – as pointed out by Abramovitz, Putnam and others – also depend on social characteristics, such as tolerance, honesty, trust and civic engagement. The argument that social factors of this type may matter for economic development is, as mentioned above, widely accepted. The problem is rather how to measure such factors. One possible source of information that has been exploited to throw some light on the issue is the 'World Value Survey'. Stephen Knack and Philip Keefer (1997) used such data to analyse the relationship between trust, norms of civic behaviour and membership in groups on the one hand, and economic growth on the other, for a sample of 29 (mostly developed) countries. The limited time and country coverage of these data has until recently precluded its extension to a sizeable part of the developing world. This has improved a lot, however, over the last few years. I shall return to this issue in the next section.

Openness (or interaction) across country borders is often taken to facilitate technology transfer (spillovers) and stimulate innovation. This issue is particularly emphasized in work inspired by the 'new growth theories' (Grossman and Helpman, 1991; Coe and Helpman, 1995; Coe et al., 1997). The applied literature on the subject has mostly focused on four channels of technology transfer across country borders: trade, foreign direct investment, migration and licensing (for overviews see Cincera and van Pottelsberghe, 2001; Keller, 2004). Some of these data sources are nevertheless in scarce supply for developing countries.

Given the relatively large number of potentially useful indicators, there is a lot of information to exploit when attempting to use these data to measure the various capabilities identified in the literature. One of the key challenges is how to combine this rich information into a smaller number of dimensions (for example, capabilities) with a clear-cut economic interpretation. The most widely used approach to construct composite variables is to select relevant indicators and weigh them together using predetermined (usually equal) weights (Archibugi and Coco, 2005). The problem in this case is that the choice of weights tends to be arbitrary. An alternative approach, pioneered by Adelman and Morris (1965, 1967), uses so-called 'factor analysis' (Basilevsky, 1994) to advise on such questions. This method is based on the very simple idea that indicators referring to the same dimension of reality are likely to be strongly correlated, and that one may use this insight to reduce the complexity of a large data set (consisting of many indicators) into a small number of composite variables, each reflecting a specific dimension of variance in the data.

Fagerberg and Srholec (2008) used factor analysis on data for 115 countries and 25 indicators between 1992 and 2004. The analysis led to the selection of four principal factors, jointly explaining about three-quarters of the total variance of the set of indicators. The first (and quantitatively most important) of these factors loads highly on several indicators associated with 'technological capability', such as patenting, scientific publications, ICT infrastructure, ISO 9000 certifications, and access to finance. The first factor, however, also correlates highly with education, so it cuts across the distinction in the literature between 'technological' (Kim, 1997) and 'social' capabilities (Abramovitz, 1986). Fagerberg and Srholec suggest interpreting it as a synthetic measure of the capabilities (or 'factors') influencing the 'development, diffusion and use of innovations', quoting Edquist (2004)'s definition of an innovation system (hence the name 'innovation system' for this factor). Figure 1.3 plots the innovation system factor score against GDP per capita for the countries covered by their investigation. The graph shows that there is a very close correlation between the 'innovation system variable' and economic development as reflected in GDP per capita. The deviations from the regression line primarily come from a group of resource-rich economies (Organization of the Petroleum Exporting Countries [OPEC] for instance), having slightly higher GDP-per-capita levels than the quality of their innovation systems would indicate, and some of the former centrally planned economies for which it is the other way round.[15]

The second factor identified by Fagerberg and Srholec loads high on various aspects reflecting the quality of 'governance', such as adherence to property rights, a well-functioning judicial system, low corruption and a

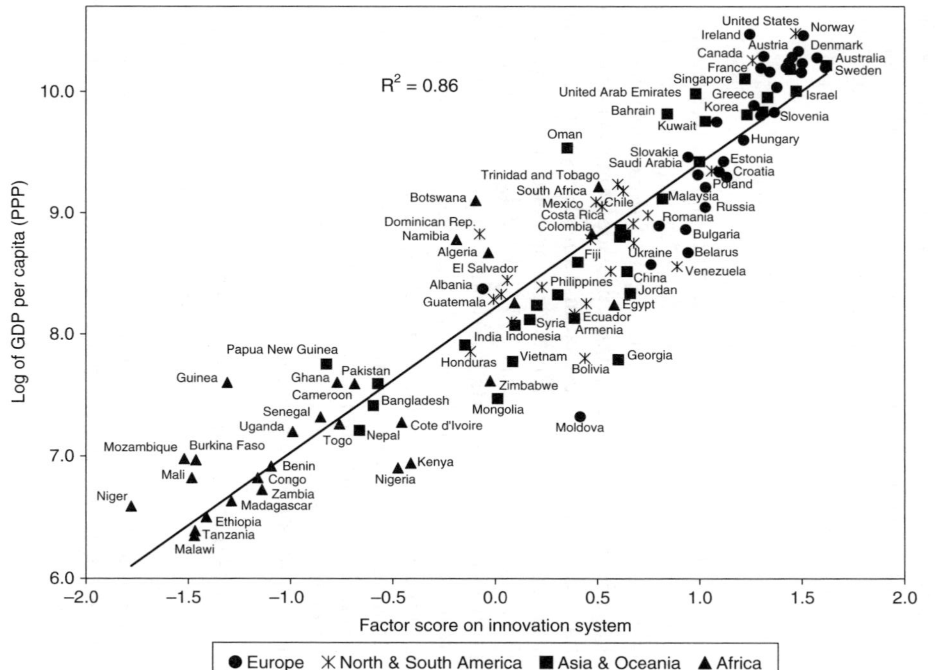

Source: Fagerberg and Srholec (2008). Reprinted from *Research Policy*, **37** (9), Jan Fagerberg and Martin Srholec, 'National Innovation Systems, Capabilities and Economic Development', pp. 1417–23 (October 2008), with permission from Elsevier.

Figure 1.3 GDP per capita and innovation system (2002–04)

favourable environment for business. As in the previous case, this factor score correlates positively with the level of economic development. The third factor, in contrast, loads particularly high on indicators reflecting the character of the 'political system'. Countries with political systems that are close to those of the Western world rank high on this dimension, while countries with systems that differ from Western democratic ideals get a low mark. In contrast to the two previous cases, however, the character of the political system is not closely correlated with levels of development. The same holds for the fourth factor identified by Fagerberg and Srholec, reflecting the degree of 'openness' to trade and foreign direct investment.[16]

The finding that economic development and capability building go hand in hand is suggestive. But correlation, it may be noted, is in itself no proof of causation, and since many of the relevant data sources used to measure capability building have existed only for a few years (and in some cases for a single year only), there is limited scope for causality testing. Nevertheless, Fagerberg and Srholec (2008) provide some evidence (in the form of multivariate tests), summarized in Table 1.1, supporting the proposition that capability building affects development positively. The period covered by the investigation was 1992 to 2004. In the first test included in the table, the capabilities (factor scores) from the beginning of the period are regressed against the level of development as measured by GDP per capita at the end of the period. While the innovation systems and governance factors were found to be significantly correlated with the level of development one decade later, the same did not hold for the character of the political system and openness to trade and foreign capital. This is consistent with the results referred to above (see Fagerberg and Srholec, 2008).

Can the implications from the above analysis be sustained in a dynamic framework? Many contributions to the empirical literature on cross-country differences in growth performance, despite theoretical differences, share a common empirical framework. So-called Barro regressions (Barro, 1991) consist of regressing initial GDP per capita and a number of other factors that may be deemed relevant against economic growth. In this framework, the GDP per capita variable measures the potential for catch-up (or convergence), while the other variables represent factors that are assumed to 'condition' the ability to exploit this potential. The second column in Table 1.1 reports the results of such an exercise with the initial levels and changes in the capability measures identified by Fagerberg and Srholec as conditional variables. The results are very similar to those obtained for levels: while both the levels and changes in the innovation system and governance factors seem to affect economic growth

Table 1.1 Capabilities and GDP per capita

Variable	Level of GDP per capita, average 2002–04	Growth of GDP per capita, annual average 1992–2004	Growth of GDP per capita, annual average 1992–2004, stepwise regression excl. the poorest half
Log of initial GDP per capita		−0.76 (2.16)*	−0.89 (3.39)**
Innovation system	0.85 (18.14)**	0.74 (2.28)*	0.56 (2.07)*
Δ innovation system		0.48 (4.67)**	0.30 (2.55)*
Governance	0.16 (3.35)**	0.39 (2.68)**	0.43 (2.34)*
Δ governance		0.38 (3.87)**	NS
Political system	−0.04 (1.08)	0.07 (0.57)	0.34 (2.71)**
Δ political system		0.12 (1.32)	0.24 (2.08)*
Openness	0.04 (1.07)	0.07 (0.64)	0.37 (3.12)**
Δ openness		0.03 (0.20)	NS†
Geography, nature and history	No	No	Yes
R^2	0.90	0.30	0.73
Observations	115	115	57

Notes: *, ** denote significance at the 5 and 1 per cent level, respectively. Standardized variables were used in the estimates (beta coefficients reported). The absolute value of robust *t*-statistics are in brackets. The capabilities (independent variables) are the lagged levels (factor scores) from the period 1992–94, while the changes in these capabilities are the differences in the levels (factor scores) between 2002–04 and 1992–2004. † NS = not significant.

Source: Based on Fagerberg and Srholec (2008), Tables 3–4.

favourably, there is very little support for the same in the case of the character of the political system and openness to trade and foreign capital.[17]

Capability building may also be influenced by long-run factors related to the history of the country (Acemoglu et al., 2001, 2002), its geography or natural resources (Gallup et al., 1999; Masters and McMillan, 2001; Bloom et al., 2003; Alesina et al., 2003; Sachs et al., 2004). Failing to take this into account may lead to biased inferences (with respect to policy, for instance). Fagerberg and Srholec (2008) found that unfavourable factors related to history, geography and natural resources did indeed influence the possibility of developing a well-working innovation system in a negative way. They pointed to this as an argument for continuing development aid, because it confirmed that some countries are much worse off than others for reasons beyond the control of people living today.

Nevertheless, the results reported in Fagerberg and Srholec (2008) also suggest that the estimated impact of the openness and political system variables may be sensitive to the composition of the sample and selection variables. The last column in Table 1.1 reports what happens if half of the sample (the poorest countries) is left out of the investigation, while a number of assumedly unfavourable factors related to history, geography and natural resources are added. The most striking difference compared to the full sample is that in this case the political system (degree of Westernization) and openness to imports and foreign capital seem to have a positive impact. Thus, it is primarily among the richer countries that the character of the political system and openness to trade and FDI matter for economic performance; for the poor part of the world, the evidence is much less convincing.

WHAT IS THE 'OPENNESS' THAT MATTERS?

The finding presented above – also corroborated by other recent research[18] – that differences in openness do not discriminate between developing countries that make it and those that fail, requires further questioning. It undoubtedly runs against the intuition of many economists and may thus be seen as surprising. Note, however, that following traditional economic theorizing on international trade, differences in openness to trade should not necessarily be expected to have long-run growth effects. Although improved access to trade may give room for increased specialization and, hence, improved productivity, this is essentially supposed to be a once-and-for-all effect (Robson, 1987). Similarly, although traditional growth theory would posit that investment is good for growth (Solow, 1956), it would not really matter where it came from.

The theoretical basis for assuming a positive impact of openness – particularly with respect to trade and FDI – on growth rests, as pointed out earlier, much more on the so-called 'new growth theories' developed by Paul Romer and others from the 1980s onward (Romer, 1990; Aghion and Howitt, 1992). These theories depart from the traditional focus in economic theory on factor accumulation, replacing it with knowledge as the most important driver of economic growth. From this perspective, openness to trade and FDI may be of importance if they have effects on knowledge flows. To what extent that is the case is a matter of controversy, as pointed out in the introduction of this chapter. As for trade, there are some reasons to believe that it might affect knowledge flows positively.

This, however, is arguably only one among several possible channels for such flows, and probably, given recent advances in telecommunications and the internet, not the most important. Regarding capital flows, and FDI in particular, the evidence seems to suggest that the knowledge flows associated with such investments are not very extensive in developing country environments. It appears that the extent of such flows depends much on the sophistication of the environment at the receiving end, which implies that it is in the developed countries that such flows matter most for knowledge transfer (for an overview, see Fagerberg et al., 2010). This is consistent with the findings discussed in the previous section.

As emphasized above, it is thus not enough to have access to ideas. One also has to be able to exploit them. So even if, say, trade and FDI open up possibilities for access to knowledge, this may not matter much for development if the capacity to exploit those opportunities is not sufficiently developed. This is the most likely explanation for the failure of most developing countries to profit from the opportunities generated by the progress of the global knowledge economy. Arguably, one might relate this lack in capacity to lack in 'openness', but in a more fundamental way, such as the openness to new ideas, people carrying those ideas, and so on.

In an attempt to throw some light on these matters, I will now discuss three types of openness (other than trade and FDI) that may be important for development. The first is *openness to ideas*, for example, the ability to identify, access, implement and develop knowledge. This type of openness is related to the 'technological capabilities' emphasized by Kim and others. As discussed above, however, the openness of society to entrepreneurs carrying new ideas also has to do with the character of institutions, governance and values in each country – the type of issues, for example, that Abramovitz subsumed under the heading 'social capabilities'. In exploring this issue, I find it useful to distinguish between *openness to business* and *openness to people*. The former refers to how new business initiatives (and existing ones too) are treated by the system of governance in the country. The latter, *openness to people*, has to do with the extent to which people with different characteristics (origin, gender, sexual orientation, and so on) are offered equal opportunities in the economic sphere and are able to work together. Arguably, a society that for some reason discriminates against a large part of the talent pool of its population will be at a loss when it comes to development.

Richer data than those underlying the discussion in the previous section are needed to explore the interrelationships between these three aspects of openness and development, in particular when it comes to social values. Drawing on Fagerberg and Srholec (2009), I will therefore focus on a more limited sample consisting of 75 countries, the majority of which are low or medium income. Since the time series for many relevant indicators are short, the focus here is on recent evidence, indicating that it is difficult to discuss causality on the basis of these data. In each case a number of relevant indicators were identified. These were then weighed together through factor analysis. An advantage of this method in the present context is its capacity to test the extent to which indicators allegedly reflecting the same dimension of reality are in fact strongly correlated. The results of this exercise are illustrated in Figures 1.4 to 1.6, which in each case plot the relevant factor score against the level of economic development (GDP per capita).[19] The figures also include the results of the relevant factor analysis including the indicators/variables used in each case.[20]

Openness to ideas is assumed to depend on the quality of a country's science base, as reflected in publications in scientific journals, international patent applications (PCT), R&D expenditure, advanced training (as captured by enrolment in doctoral programmes), science and engineering (S&E) education, the share of professionals and technicians in employment, use of quality standards (ISO) and trademarks and, finally, access to a state-of-the-art ICT infrastructure. The result, reported in the upper left quadrant of Figure 1.4 shows that all indicators taken into account by the analysis are strongly correlated with the resulting measure. The figure also plots *openness to ideas* against GDP per capita (in terms of purchasing power parity [PPP]) for the countries included in the analysis. The correlation is very close indeed: about 85 per cent of the variation in GDP per capita may be 'explained' by differences in *openness to ideas*.

Openness to business, in contrast, reflects how easy it is to set up (or close) a business or to protect intellectual property rights (IPRs) if law and order is adhered to; it also shows the extent to which corruption is a problem. This may be said to reflect the 'innovation friendliness' of governance in a given country. As shown in Figure 1.5, this type of openness is also strongly correlated with economic development. This also holds for *openness to people*, which is a measure of the openness of society to people with different characteristics (origin, gender, sexual orientation), the degree of trust among the citizens and their willingness to participate in civic activities (such as signing a petition). Note that the countries with the highest recorded values for these aspects of openness are not the ones usually found in such comparisons, such as the United States or Japan, but a group of small, high-income countries from northern Europe. It may also be noted that there is a group of (overwhelmingly Muslim) countries in Africa and Asia that score very low on 'openness to people', mainly because of widespread negative attitudes towards inclusion on equal terms of women, homosexuals and immigrants into society (Figure 1.6). Such

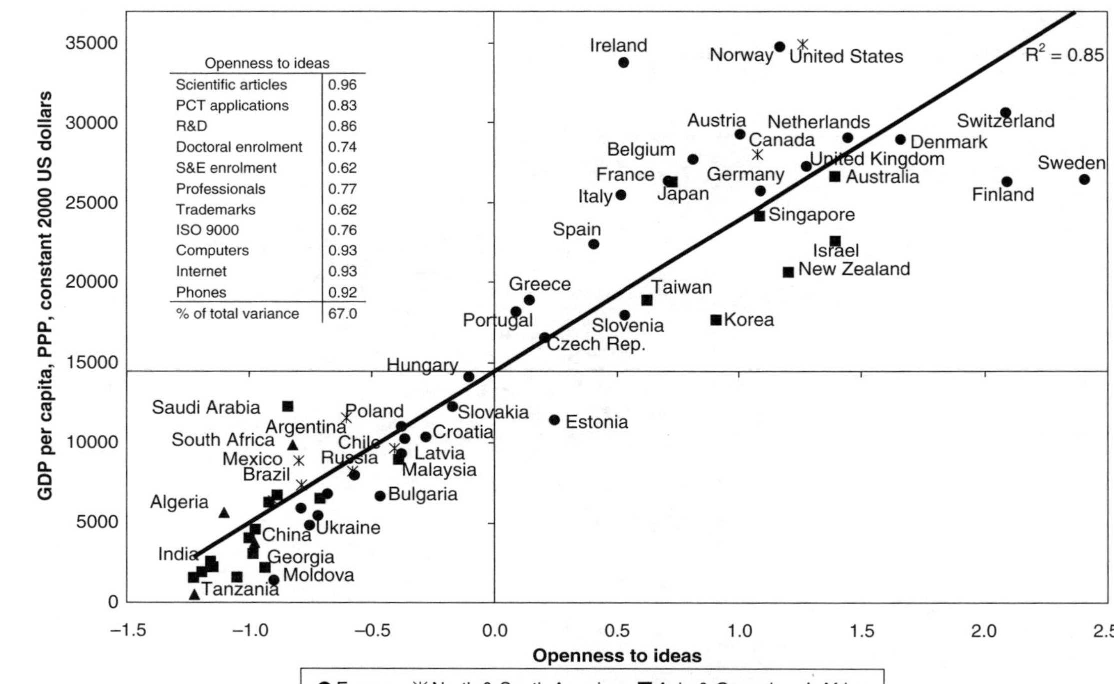

Source: Fagerberg and Srholec (2009).

Figure 1.4 Openness to ideas (75 countries, 2002–04)

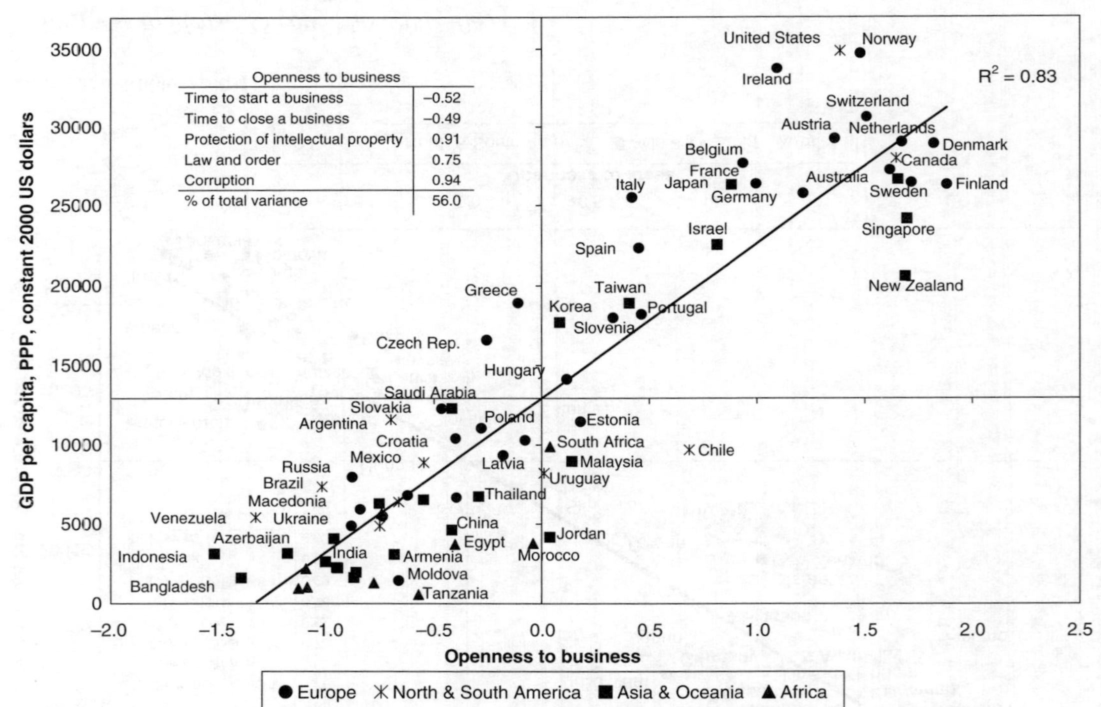

Source: Fagerberg and Srholec (2009).

Figure 1.5 Openness to business (75 countries, 2002–04)

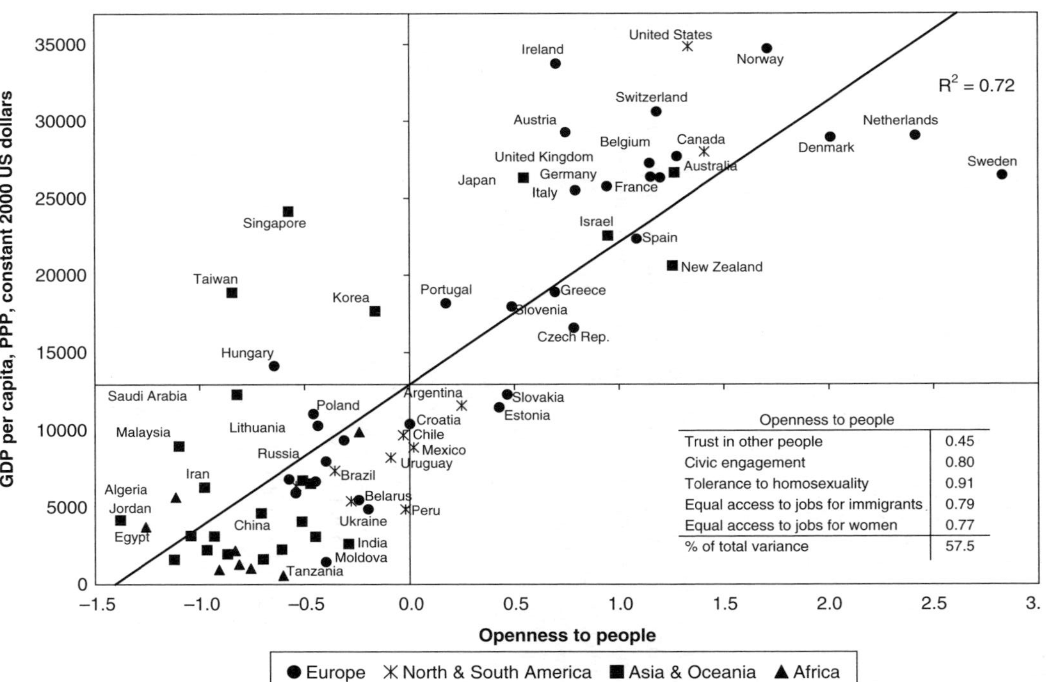

Source: Fagerberg and Srholec (2009).

Figure 1.6 Openness to people (75 countries, 2002–04)

observations beg further questioning about the role of deeper social and political factors in the long-run development of such countries.

CONCLUSIONS

The global division of labour is changing. China, India and a number of other countries from the developing world have increased their presence in the global economy during the last decade. Nevertheless, this is, as pointed out in the introduction to this chapter, far from a uniform tendency. Many, if not most, developing countries fail to mimic this performance, and global inequality, whether measured between countries or at the individual level, is on the rise. The pressing problem, from a policymaker's point of view, is how to identify policies that can help change these trends.

For a long time, the standard developed-country advice (the so-called Washington Consensus) to policymakers in the developing world was to replicate the institutions and policies – particularly with respect to trade and foreign investments – already in place in the developed part of the world (for example, the United States). It is now clear, however, that this advice was based more on ideology and (widely shared) beliefs than on solid empirical evidence. In fact, the evidence presented in this chapter and in other recent research clearly shows that developing countries that adopt Western-type institutions and practise openness to international trade and FDIs do not perform better than those that do not. As pointed out by Ha-Joon Chang (2002), several countries that have succeeded in catching up have done exactly the opposite of what the Washington Consensus would suggest.

What can one learn from all this? To start, policy advice should not solely be based on ideological concerns: it should be evidence based. So what does the evidence tell us about the challenges facing developing countries today? The global knowledge economy presents developing countries with both opportunities and challenges: opportunities, because there is an enormous amount of knowledge out there to exploit, and challenges, because it is not at all easy to succeed in doing so. Successful exploitation of knowledge requires technological capabilities that cannot be taken for granted. Therefore, creation of such capabilities should be at the centre of attention of policymakers in the developing world. The evidence clearly suggests that countries that succeed in doing so are the ones that manage to escape the vicious circle of poverty, disease and social and political unrest that characterize many countries in the developing world today (Fagerberg and Srholec, 2010).

The emphasis placed here on technological capabilities should not be seen as suggesting that there is an easy 'technological quick fix' to the problem of underdevelopment. Firm-level technological capabilities do not develop in a vacuum. Such capabilities extend beyond the individual firm to the broader network of firms, organizations and institutions in which the firm is embedded. Moreover, there is a strong correlation and, arguably, interdependence between technological capabilities of firms and the character of the broader social, political and economic environment in which they operate, what Abramovitz had in mind with the notion of 'social capabilities' (Fagerberg and Srholec, 2010). The significance of this extends far beyond familiar topics such as the importance of education, infrastructure, access to finance, and the maintenance of law and order. It also has to do with the openness of society to new ventures and its ability to mobilize the talent of its own population to participate in such undertakings. As mentioned above, countries that fail to do so, because of, say, culturally inherited disrespect for certain parts of the population based on ethnicity, gender or religion, are likely to lag in the development process. Hence, successful development will require the advancement of both technological and social capabilities, and the latter may be as challenging as the former.

NOTES

1. This chapter draws on joint work with Martin Srholec, and I am grateful for his permission to use it here. The chapter has also benefited from comments and suggestions from the commentator and other participants of the Cournot Centre conference, 'The New International Division of Labour', held 12–13 November 2009. Remaining errors are my own.
2. Recent analyses by Branko Milanovic (2009) based on revised estimates of GDP deflators confirm the long-run trend towards divergence across countries, but also provide evidence of a possible trend break around the turn of the millennium. His analysis stops in 2006, however, and as he points out, it is too early to conclude definitively on the subject.
3. It might be argued that while possibly true for countries, this might not apply for individuals across the globe, since some of the countries whose income per capita has grown fast recently are in fact very populous. Nevertheless, income differences within large, fast growing countries, such as China, have also increased dramatically during the process, so the outcome for global inequality at the individual level is far from obvious. In fact, recent analyses (see Milanovic, 2009) indicate that the differences across individuals across the globe have increased over the last two decades.
4. Josef Schumpeter had already in *The Theory of Economic Development* (1934 [1911]) suggested that an economy with no innovation (given knowledge, behaviour, and so on) would be in a stationary state (constant productivity). He called this state 'the circular flow'. This suggestion was met with strong criticism at the time. In 1956, however, Solow published a formal model that proved that this proposition would hold (in equilibrium).

5. The term 'Washington Consensus' was coined in 1989 by John Williamson to describe a set of policy prescriptions that he thought institutions such as the IMF, World Bank, and the US Treasury should promote in their relationships with developing countries. As Williamson has pointed out, however, the term subsequently came to be used as a synonym for 'market fundamentalism'. For an overview see http://en.wikipedia.org/wiki/Washington_consensus.
6. It has been shown that the relationship between openness to trade (exports) and economic growth differs a lot across time. For long periods, the relationship has been found to be insignificant or even negative (Vamvakidis, 2002).
7. See, for example, Abramovitz (1986) and Cohen and Levinthal (1990).
8. For a good overview see Foray (2004).
9. Adelman and Morris saw economic development as contingent on broader social and political changes accompanying the transition from a traditional (rural) way of life, based on a high degree of self-sufficiency, to a modern industrialized society characterized by market relationships and new forms of institutions and governance.
10. Putnam defines 'social capital' as 'features of social organization, such as trust, norms and networks, that can improve the efficiency of society by facilitating coordinated actions' (Putnam, 1993, p. 167). In sociology, the term is often used as an attribute of individuals, not as a characteristic of communities, as in the tradition of Putnam. For an overview and discussion of different usages of the term, see Portes (1998).
11. Firms' own judgements about their innovativeness (innovation counts) might be another possible source of information, but such data are only available for a limited number of countries and time spans. See Fagerberg et al. (2010) for more information on this data source.
12. The importance of education and skills is emphasized repeatedly in the economic literature. For an overview see Krueger and Lindahl (2001).
13. For details on these indicators/sources see Fagerberg and Srholec (2008, 2009).
14. To measure the latter (differences in political system) one could, for example, use variables reflecting the degree of democracy versus autocracy, the extent of checks and balances in the political system, the degree of competition for posts in the executive branch and legislature, and the extent of political rights and civil liberties. Since Western democracies will tend to have high values on most of these variables, a possible approach might be to measure in such a case the degree of 'Westernization' of a country's institutions.
15. Fagerberg and Srholec's study indicates that the most advanced innovation systems are to be found in smaller countries (in terms of population) such as Australia, Denmark and Norway. These three countries, it may be noted, are low by international standards on patents and R&D. Fagerberg and Srholec (2008) suggest that the explanation for this difference may be that these countries have well-developed capabilities for exploiting knowledge.
16. As noted, this is a factor that is deemed particularly important by followers of the 'new growth theory'. The results reported by Fagerberg and Srholec (2008) indicate, however, that 'openness' to trade and FDI is uncorrelated with economic development. This holds irrespective of whether country size is controlled for or not.
17. The possibility that economic growth in some sense affects capability building (or some aspects of it) cannot be excluded a priori. Fagerberg and Srholec (2008) tested for the possibility of an endogeneity bias in the estimates, because of a possible feedback from economic growth on capability changes, using the Hausman (or Durbin–Wu–Hausman) procedure (for further details see Wooldridge, 2002, pp. 118–22). The test failed to detect evidence of endogeneity bias.
18. See the introduction to this chapter and the references therein.
19. The GDP per capita figures in Figures 1.4 to 1.6 are averages over the years 2000–04, measured in constant (2000) international USD, using purchasing power parity rates (PPP).
20. A common assumption in factor analysis is that for a factor to be retained, it should

explain at least as much of the total variance as an average indicator; that is, the factor should have 'eigenvalue' above one. In the estimates reported here, only one factor with an eigenvalue above one was identified (see Fagerberg and Srholec, 2009, for details).

REFERENCES

Abramovitz, M. (1986), 'Catching up, forging ahead, and falling behind', *Journal of Economic History*, **46**, pp. 386–406.

Abramovitz, M. (1994), 'The origins of the post-war catch-up and convergence boom', in J. Fagerberg, B. Vespagen and N. von Tunzelman (eds), *The Dynamics of Technology, Trade and Growth*, Aldershot, UK and Brookfield, USA: Edward Elgar, pp. 21–52.

Acemoglu, D., S. Johnson and A. Robinson (2001), 'The colonial origins of comparative development: an empirical investigation', *American Economic Review*, **91**, pp. 1369–401.

Acemoglu, D., S. Johnson and A. Robinson (2002), 'Reversal of fortune: geography and institutions in the making of the modern world income distribution', *Quarterly Journal of Economics*, **117**, pp. 1231–94.

Adelman, I. and C.T. Morris (1965), 'A factor analysis of the interrelationship between social and political variables and per capita gross national product', *Quarterly Journal of Economics*, **79**, pp. 555–78.

Adelman, I. and C.T. Morris (1967), *Society, Politics and Economic Development*, Baltimore, MD: The Johns Hopkins Press.

Adler, J. (1965), *Absorptive Capacity and Its Determinants*, Washington, DC: Brookings Institution.

Aghion, P. and P. Howitt (1992), 'A model of growth through creative destruction', *Econometrica*, **60**, pp. 323–51.

Alesina, A., A. Devleeschauwer, W. Easterly, S. Kurlat and R. Wacziarg (2003), 'Fractionalization', *Journal of Economic Growth*, **8**, pp. 155–94.

Amsden, A.H. (1989), *Asia's Next Giant: South Korea and Late Industrialization*, New York: Oxford University Press.

Archibugi, D. and A. Coco (2005), 'Measuring technological capabilities at the country level: a survey and a menu for choice', *Research Policy*, **34**, pp. 175–94.

Arrow, K. (1972), 'Gifts and exchanges', *Philosophy and Public Affairs*, **1** (4), pp. 343–62.

Barro, R.J. (1991), 'Economic growth in a cross section of countries', *Quarterly Journal of Economics*, **106**, pp. 407–43.

Basilevsky, A. (1994), *Statistical Factor Analysis and Related Methods: Theory and Applications*, London: John Wiley & Sons.

Bell, M. and K. Pavitt (1993), 'Technological accumulation and industrial growth: contrasts between developed and developing countries', *Industrial Corporate Change*, **2**, pp. 157–210.

Bloom, D.E., D. Canning and J. Sevilla (2003), 'Geography and poverty traps', *Journal of Economic Growth*, **8**, pp. 355–78.

Chang, Ha-Joon (2002), *Kicking Away the Ladder: Development Strategy in Historical Perspective*, London: Anthem Press.

Cincera, M. and B. van Pottelsberghe de la Potterie (2001), 'International R&D spillovers: a survey', *Cahiers Economiques de Bruxelles*, **169**, pp. 3–32.

Coe, D. and E. Helpman (1995), 'International R&D spillovers', *European Economic Review*, **39**, pp. 859–87.

Coe, D., E. Helpman and A.W. Hoffmaister (1997), 'North–South R&D spillovers', *Economic Journal*, **107**, pp. 134–49.

Cohen, W.M. and D.A. Levinthal (1990), 'Absorptive capacity: a new perspective on learning and innovation', *Administrative Science Quarterly*, **35** (1), pp. 128–52.

Denison, E.F. (1967), *Why Growth Rates Differ*, Washington, DC: Brookings Institution.

Eckaus, R.S. (1973), 'Absorptive capacity as a constraint due to maturation processes', in J. Bhagwati and R.S. Eckaus (eds), *Development and Planning: Essays in Honour of Paul Rosenstein-Rodan*, London: Allen & Unwin, pp. 79–108.

Edquist, C. (2004), 'Systems of innovation: perspectives and challenges', in J. Fagerberg, D. Mowery and R. Nelson (eds), *The Oxford Handbook of Innovation*, Oxford: Oxford University Press, pp. 181–208.

Fagerberg, J. and M. Srholec (2005), 'Catching up: what are the critical factors for success?', Working Papers on Innovation Studies 20050401, Centre for Technology, Innovation and Culture, University of Oslo, available at: http://ideas.repec.org/p/tik/inowpp/20050401.html (accessed 23 May 2010).

Fagerberg, J. and M. Srholec (2008), 'National innovation systems, capabilities and economic development', *Research Policy*, **37**, pp. 1417–35.

Fagerberg, J. and M. Srholec (2009), 'Innovation systems, technology and development: unpacking the relationships', in B.A. Lundvall, K.J. Joseph and C. Chaminade (eds), *Handbook of Innovation Systems and Developing Countries*, Cheltenham, UK and Northhampton, MA, USA: Edward Elgar, pp. 83–115.

Fagerberg, J. and M. Srholec (2010), 'Knowledge, capabilities and the poverty trap: the complex interplay between technological, social and geographical factors', in P. Meusburger, J. Glückler and E. Wunder (eds), *Knowledge and Economy*, Dordrecht: Springer, forthcoming.

Fagerberg, J., M. Srholec and B. Verspagen (2010), 'Innovation and economic development', in B. Hall and N. Rosenberg (eds), *Handbook of the Economics of Innovation*, Amsterdam: North Holland, pp. 833–72.

Foray, D. (2004), *The Economics of Knowledge*, Cambridge, MA: MIT Press.

Gallup, J.L., J.D. Sachs and A. Mellinger (1999), 'Geography and economic development', Harvard University, CID Working Paper No. 1/1999.

Görg, H. and D. Greenaway (2004), 'Much ado about nothing? Do domestic firms really benefit from foreign direct investment?', *The World Bank Research Observer*, **19**, pp. 171–97.

Grossman, G.M. and E. Helpman (1991), *Innovation and Growth in the Global Economy*, Cambridge, MA: MIT Press.

Hayek, F.A. (1945), 'The use of knowledge in society', *American Economic Review*, **35**, pp. 519–30.

Heston, A., R. Summers and B. Aten (2002), *Penn World Table Version 6.1*, Center for International Comparisons at the University of Pennsylvania (CICUP).

Johnson, C.A. (1982), *MITI and the Japanese Miracle: The Growth of Industrial Policy*, Stanford, CA: Stanford University Press, pp. 1925–75.

Keller, W. (2004), 'International technology diffusion', *Journal of Economic Literature*, **42**, pp. 752–82.

Kim, L. (1980), 'Stages of development of industrial technology in a developing country: a model', *Research Policy*, **9**, pp. 254–77.

Kim, L. (1997), *Imitation to Innovation: The Dynamics of Korea's Technological Learning*, Cambridge, MA: Harvard Business School Press.

Knack, S. and P. Keefer (1997), 'Does social capital have an economic payoff? A cross-country investigation', *The Quarterly Journal of Economics*, **112**, pp. 1251–88.

Krueger, A. and M. Lindahl (2001), 'Education for growth: why and for whom?', *Journal of Economic Literature*, **39**, pp. 1101–36.

Lall, S. (1992), 'Technological capabilities and industrialization', *World Development*, **20**, pp. 165–86.

Lundvall, B.A. (ed.) (1992), *National Systems of Innovation: Towards a Theory of Innovation and Interactive Learning*, London: Pinter Publishers.

Masters, W.A. and M.S. McMillan (2001), 'Climate and scale in economic growth', *Journal of Economic Growth*, **6**, pp. 167–86.

Milanovic, B. (2009), 'Global inequality recalculated: the effect of new 2005 PPP estimates on global inequality', Policy Research Working Paper Series 5061, The World Bank.

Portes, A. (1998), 'Social capital: its origins and applications in modern sociology', *Annual Review of Sociology*, **24**, pp. 1–24.

Putnam, R. (1993), *Making Democracy Work*, Princeton, NJ: Princeton University Press.

Robson, P. (1987), *The Economics of International Integration*, 3rd edn, London: Allen & Unwin.

Rodrik, D., A. Subramanian and F. Trebbi (2004), 'Institutions rule: the primacy of institutions over geography and integration in economic development', *Journal of Economic Growth*, **9**, pp. 131–65.

Romer, P.M. (1990), 'Endogenous technological change', *Journal of Political Economy*, **98** (5), pp. 71–102.

Romijn, H. (1999), *Acquisition of Technological Capabilities in Small Firms in Developing Countries*, Basingstoke: Macmillan Press.

Sachs, J.D., J.W. McArthur, G. Schmidt-Traub, M. Kruk, C. Bahadur, M. Faye and G. McCord (2004), 'Ending Africa's poverty trap', *Brookings Papers on Economic Activity*, **1**, pp. 117–240.

Schumpeter, J. (1934/1911), *The Theory of Economic Development: An Inquiry into Profits, Capital, Credit, Interest and the Business Cycle* [*Theorie der wirtschaftlichen Entwicklung*], translated by Redvers Opie, Cambridge, MA: Harvard University Press.

Solow, R.M. (1956), 'A contribution to the theory of economic growth', *Quarterly Journal of Economics*, **70** (1), pp. 65–94.

Vamvakidis, A. (2002), 'How robust is the growth–openness connection: historical evidence', *Journal of Economic Growth*, **7**, pp. 1381–438.

Wade, R. (1990), *Governing the Market: Economic Theory and the Role of Government in East Asian Industrialization*, Princeton, NJ: Princeton University Press.

Woolcock, M. and D. Narayan (2000), 'Social capital: implications for development theory, research, and policy', *World Bank Research Observer*, **15**, pp. 225–50.

Wooldridge, J.M. (2002), *Econometric Analysis of Cross Section and Panel Data*, Cambridge, MA: MIT Press.

2. How global is foreign direct investment and what can policymakers do about it? Stylized facts, knowledge gaps, and selected policy instruments[1]

Peter Nunnenkamp

INTRODUCTION

Foreign direct investment (FDI) is a major driving force of globalization. Worldwide FDI stocks (in current prices) soared from US$700 billion in 1980 to almost US$15 trillion in 2008.[2] In contrast to the vagaries of international financial markets, booming FDI is widely believed to offer access to capital, technology and know-how for an increasing number of host countries, thereby providing them with better chances to integrate themselves into the global division of labour.

Even sharp critics of financial globalization and capital account liberalization advocate opening up to FDI. According to Joseph Stiglitz (2000, p. 1076):

> the argument for foreign direct investment . . . is compelling. Such investment brings with it not only resources, but technology, access to markets, and (hopefully) valuable training, an improvement in human capital. Foreign direct investment is also not as volatile – and therefore as disruptive – as the short-term flows.

Institutions such as the United Nations, which not very long ago passed extremely critical judgements on multinational enterprises (MNEs), now expect these enterprises to promote economic development in emerging markets, and even help the fight against absolute poverty in the neediest host countries.[3] The UN summit on Financing for Development in Monterrey in 2002 concluded that creating the necessary conditions to facilitate FDI inflows is a central challenge for developing countries, particularly the poorest among them.

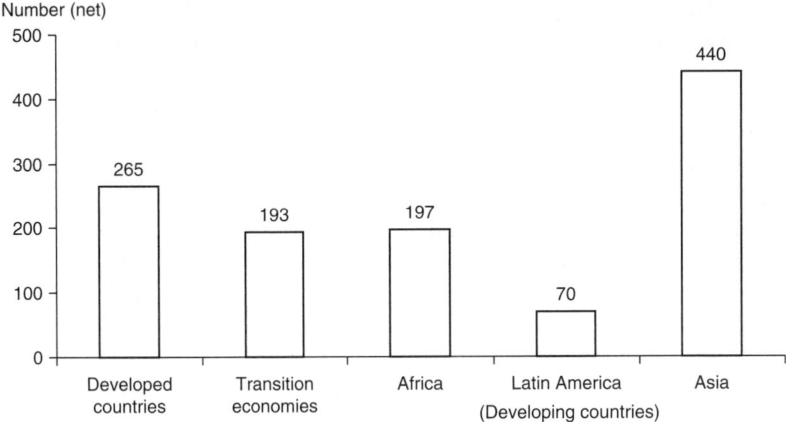

Source: UNCTAD (http://stats.unctad.org/FDI/).

Figure 2.1 Changes in national FDI policies (number of 'more favourable' minus 'less favourable'), 2000–06

Ever more countries have entered the fierce worldwide competition for FDI. The account of changes in national FDI policies by the United Nations Conference on Trade and Development (UNCTAD) reveals that almost 90 per cent of the measures taken by all countries in 2000–06 were 'more favourable' to FDI, for example, by relaxing foreign ownership restrictions, abolishing sector-specific restrictions and offering incentives. During the same period, African countries implemented 238 policy changes in favour of FDI, representing 18 per cent of such changes that took place worldwide, while just 41 measures were 'less favourable' to FDI (Figure 2.1).

FDI nevertheless continues to be concentrated in some fairly advanced and large host countries (see the next section). The competition for FDI may be global, but its distribution is in striking contrast with the notion of global production sharing via FDI. Perhaps still more surprisingly, there are few undisputed insights on which policymakers in developing host countries can rely when attempting to attract FDI – the burgeoning literature on FDI determinants notwithstanding (see the third section). The fourth section summarizes some recent studies based on a common research strategy, which focus on disputed (unilateral and bilateral) policy instruments and attempt to overcome critical shortcomings in previous literature. Analysing the determinants of FDI for a large panel of host countries, including those that have been sidelined so far, offers new insights for

FDI to become a more global phenomenon. Nonetheless, this is just one step towards another set of tricky questions (see the final section).

HOW GLOBAL IS FDI?

Laza Kekic (2009) expected that, for the first time ever, emerging markets were set to attract more than half of global FDI inflows in 2009. Kekic speculated that this 'distinct shift in the pattern of FDI' may indicate that 'practice may be catching up to [the] theory', according to which capital should flow from capital-abundant rich countries to capital-scarce poor countries.

The 'distinct shift' is largely a result, however, of the financial crisis in 2008–09 and may prove short-lived as soon as mergers and acquisitions among firms based in the most advanced economies recover. All developing and transition economies taken together attracted one-third of worldwide FDI flows during the three years preceding the crisis, which was slightly *below* their share in 1992–94. Longer-term trends in FDI stocks clearly contradict the view of FDI being redirected from richer to poorer countries (Figure 2.2). During the 1980s, the share of all developing countries actually declined (from more than 40 per cent to less than 30 per cent). Subsequently, the small group of developed countries persistently absorbed more than two-thirds of worldwide FDI stocks, even though

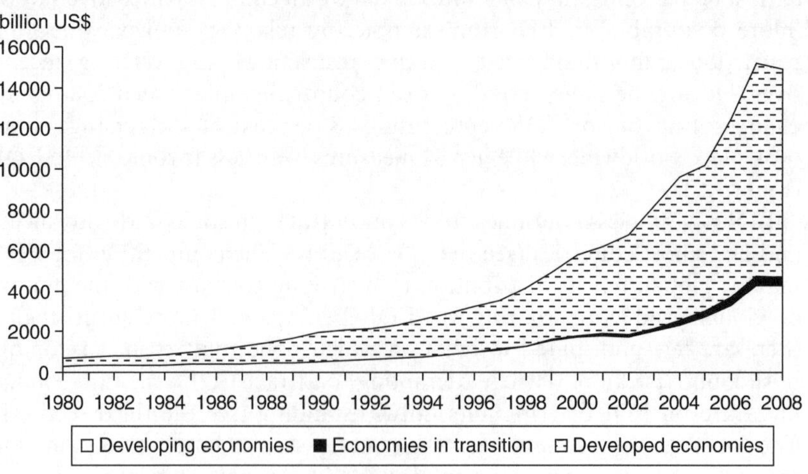

Source: UNCTAD (http://stats.unctad.org/FDI/).

Figure 2.2 Composition of worldwide FDI stocks, 1980–2008

transition countries in Central and Eastern Europe emerged as new competitors for FDI.

The distribution of FDI is heavily skewed also among developing and transition economies. The strong concentration of FDI stocks in a few large and fairly advanced developing countries persists. The 20 top performers accounted for more than 80 per cent of FDI stocks in all developing countries at the beginning of the 1990s, at the turn of the century, and still in 2007. Throughout this period, the top 20 consisted mainly of host countries offering huge market potential, notably mainland China, Brazil and Indonesia, and high-income economies such as Hong Kong, Singapore and South Korea.

It is not only at the top of the pyramid that the skewed distribution of FDI among developing countries persists. Rather, the ranking of all 161 economies that UNCTAD lists under 'developing economies' has hardly changed since 1990. A simple correlation exercise based on FDI stock data in 1990, 2000 and 2007 results in extremely high Spearman rank coefficients of 0.83 (1990 versus 2007) and 0.94 (2000 versus 2007).

The above-noted Monterrey Consensus mentions the least developed countries (LDCs), small island states as well as landlocked developing countries as those groups most in need of FDI to achieve national development priorities. UNCTAD has traced the development of inward FDI stocks for these and related sub-groups of developing countries over several decades. As Table 2.1 shows, their shares in worldwide FDI stocks have hardly increased from the typically extremely low starting levels in 1980. At first sight, the group of low-income countries appears to be

Table 2.1 Share of selected groups of developing countries in worldwide FDI stocks (%), 1980–2007

	1980	1990	2000	2007
Low-income developing countries	2.9	3.4	6.2	4.8
Low-income developing countries, excluding China	2.7	2.3	2.9	2.7
Least developed countries	0.8	0.5	0.7	0.7
Landlocked developing countries	0.4	0.3	0.6	0.7
Small island developing states	0.6	0.4	0.4	0.3
Structurally weak, vulnerable and small economies	2.7	1.8	1.9	1.7
Heavily indebted poor countries	0.8	0.6	0.6	0.6

Note: Country groups according to UNCTAD definitions.

Source: UNCTAD (http://stats.unctad.org/FDI/).

an exception. The increasing share for this group is exclusively a result, however, of booming FDI in mainland China.

WHAT PREVIOUS LITERATURE CAN(NOT) TELL

The driving forces of FDI have received a lot of attention from economists. Nevertheless, the existing literature is not useful for the large number of potential host countries that have been sidelined by MNEs in the past. There are several reasons for this. Part of the literature is designed in a way that largely eschews policy relevance. Most empirical studies on location choice provide only limited insights into the effectiveness of specific policy instruments. In particular, data constraints often result in small and unrepresentative samples, so empirical findings are likely to be biased.

Recent research focuses on the varying FDI motivations to develop the theory and estimation of general equilibrium models of MNEs.[4] The distinction between horizontal and vertical FDI has been a major step in this direction. The well-known knowledge-capital model of MNEs developed by David Carr et al. (2001) integrates these two major types into a single theoretical framework: horizontal MNEs with similar production activities in their home and host countries, and vertical MNEs with segmented value chains and headquarter services in the (more advanced) home country.

Essential elements of the knowledge-capital model include the size of home and host country markets, relative skill endowments, as well as interactions, for example, between size and endowment differences of the host and home countries. The model also considers trade and investment costs, that is, factors that can be shaped by economic policymakers. The focus, however, clearly remains on 'the primary long-run determinants of FDI location' (Blonigen, 2005, p. 392), rather than the effectiveness of different policy options to stimulate FDI inflows. For instance, horizontal FDI is expected to be concentrated among countries that are relatively similar in both size and relative factor endowments.

In principle, the knowledge-capital model provides a theoretically sound foundation that could be 'augmented' by more specific policy variables in order to assess the chances of a broad spectrum of host countries to attract FDI. This approach has several problems, however. Some of the above-noted elements of the model are hard to capture in the context of a large panel of host countries.[5] Especially for low-income countries, data on skill endowments are often not available for sufficiently long periods of time. In addition to data constraints, Peter Egger and Valeria Merlo (2007) argue that empirical models based on Carr et al. (2001) perform less well in panel settings.[6] Therefore, the research reported in the next section employs simple gravity-type models on the determinants of FDI.[7]

Earlier cross-country studies tended to be less demanding in terms of econometrics and data. Yet reviews of this quantitatively important strand of the literature invite the conclusion that little has been achieved in providing developing countries with reliable policy advice to attract FDI. In the 1990s, Kwang Jun and Harinder Singh (1996, p. 70) concluded that a consensus on the major determinants of FDI has been 'elusive'. Avik Chakrabarti (2001) applied extreme bounds analysis to determine which coefficients of the explanatory variables used in cross-country studies on possible FDI determinants are 'robust' and which are 'fragile' to small changes in the conditioning information set. His results signify that, for each of the policy-related variables under consideration, 'one can find a significant coefficient of the theoretically predicted sign only by selectively adding and combining explanatory variables as there is not enough independent variation in any of these variables to explain cross-country differences in FDI' (Chakrabarti, 2001, p. 105). Purchasing power in host-country markets proved to be the only robust explanatory variable positively related to FDI inflows.

Chakrabarti's findings are not particularly encouraging for economic policymakers looking for effective means to attract FDI. FDI determinants such as market size, local endowment of resources sought after by MNEs, or geographical and cultural proximity to major source countries are beyond the realm of short-term policymaking, either because these factors are unalterable or because changing them is a very long process. Nevertheless, pure cross-country studies are inherently flawed and not well-suited to identify effective policy instruments as the time dimension is completely missing.[8]

On the other hand, earlier panel analyses typically suffer from small and unrepresentative host-country samples. The pooled cross-country and time-series model estimated by Jun and Singh (1996) covers just 31 host countries. Low-income countries are scarcely represented in their sample, which renders it almost impossible to assess the chances of developing countries to attract FDI. Likewise, the panel analysis of Victor Gastanaga et al. (1998, p. 1310) hardly fills the gap in 'research on the effects of policy variables on FDI, especially with respect to LDCs'. Their sample is also small and biased against low-income countries, accounting for just ten out of 49 sample countries.

To summarize, it seems that two conditions have to be met for empirical studies on FDI determinants to offer relevant insights for policymakers in developing countries. First, the focus should be on variables that are amenable to policymaking, while controlling for market and endowment-related factors that tend to be stable in the short run. Second, sample selection bias must be avoided by including essentially all small and poor countries, even if many of these countries received little FDI or none at all. Howard Shatz's (2003, p. 118) observation provides an important starting point for the studies summarized in the following section: nearly all research on foreign direct investment focuses on the winners, countries that have achieved at least some success in attracting FDI. This is a significant problem since policy advice is most often sought by the countries that are excluded from analysis.

NEW INSIGHTS FROM RECENT STUDIES ON BILATERAL FDI

Common Features of the Gravity-Type Models

With several co-authors, I revisited some disputed policy issues in a number of recent papers that are based on a fairly simple approach. The simplicity of the underlying gravity-type models makes it possible to overcome, or at least minimize, the sample selection bias that, in my view, characterizes almost all previous studies on related policy issues.

The following studies employ the largest possible panel of bilateral FDI relations, covering (1) old and new sources of FDI and (2) potential host countries that failed to attract (much) FDI. By including non-OECD sources of FDI, they partly capture the recent surge of FDI flows from developing countries to other developing countries.[9] In that way, the studies take into account that the driving forces of FDI from non-OECD sources may differ from those of the traditional sources of FDI. Compared to US or German FDI, for example, FDI from source countries such as Singapore and Taiwan is more concentrated in lower-wage host countries, which could imply that cost motives play a relatively prominent role (Ellingsen et al., 2006; Liu and Nunnenkamp, 2009).

Coverage matters even more for the host countries of FDI. As noted before, previous research often suffers from sample selection bias by focusing on host countries that attracted sufficiently high FDI to be listed in officially published statistics on FDI. To avoid such a bias and provide meaningful policy advice, the sample of host countries used here includes a large number of small and poor economies that have received little or zero FDI inflows in the past.[10] In fact, the share of zero observations is large in all analyses to follow; it represents, for example, about 70 per cent of all observations in Busse et al. (2010a). Therefore, the studies apply several estimation methods, including non-linear estimations, and perform extensive robustness tests related to the treatment of zero observations.

The studies summarized in the following paragraphs have some more common features. The interpretation of results is mainly from a developing-country perspective. It is primarily for these host countries that policy instruments such as bilateral investment treaties (BITs) may compensate for less developed local institutions and may, thus, help attract FDI. The period of observation typically ranges back to the late 1970s, so that the time dimension is sufficiently long. Possible endogeneity of (unilateral and bilateral) policy variables is accounted for, typically by performing general method of moments (GMM) estimations.

All estimations reported below include a standard set of controlling variables.[11] In particular, the size and growth of host-country markets enter as possible determinants of horizontal FDI. Standard determinants of vertical FDI include the difference in per capita income between the source and the host country as well as openness to trade of the host country (proxied by the sum of imports and exports in per cent of GDP). Economic and political stability concerns that are widely believed to discourage FDI are captured by the rate of inflation in the host country and some measure of the quality of local institutions, such as institutional constraints limiting the political discretion of the executive branch.

The standard set of FDI determinants is augmented in alternative ways. The focus is on unilateral and bilateral measures that are relatively easily amenable to policymaking in (potential) host countries, but whose effectiveness in stimulating FDI inflows has remained disputed. Among bilateral measures, BITs and double taxation treaties (DTTs) are addressed in the first two studies by Matthias Busse et al. (2010a) and Fabian Barthel et al. (2010). Unilateral policy options with respect to labour rights and gender disparity in education are analysed in Busse et al. (2010b) as well as Busse and Nunnenkamp (2009).

Bilateral Instruments: BITs and DTTs

The effectiveness of bilateral measures is often dismissed in earlier studies. Mary Hallward-Driemeier (2003) finds little evidence that BITs have stimulated bilateral FDI flows from OECD countries to developing countries. Her sample of 31 host countries is rather small, however. Jennifer Tobin and Susan Rose-Ackerman (2005, 2006) reject the view that BITs are a substitute for a favourable local business environment. Eric Neumayer and Laura Spess (2005) cover a relatively broad sample of host countries. Using aggregate FDI inflows from all sources, rather than bilateral flows,

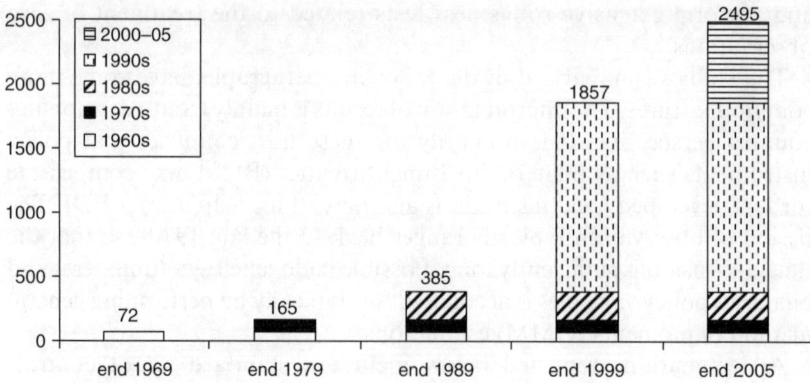

Source: UNCTAD (http://www.unctadxi.org/templates/DocSearch____779.aspx), as presented in Busse et al. (2010a).

Figure 2.3 Number of BITs concluded, 1969–2005

they find that developing countries that had agreed to a larger number of BITs attracted higher FDI inflows.

Indeed, policymakers in developing countries have increasingly pinned their hopes on BITs to improve their chances in the worldwide competition for FDI. The overall number of BITs concluded worldwide surpassed 2500 in 2006 (Figure 2.3). In addition to unilateral liberalization of FDI-related regulations, host countries have committed themselves through BITs in a legally binding way to grant foreign investors various rights that reduce uncertainty with respect to entry and exit conditions, post-entry operations as well as dispute settlements. Unilateral measures are non-binding and suffer from time-inconsistency problems (Neumayer and Spess, 2005). Theoretically, BITs would be superior to unilateral liberalization if attracting FDI were a one-time game. The host country could then easily renege on unilateral promises concerning the treatment of FDI once the foreign investor realized the sunk costs associated with locating in the host country. In reality, however, attracting FDI amounts to a repeated game in which the host country strives for continuous inflows of FDI from investors who are aware of its past behaviour. In other words, reversing unilateral liberalization once some FDI is 'locked in' would come at the cost of deterring future inflows.

Busse et al. (2010a) control for unilateral capital account liberalization, which coincides with the conclusion of BITs, in order not to overestimate the effects of (ratified) BITs on FDI. The dependent FDI variable is measured as the share attracted by a specific (developing) host country in total FDI flows from a particular source country to all 83 (developing) host countries in the sample. This measure of relative attractiveness is preferred as it relates to the theoretical model of Zachary Elkins et al. (2006), according to which host countries ratify BITs to divert FDI away from competing host countries.[12]

Major results of the fixed-effects ordinary least squares (OLS) estimations are presented in Table 2.2. It can be seen that most of the controlling variables have expected signs and are statistically significant. For instance, FDI is clearly flowing to larger markets, *ln (GDP)*. At the same time, one finds evidence for vertical FDI, reflected in *ln (DiffGDPpc)*. Higher economic instability, proxied by *ln (Inflation)*, is associated with lower FDI flows, while better institutions, *PolCon*, are associated with higher FDI flows.

Turning to the explanatory variable of principal interest, the coefficient of the dummy variable *BIT* is significantly positive at the 1 per cent level, even though the existence of other bilateral and plurilateral treaties, *DTT* and regional trade agreements (*RTA*), is controlled for. Calculating the economic impact of *BIT*, the results reported in column 1 imply that, at the mean, the ratification of BITs with all source countries would raise the host country's share in FDI flows from all source countries by almost 35 per cent.[13] This effect weakens only slightly when adding unilateral capital account liberalization, *CapOpen*, as an additional controlling variable (column 2). Furthermore, Busse et al. (2010a) interact the BIT variable with institutional development and capital account liberalization to check whether BITs may substitute for unilateral measures to promote FDI (columns 3 and 4). There is some evidence to this effect: BITs turn out to be more effective in stimulating FDI under conditions of higher investor uncertainty because of greater political discretion of the executive branch in the host country (reflected in lower values of *PolCon*).

Busse et al. (2010a) checked the robustness of these results in several respects (not shown in the table). First, they estimated non-linear (Tobit as well as Poisson pseudo-maximum-likelihood) models since OLS might produce biased results because of the large number of zero observations. Independent of the choice of models, the effect of BITs always remains positive and significant at the 5 per cent level or better. Second, they accounted for possible endogeneity of the ratification of BITs (and most of the controlling variables) by performing system GMM estimations. Arguably, investors press for better protection of their assets held abroad, resulting in reverse causation with FDI, thus inducing the conclusion of BITs. Indeed, the coefficients of *BIT* are typically smaller in the GMM regressions, indicating that the fixed-effects estimations tend to overstate the impact of BITs. Nevertheless, the GMM approach corroborates that ratifying BITs leads to higher FDI inflows.

Table 2.2 Fixed-effects OLS estimation results on the effects of BITs on bilateral FDI flows

Dependent variable	(1)	(2)	(3)	(4)
	ln (FDI share), including zero observations			
BIT	0.106***	0.0899***	0.226***	0.0985***
	(3.37)	(2.77)	(4.23)	(2.91)
ln (GDP)	0.193***	0.201***	0.193***	0.200***
	(5.46)	(5.16)	(5.05)	(5.14)
ln (DiffGDPpc)	0.00824***	0.00884***	0.00863***	0.00883***
	(3.54)	(3.51)	(3.43)	(3.51)
Growth	0.00114	0.00102	0.000882	0.00106
	(1.21)	(1.05)	(0.91)	(1.09)
ln (Inflation)	−0.00710*	−0.00763*	−0.00880**	−0.00783**
	(−1.92)	(−1.91)	(−2.21)	(−1.97)
Openness	0.000241	0.000415	0.000454	0.000382
	(0.74)	(1.20)	(1.31)	(1.11)
RTA	0.180***	0.167**	0.177**	0.172**
	(2.68)	(2.43)	(2.57)	(2.49)
PolCon	0.110***	0.114***	0.172***	0.115***
	(3.19)	(3.21)	(4.66)	(3.23)
DTT	0.105**	0.0809*	0.0832*	0.0803*
	(2.22)	(1.64)	(1.68)	(1.65)
CommonCurrency	0.112	0.103	0.115	0.105
	(1.47)	(1.36)	(1.52)	(1.39)
CapOpen		0.0114**	0.0118**	0.0157***
		(1.97)	(2.04)	(2.73)
PolCon×BIT			−0.400***	
			(−3.47)	
CapOpen×BIT				−0.0247
				(−1.56)
Observations	14077	13747	13747	13747
Country pairs	2313	2313	2313	2313
R^2 (within)	0.02	0.02	0.02	0.02

Notes: *t*-values, reported in parentheses, are corrected for heteroskedasticity; coefficients for the year dummies are not shown; likewise, host-year and source-year effects are always included but not displayed; ***, ** and * denote significance at the 1, 5 and 10% level, respectively.

Source: Own estimations, adapted from Busse et al. (2010a).

These findings suggest that policymakers have used an effective means of promoting FDI by concluding BITs. When replicating the estimations for sub-groups of developing host countries, BITs turn out to be effective in promoting FDI in both low- and middle-income countries. Some ambiguities nevertheless remain. On the one hand, excluding the group of transition countries from the sample considerably diminishes the effect of BITs, suggesting that overall results are largely driven by the experience of transition countries. On the other hand, the size of the *BIT* coefficient increases when excluding the large number of zero observations for the dependent FDI variable. This may indicate that BITs help less in countries that appear to be totally unattractive (and, thus, have zero inflows).

In a closely related study, Barthel et al. (2010) put particular emphasis on the effectiveness of DTTs. The starting points are very similar to those of the study on BITs. The increase in the number of DTTs resembles that of BITs, with 2350 DTTs in force at the end of 2007. All the same, the effectiveness of DTTs in stimulating FDI is open to question. According to Peter Egger et al. (2006, p. 902), 'one of the most visible obstacles to cross border investment is the double taxation of foreign-earned income'. Bruce Blonigen and Ronald Davies (2005, p. 530) suspect, however, that 'recent treaties are not geared toward the promotion of FDI but rather toward reductions in tax evasion'. Preventing 'double non-taxation' (Barthel et al., 2010) in this way may even discourage FDI.

Also similar to BITs, previous empirical evidence on the FDI effects of DTTs is highly inconclusive. On the one hand, studies using bilateral FDI data typically suffer from small and unrepresentative host-country samples. In particular, lacking or insufficient coverage of developing host countries may explain why these studies tend to find negative effects (see, for example, Blonigen and Davies, 2005; Egger et al., 2006). On the other hand, the results of studies using aggregate FDI data for larger samples tend to be more benign. For instance, Eric Neumayer (2007) shows that host countries that had signed a larger number of DTTs with OECD source countries attracted higher FDI stocks and flows. Note, however, that Neumayer (2007) failed to find a positive effect of DTTs on FDI in low-income developing countries.

Barthel et al. (2010) are the first to employ bilateral FDI stock data for a large and representative sample of 30 source countries and 105 host countries (including 84 developing countries), largely based on data from UNCTAD's Data Extract Service. With the exception that Barthel et al. use FDI stocks and a slightly shorter list of controlling variables, their research design is similar to that of Busse et al. (2010a). First, they estimate a static model with pair-wise fixed effects.[14] The DTT dummy turns out to be significantly positive at the 1 per cent level. The average quantitative effect is substantial: a DTT entering into force increases bilateral FDI stocks by 27 per cent. Next, the lagged dependent variable is added to the list of explanatory variables. This dynamic model reveals a similarly large long-run effect of 31 per cent. Finally, a GMM estimator is applied to account for possible endogeneity of DTTs (and other explanatory variables). In this step of the analysis, the DTT dummy is replaced by the number of years of the DTT being in force. Nevertheless, DTTs still have a positive effect on bilateral FDI stocks.

From the perspective of developing host countries, it is most interesting to note that Barthel et al. (2010) clearly reveal how seriously distorted the picture on the effectiveness of bilateral arrangements might be when the estimations are based on small and unrepresentative samples. The effect of DTTs is no longer positive when replicating the above analysis for the small samples used by Blonigen and Davies (2005) or by Egger et al. (2006). In other words, developing countries need to be sufficiently represented in the sample to identify DTTs as an effective means through which policymakers may promote FDI. This does not necessarily imply that DTTs are equally effective in various sub-groups of developing countries. Indeed, the robustness tests performed by Barthel et al. indicate that the positive effect of DTTs on FDI stocks in low-income developing countries is sensitive to the choice of the model. This is in contrast to the corresponding estimation for middle-income developing countries, and also to the results on the BITs reported above.[15]

Unilateral Policies with Regard to Labour Rights and Gender Discrimination

Very few low-income countries belong to the top 50 signatories of BITs or DTTs (in terms of the number of BITs and DTTs, respectively; UNCTAD, 2006, p. 279). This may be partly because advanced source countries of FDI are less eager to enter into bilateral negotiations with these countries, compared to host countries offering larger markets with more purchasing power. The United States, for instance, had just nine BIT partners in 2009 that the World Bank classified as low-income countries, while 33 BIT partners belonged to the middle-income group. At the same time, low-income countries themselves may be reluctant to spend scarce administrative resources on bilateral negotiations resulting in BITs or DTTs whose promotional FDI effects are questionable.

In this context, I address two distinct unilateral measures through which developing countries, and particularly the poorer countries among them, may have attempted to lure MNEs. Busse et al. (2010b) augment the basic gravity-type model outlined above by considering the host countries' policy with regard to labour rights, in addition to the standard controlling variables, as well as BITs and unilateral capital account liberalization. Busse and Nunnenkamp (2009) augment the basic model by evaluating the FDI effects of gender discrimination in education.

The motivation of both papers is similar. Poor and small host countries may have little to offer to attract FDI – except perhaps abundant and cheap labour. Hence, policymakers in these countries may keep labour costs in check in order to benefit from the relocation of labour-intensive production lines to lower-wage countries. Conversely, globalization critics are concerned that, by aggressively competing for FDI, policymakers in developing countries engage in a race to the bottom with respect to social standards, worker rights and gender equality.

Previous evidence is inconclusive on whether FDI, in order to reduce labour costs, goes where social standards are low, worker rights repressed and labour markets unrestricted. Violations of basic civil liberties and core labour standards appear to *reduce* FDI (Kucera, 2002; Harms and Ursprung, 2002; Busse, 2003). On the other hand, the literature discussing specific aspects of labour market regulations finds that host countries with more flexible labour markets attract more FDI (see for example, Görg, 2005; Javorcik and Spatareanu, 2005). Similar to the above reasoning on bilateral treaties, the latter studies can hardly be relied on when advising policymakers in developing countries. The sample of Beata Javorcik and Mariana Spatareanu (2005) is restricted to 19 European host countries where labour market flexibility, notably the ease of dismissal, is shown to be associated with higher FDI. Likewise, the finding of Holger Görg (2005) that stricter employment protection discourages US (manufacturing) FDI relates to a small sample of 33 host countries in which India represents the only low-income country.

By contrast, the following GMM estimations are based on FDI flows to a sample of 82 low- and middle-income host countries during the period 1984–2004. The explanatory variable of interest, labour rights (*LabR*), captures the presence and actual adherence to legal rights of workers to organize, bargain collectively and strike. It records 37 specific violations of such rights ranging from the absence of legal rights to limitations and the breach of legal obligations by governments and employers.[16] Higher scores reflect stronger labour rights in the host country of FDI. The sign of *LabR* should be negative if repressed labour rights are associated with higher FDI inflows. The counterhypothesis applies if MNEs are under strict public scrutiny to show good corporate conduct concerning workers and, therefore, shy away from host countries with pervasive social injustice (Neumayer and De Soysa, 2006).

Not surprisingly, FDI proves to be strongly path dependent; most

Table 2.3 GMM estimation results on the effects of labour rights on bilateral FDI flows

Model	I	II	III	IV	V
Full developing country sample					
1. *LabR*, host country	0.00697*** (5.16)	0.00522*** (4.18)	0.00405*** (2.82)	0.00293** (2.19)	0.00457** (2.44)
2. *LabR*, difference host minus source country	0.00419*** (4.82)	0.00379*** (4.59)	0.00329*** (3.52)	0.00284*** (3.13)	0.00302* (1.78)
Reduced samples (with *LabR*, host country)					
3. Excluding Brazil, China, India and Indonesia	0.00674*** (4.84)	0.00473*** (3.83)	0.00330** (2.34)	0.00295** (2.35)	0.00345* (1.84)
4. Middle-income host countries	0.00623*** (3.29)	0.00590*** (3.19)	0.00723*** (3.58)	0.00470*** (2.58)	0.00932*** (3.20)
5. Low-income host countries	0.00162 (1.56)	0.00198* (1.94)	0.00193* (1.83)	0.00175* (1.75)	0.00436*** (3.55)
Observations	11745	11546	10690	10690	4181
Country pairs	2287	2287	2175	2175	861
Sargan (*p*-value)[a]	0.12	0.15	0.13	0.14	0.01
AB 2 (*p*-value)[b]	0.14	0.14	0.16	0.16	0.52
Instruments	285	325	352	352	300

Notes:
Estimation based on one-step system-GMM estimator with robust standard errors; corresponding *z*-values are reported in parentheses; ***, **, * significant at 1, 5, and 10% level, respectively.
Models I–V differ only by the list and specification of controlling variables; coefficients of controlling variables, including the lagged dependent, are not reported, but are available on request. Host-year and source-year effects and time dummies are always included.
All test statistics refer to the estimation for the full developing country sample with *LabR* reported in line 1.
a Sargan test of overidentification.
b Arellano-Bond test that second-order autocorrelation in residuals is 0; first-order autocorrelation is always rejected.

Source: Own estimations, adapted from Busse et al. (2010b).

controlling variables are statistically significant with the expected sign (not shown). The labour rights variable is significantly positive in all specifications reported in Table 2.3. If it is at all possible to prevent rising labour costs by repressing worker rights and, thereby, lure MNEs, the findings clearly suggest that this effect was dominated by other factors. Rather,

MNEs appear to prefer host countries where labour rights are respected, possibly because they are concerned about their reputation regarding corporate conduct. This result holds when additionally controlling for centralized wage bargaining in the host country (model V). In fact, there is no evidence for the widely held view that FDI is discouraged by centralized bargaining.[17] Furthermore, calculating the long-run effect of an improvement in labour rights by one standard deviation results in a quantitatively relevant increase in the FDI share by almost 20 per cent (in model I).

It is mainly for relatively advanced developing host countries that better labour rights enforcement is associated with higher FDI. This can be seen when separating the overall sample into low- and middle-income countries. Nevertheless, it does not pay even for low-income countries to repress labour rights, although this sub-group in particular may have little to offer apart from cheap labour to attract FDI.

Busse and Nunnenkamp (2009) reach similar conclusions on gender disparity as a possible determinant of FDI flows to developing countries.[18] On the one hand, gender disparity in education may stimulate FDI by offering cost advantages if it leads to lower average wages at a given level of labour productivity. On the other hand, FDI may be discouraged if foreign investors increasingly rely on local availability of skilled labour, which gender disparity in education is likely to constrain. A similar trade-off has been addressed by Shatz (2003), even though he does not consider gender disparity. Shatz (2003, p. 118) finds that better educated workers attract more FDI, and rejects the counterhypothesis according to which FDI is undertaken 'in countries with low levels of education to escape the high compensation costs with which higher levels of education and skill are associated'.

Busse and Nunnenkamp (2009) perform Tobit estimations of the standard gravity-type model, which is augmented by educational variables, including different measures of gender disparity in education (proxied by average years of schooling). They chose this somewhat indirect approach of assessing the FDI effects of gender disparity, because disparity measures that directly capture wage costs, labour productivity and the qualification of the workforce by gender are unavailable or subject to serious data constraints. Kucera (2002) appears to be the only previous study that addresses gender-specific education as a determinant of FDI. He finds a positive effect of (relative) female educational attainment. This effect, however, is statistically significant only when high-income host countries are included in the sample. Moreover, Kucera's analysis is purely cross-sectional. By contrast, Busse and Nunnenkamp (2009) perform dynamic panel estimations focusing on 77 developing host countries and covering the period 1984–2004.

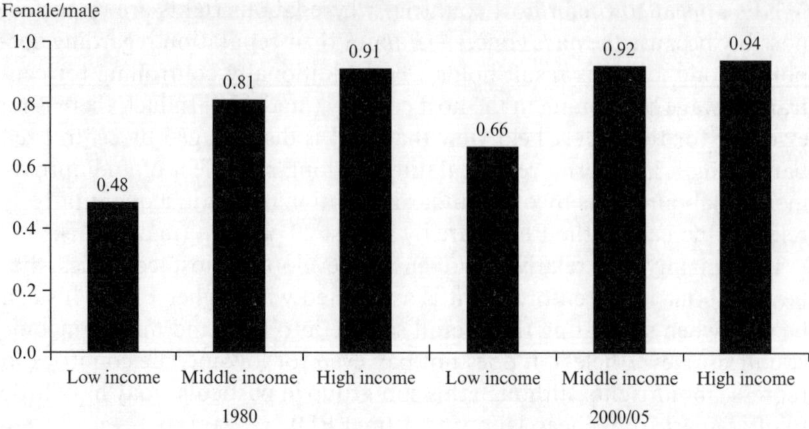

Notes: Average years of schooling at all levels combined: females divided by males; 2000/05 represents the average for 2000 and 2005.

Sources: Robert J. Barro and Jong-Wha Lee (2001) and UNESCO; as presented in Busse and Nunnenkamp (2009).

Figure 2.4 Gender disparity in schooling, 1980 and 2000/2005 in low-, middle- and high-income countries

Gender gaps in education tend to be particularly wide in low-income countries, even though the gap has narrowed since 1980 (Figure 2.4). The estimation results strongly suggest that further narrowing these gaps would *increase* FDI inflows (Table 2.4).[19] In other words, it would be counterproductive if policymakers in developing countries entered into a race to the bottom, not only by lowering corporate taxation, but also by being lenient about the still widespread gender gaps in education. Nevertheless, one cannot rule out that gender discrimination in education has a positive effect on cost-oriented FDI decisions of MNEs by keeping wages in the host country low. This effect appears to be minor, however, compared to the discouraging effect that gender discrimination has on FDI by limiting the pool of qualified local labour.

There are some indications that policy choices are less obvious precisely where gender gaps are most pronounced and FDI tends to be lowest. Most notably, the win–win situation of less gender disparity going along with more FDI is confined to middle-income countries. The insignificantly positive effect of gender disparity on FDI in low-income countries may be attributed to the prominence of specific types of FDI relying less on qualified local labour; resource-oriented FDI in the primary sector of low-

Table 2.4 Tobit estimation results on the effects of gender disparity in education on bilateral FDI flows

Dependent variable	ln (FDI share)
Full sample	
Education, all levels	−0.0496***
	(0.0090)
Primary education	−0.0701***
	(0.015)
Secondary education	−0.135***
	(0.023)
Tertiary education	−0.372***
	(0.090)
Sub-samples (education, all levels)	
Middle-income countries	−0.0655***
	(0.013)
Low-income countries	0.00653
	(0.011)
Developed source countries	−0.0619***
	(0.010)
Developing source countries	−0.00336
	(0.019)

Notes:

To save space, I only report the results for the variable on inequality in education.
Marginal effects, computed at the mean; standard errors in parentheses; *** significant at 1% level; ** significant at 5% level; * significant at 10% level.
The *p*-values of the Wald χ^2 test for the null hypothesis that all explanatory variables equal zero are always statistically significant at the 1% level (not reported).

Source: Own estimations, adapted from Busse and Nunnenkamp (2009).

income countries is a case in point. Moreover, low-income host countries may attract FDI primarily from other developing countries. Investors based there appear to care less about gender inequality in education than investors from advanced source countries (see the bottom lines of Table 2.4). Finally, additional estimations performed for gender disparity at different levels of education indicate that positive effects on FDI are considerably weaker at the primary level than at the secondary and tertiary levels. This may involve a dilemma facing policymakers in low-income countries, where policies to narrow gender gaps would have to first target primary education. All the same, even for low-income countries, it would not pay – in terms of higher FDI inflows – to maintain gender gaps in education.

SUMMARY AND EXTENSIONS

Recent empirical contributions to the literature on the determinants of FDI departed from two observations. First, FDI is still far from being a truly global phenomenon. Many countries have failed to attract much FDI – in particular those developing countries where capital, technology transfers and know-how would be needed most urgently to take part in the international division of labour. Second, one knows surprisingly little on how to improve this situation and spread the benefits FDI may bring to a larger number of host countries. A large part of empirical research on the driving forces of FDI is of limited use to policymakers in countries that have been sidelined by MNEs in the past.

The aim of the empirical studies summarized above is to help improve the chances of developing countries to integrate themselves into the international division of labour. Two preconditions are necessary for empirical research to be of policy relevance in countries that have had little success so far in the fierce worldwide competition for FDI: (1) the list of explanatory variables must go beyond factors that are more or less unalterable for policymakers (such as natural resource endowments and the size of local markets); (2) analyses must not be restricted to the 'winners', that is, host countries that have achieved at least some success in attracting FDI. Policy advice is most often sought by countries that are not even listed in many FDI statistics (Shatz, 2003).

I have identified a few policy instruments that appear to be effective in promoting FDI flows to developing countries, in contrast to the findings of earlier studies that were based on small and unrepresentative samples. At the same time, there are some indications that it may be harder for poorer countries to make themselves more attractive to foreign investors. FDI promotion through bilateral treaties appears to be less effective in low-income countries (DTTs) or in countries that have not previously received any FDI (BITs). Note also that DTTs and BITs involve costs for the host countries that cannot be captured in cross-country analyses. Bilateral negotiations absorb scarce administrative resources. Giving up national sovereignty could adversely affect public budgets. For instance, concluding DTTs involves tricky choices for low-income countries when FDI effects are relatively weak and losses in tax revenues loom large (considering that taxes on cross-border transactions often account for a large share of government revenues in poor countries).

For the two unilateral measures considered here, win–win situations again are less likely for countries lagging behind in the worldwide competition for FDI. While there is no evidence that MNEs prefer low-income countries where labour rights are violated, the link between labour rights and FDI is clearly positive only for more advanced developing countries. Similarly, the win–win situation of less gender discrimination and more FDI is confined to developing countries with relatively high per capita incomes.

There are various other unilateral measures that should receive more attention in policy-oriented research on FDI determinants. Empirical analyses typically control for some broadly defined institutional conditions in the host countries. The link between institutional development and FDI inflows is often shown to be positive, resulting in calls for better local governance to attract FDI. It might be more useful to focus on specific institutional aspects that appear to be particularly relevant in the context of FDI and more easily amenable to policy than general governance issues.[20] The protection of intellectual property rights (IPR) provides a case in point. From simple inspection of the widely used Ginarte–Park index on IPR, it appears that IPR protection is correlated positively with FDI and also with the ratio of FDI inflows to host-country imports of manufactured goods. This may indicate that stronger IPR provide incentives for MNEs to prefer FDI over exporting. It remains to be analysed, however, if and to what extent stronger IPR would attract FDI to developing countries once other factors are appropriately controlled for.

The set of bilateral instruments may be more limited. Future research in this area should pay more attention to the contents of bilateral treaties. The proliferation of BITs and DTTs could result in diminishing returns in the sense that the mere existence of a treaty will no longer be a distinctive factor signalling the host country's readiness to protect foreign investors (Tobin and Rose-Ackerman, 2006). Hence, the future effectiveness of BITs, for example, may increasingly depend on whether the 'new generation' of BITs involves more binding commitments. To capture this effect, the common, though extremely unrealistic, assumption of homogeneous BITs has to be relaxed. Three aspects of heterogeneity seem to be of particular importance: (1) BITs with explicit provisions relating to the pre-establishment phase should be treated differently from those granting protection only after establishment; (2) BITs with pervasive provisions related to performance requirements may be separated from those without such provisions; and (3) BITs including investor–state arbitration should be distinguished from those limited to state-to-state arbitration.

In summary, various questions on the effectiveness of specific policy instruments in attracting FDI remain to be addressed. Slightly paraphrasing the 'new' UN Consensus achieved in Monterrey: creating the necessary conditions to facilitate FDI flows to developing countries, particularly the poorest among them, will remain a central challenge for some time. Moreover, another set of tricky questions has to be resolved for FDI to help developing host countries catch up economically and reduce poverty. Attracting FDI may prove to be the easy part, compared to creating a host-country environment in which the, as of now, widely perceived benefits of FDI could actually be reaped.

NOTES

1. This contribution relies heavily on joint research with several co-authors. In particular, I would like to thank Matthias Busse, Jens Königer and Mariana Spatareanu for a most productive cooperation.
2. See UNCTAD, http://stats.unctad.org/fdi/.
3. As *The Economist* (27 January 2000) noted, multinational enterprises were 'widely denounced as big, irresponsible, monopolistic monsters' in the 1970s. By contrast, the UN stated in 2002 that FDI flows are 'vital complements to national and international development efforts', contributing 'toward financing sustained economic growth over the long term' (http://www.un.org/esa/ffd/monterrey/MonterreyConsensus.pdf).
4. See Blonigen (2005) for a detailed review.
5. Note that the estimation results in Carr et al. (2001) are based on bilateral US–FDI relations with just 36 countries.
6. Specifically, the interaction terms of the knowledge-capital model lead to multicollinearity among the regressors, which Egger and Merlo (2007) consider to be particularly harmful in the time dimension of FDI panel data.
7. The gravity models appeared to lack theoretical foundation and were 'not held in very high standing by most of the profession for decades' (Blonigen, 2005, p. 393). Nevertheless, this type of model 'is arguably the most widely used empirical specification of FDI' (Blonigen et al., 2007, p. 1309) and has proven to fit FDI data fairly well.
8. The Extreme Bounds Analysis of Chakrabarti (2001) is based on data for a single year (1994).
9. Coverage of new FDI sources remains far from complete, however. Most notably, data are missing for Chinese FDI outflows.
10. While this information is often not available from published FDI statistics, UNCTAD's Data Extract Service offers extensive data on bilateral FDI for researchers to purchase.
11. I do not discuss the results for controlling variables in any detail here to save space. Detailed results are presented in the papers underlying this summary assessment and are available on request.
12. At the same time, Busse et al. (2010a) control for other bilateral and plurilateral treaties such as regional trade agreements and DTTs.
13. See Busse et al. (2010a) for the details of this calculation.
14. Detailed results are not shown here to save space.
15. On the other hand, the effect of DTTs hardly depends on whether or not transition countries are included in the sample. This finding is also somewhat in conflict with what Busse et al. (2010a) found for BITs.
16. The data were kindly made available by Layna Mosley. See Kucera (2002) as well as Mosley and Uno (2007) for a detailed account. For our sample of countries, *LabR* has a mean of 22.3 and a (within) standard deviation of 4.36, and ranges from 2.5 to 37. Controlling variables are essentially as in Busse et al. (2010a), including a dummy for the existence of BITs. The dependent variable is also defined as in Busse et al. (2010a).
17. Major results also hold when redefining the labour rights variable so as to reflect the difference in *LabR* between the host and the source country (line 2 in Table 2.3).
18. In contrast to international trade, the vast literature on the determinants of FDI has generally been gender blind (Braunstein, 2006).

19. At the same time, Busse and Nunnenkamp (2009) corroborate Shatz (2003) in that average years of schooling of both sexes together are associated with higher FDI (not shown).
20. See Blonigen (2005, p. 390) for a similar line of reasoning with respect to institutions and FDI.

REFERENCES

Barro, Robert J. and Jong-Wha Lee (2001), 'International data on educational attainment: updates and implications', *Oxford Economic Papers*, **53** (3), pp. 541–63.

Barthel, Fabian, Matthias Busse and Eric Neumayer (2010), 'The impact of double taxation treaties on foreign direct investment: evidence from large dyadic panel data', *Contemporary Economic Policy*, **28** (3), pp. 366–77.

Blonigen, Bruce A. (2005), 'A review of the empirical literature on FDI determinants', *Atlantic Economic Journal*, **33** (4), pp. 383–403.

Blonigen, Bruce A. and Ronald B. Davies (2005), 'Do bilateral tax treaties promote foreign direct investment?', in Eun Kwang Choi and James C. Hartigan (eds), *Handbook of International Trade, Volume II*, London: Blackwell, pp. 526–46.

Blonigen, Bruce A., Ronald B. Davies, Glen R. Waddell and Helen T. Naughton (2007), 'FDI in space: spatial autoregressive relationships in foreign direct investment', *European Economic Review*, **51** (5), pp. 1303–25.

Braunstein, Elissa (2006), 'Foreign direct investment, development and gender equity: a review of research and policy', UNRISD Occasional Paper 12, Geneva: United Nations Research Institute for Social Development.

Busse, Matthias (2003), 'Do transnational corporations care about labour standards?', *Journal of Developing Areas*, **36** (2), pp. 49–68.

Busse, Matthias and Peter Nunnenkamp (2009), 'Gender disparity in education and the international competition for foreign direct investment', *Feminist Economics*, **15** (3), pp. 61–90.

Busse, Matthias, Jens Königer and Peter Nunnenkamp (2010a), 'FDI promotion through bilateral investment treaties: more than a bit?', *Review of World Economics*, **146** (1), pp. 147–77.

Busse, Matthias, Peter Nunnenkamp and Mariana Spatareanu (2010b), 'Foreign direct investment and labor rights: a panel analysis of bilateral FDI flows', *Applied Economics Letters*, forthcoming.

Carr, David L., James R. Markusen and Keith E. Maskus (2001), 'Estimating the knowledge-capital model of the multinational enterprise', *American Economic Review*, **91** (3), pp. 693–708.

Chakrabarti, Avik (2001), 'The determinants of foreign direct investment: sensitivity analyses of cross-country regressions', *Kyklos*, **54** (1), pp. 89–113.

Egger, Peter and Valeria Merlo (2007), 'The impact of bilateral investment treaties on FDI dynamics', *World Economy*, **30** (10), pp. 1536–49.

Egger, Peter, Mario Larch, Michael Pfaffermayr and Hannes Winner (2006), 'The impact of endogenous tax treaties on foreign direct investment: theory and evidence', *Canadian Journal of Economics*, **39** (3), pp. 901–31.

Elkins, Zachary, Andrew T. Guzman and Beth A. Simmons (2006), 'Competing for capital: the diffusion of bilateral investment treaties, 1960–2000', *International Organization*, **60** (Fall), pp. 811–46.

Ellingsen, Gaute, Winfried Likumahuwa and Peter Nunnenkamp (2006), 'Outward FDI by Singapore: a different animal?', *Transnational Corporations*, **15** (2), pp. 1–40.

Gastanaga, Victor M., Jeffrey B. Nugent and Bistra Pashamova (1998), 'Host country reforms and FDI inflows: how much difference do they make?', *World Development*, **26** (7), pp. 1299–314.

Görg, Holger (2005), 'Fancy a stay at the "Hotel California"? The role of easy entry and exit for FDI', *Kyklos*, **58** (4), pp. 519–35.

Hallward-Driemeier, Mary (2003), 'Do bilateral investment treaties attract foreign direct investment? Only a bit . . . and they could bite', World Bank Policy Research Working Paper 3121, Washington, DC: The World Bank.

Harms, Phillipp and Heinrich W. Ursprung (2002), 'Do civil and political repression really boost foreign direct investment?', *Economic Inquiry*, **40** (4), pp. 651–63.

Javorcik, Beata and Mariana Spatareanu (2005), 'Do foreign investors care about labor market regulations?', *Review of World Economics*, **141** (3), pp. 375–403.

Jun, Kwang W. and Harinder Singh (1996), 'The determinants of foreign direct investment in developing countries', *Transnational Corporations*, **5** (2), pp. 67–105.

Kekic, Laza (2009), 'The global economic crisis and FDI flows to emerging markets', *Columbia FDI Perspectives*, **15**, New York: Vale Columbia Center on Sustainable International Investment.

Kucera, David (2002), 'Core labour standards and foreign direct investment', *International Labour Review*, **141** (1–2), pp. 31–68.

Liu, Wan-Hsin and Peter Nunnenkamp (2009), 'Domestic repercussions of different types of FDI: firm-level evidence for Taiwanese manufacturing', Working Paper 1546, Kiel Institute for the World Economy.

Mosley, Layna and Saika Uno (2007), 'Racing to the bottom or climbing to the top? Economic globalization and collective labor rights', *Comparative Political Studies*, **40** (8), pp. 923–48.

Neumayer, Eric (2007), 'Do double taxation treaties increase foreign direct investment to developing countries?', *Journal of Development Studies*, **43** (8), pp. 1501–19.

Neumayer, Eric and Indra De Soysa (2006), 'Globalization and the right to free association and collective bargaining: an empirical analysis', *World Development*, **34** (1), pp. 31–49.

Neumayer, Eric and Laura Spess (2005), 'Do bilateral investment treaties increase foreign direct investment to developing countries?', *World Development*, **33** (10), pp. 1567–85.

Shatz, Howard J. (2003), 'Gravity, education, and economic development in a multinational affiliate location', *Journal of International Trade and Economic Development*, **12** (2), pp. 117–50.

Stiglitz, Joseph E. (2000), 'Capital market liberalization, economic growth, and instability', *World Development*, **28** (6), pp. 1075–86.

Tobin, Jennifer and Susan Rose-Ackerman (2005), 'Foreign direct investment and the business environment in developing countries: the impact of bilateral investment treaties', available at: http://ideas.repec.org/p/wdi/papers/2003-587.html (accessed October 2009).

Tobin, Jennifer and Susan Rose-Ackerman (2006), 'When BITs have some bite: the political–economic environment for bilateral investment treaties', available at: http://www.law.yale.edu/documents/pdf/When_BITs_Have_Some_Bite.doc (accessed October 2009).
UNCTAD (2006), *World Investment Report 2006*, New York: United Nations.

3. Labour market frictions as a source of comparative advantage: implications for unemployment and inequality[1]

Elhanan Helpman

INTRODUCTION

Until the 1980s, studies of international trade were dominated by two sources of comparative advantage: technological capabilities and factor endowments. The former approach, originally attributed to David Ricardo, starts from the observation that sectoral relative labour productivity varies across countries, and derives from this feature implications for the structure of foreign trade. The latter approach, originally attributed to Eli Heckscher and reformulated by Bertil Ohlin, starts from the observation that endowments vary across countries, and derives from this feature implications for the structure of trade, assuming that technologies are the same in every country. While the Ricardian approach abstracts from differences in the composition of factor endowments, the Heckscher–Ohlin approach abstracts from differences in technologies. These two approaches are complementary to each other, emphasizing alternative sources of comparative advantage. Both focus, however, on explaining the structure of trade at the sectoral level, that is, on predicting which country exports food, which exports electronic products, which exports chemical products, and so forth.

As growth in world trade proceeded at a rapid pace after World War Two, and especially so in manufactures, it became apparent that this focus was not adequate, because much of world trade was taking place within industries. Namely, many countries both exported and imported food, exported and imported electronic products, and exported and imported chemical products. Moreover, it was recognized that an emphasis on differences across countries, either in technologies or factor endowments, is useful for explaining trade among countries that differ from each other, but not for explaining trade among countries that are similar to each other. Yet the majority of world trade took place (and still does) among the industrial countries, which are similar to each other, rather than between the industrial and less-developed countries, which differ substantially.

In response to these empirical observations, the analysis of trade was further enriched in the 1980s with the development of trade models that featured economies of scale and imperfect competition. Particularly successful was the integration of monopolistic competition into an otherwise standard Heckscher–Ohlin framework, thereby accounting for the existence of both intersectoral and intra-industry trade, and for large volumes of trade among similar countries. Over time, the resulting Helpman–Krugman model became the standard tool for addressing trade issues, such as the link between trade and growth, because it proved to be flexible enough for both theoretical and empirical analysis.

Despite the desirable features of the trade models from the 1980s, they turned out to be inadequate for explaining a range of new findings that emerged in the 1990s. In that decade, new firm-level data sets became available, which led to the discovery of new patterns of trade *within* industries. Of particular interest was the finding that within a sector such as food or electronics, only a fraction of firms export, and that this fraction varies greatly across industries. Moreover, within an industry, exporting firms differ systematically from non-exporters; in particular, exporters are bigger and more productive than non-exporters, they employ a different composition of workers, and they pay higher wages. These findings led to a re-examination of the monopolistic competition approach to international trade, enriching it with heterogeneous firms within industries, and to a new workhorse for trade analysis – the Melitz model.

In parallel, both theory and empirical analysis started to pay more attention to institutional determinants of comparative advantage. Scholars incorporated incomplete contracts into trade theory in order to study firm choices between outsourcing and in-house production of intermediate inputs on the one hand, and offshoring versus domestic sourcing of intermediate inputs on the other.[2] This brought to the fore the role of legal institutions in shaping comparative advantage. Indeed, differences across countries in the quality of legal systems proved to be an important determinant of trade flows.[3] Other studies examined the role of financial institutions in shaping world trade and found that differences across countries in levels of financial development had a large impact on trade flows, and that this effect was related to variation across sectors in the degree of dependence on external finance (see Manova, 2008, 2009). Finally, differences across countries in labour market characteristics shape trade structure by impacting the degree to which it pays a country to lock in resources in industries with different volatility levels (see Cuñat and Melitz, 2007).

The addition of within-industry heterogeneity and institutional factors to the toolkit of international trade analysis has enriched our ability to understand new sources of comparative advantage and, as a result, new developments in international trade and foreign direct investment (FDI). It is not my intention to review all these developments, but rather to discuss one line of inquiry in which heterogeneity within industries and differences across countries in labour market frictions play a central role. For this purpose I first review some of the insights from Melitz (2003) on trade with heterogeneous firms, followed by a discussion of search and matching frictions in labour markets; these have been introduced into the literature by Peter Diamond (1982a, 1982b) and by Dale Mortensen and Christopher Pissarides (1994). Finally, I discuss the work of Elhanan Helpman and Oleg Itskhoki (2010), and Helpman et al. (2010a, 2010b), which combine search and matching frictions in labour markets with Melitz-style firm heterogeneity in order to investigate the determinants of unemployment and inequality in trading countries. This discussion is organized around the following three questions: (1) What are the impacts of one country's labour market frictions on its trade partners? (2) How does removing trade impediments impact countries with different labour market frictions? and (3) What is the impact of trade on inequality and unemployment?

HETEROGENEOUS FIRMS WITHIN INDUSTRIES

As pointed out above, in the 1990s a number of studies examined how firms differ by trade status. Andrew Bernard and colleagues (1995) and Bernard and Jensen (1999) addressed this question with US data, and their work was followed by studies based on data from Canada, Colombia, France, Mexico, Morocco, Spain and Taiwan.[4] All these studies found that only a small fraction of firms export, that exporting firms are larger and more productive than non-exporters, and that firms exhibit persistence in their export status; namely, non-exporters persist in not exporting while exporters persist in exporting, although occasionally firms switch status. The last finding was interpreted to reflect the sunk costs of exporting, meaning that a firm has to bear a fixed cost in order to penetrate a foreign market.[5] Sanghamitra Das and colleagues (2007) found such costs to be around US$400,000 for Colombian firms.

According to the World Trade Organization (WTO) (2008, Table 5), in the United States 18 per cent of manufacturing firms exported in 2002, in

France 17.4 per cent of firms in this sector exported in 1986, in Japan this fraction was 20 per cent in 2000, and in Norway it exceeded 39 per cent in 2003. The same publication (Table 6) reports a high concentration of exports in large firms. In the United States, for example, in 2002 the top 1 per cent of firms by size controlled 81 per cent of manufacturing exports, while the top 10 per cent controlled 96 per cent. In France, the comparable numbers were 44 and 84 per cent, respectively, in 2003, and in Norway they were 53 and 91 per cent, respectively, in 2003.

Exporting firms are both larger and more productive than non-exporters. For example, in the United States exporters employ about twice as many workers as non-exporters, and the value-added per worker of exporters is 11 per cent larger than the value-added per worker of non-exporters.[6] Nevertheless, exporting firms sell abroad only a small fraction of their output.[7]

Marc Melitz (2003) develops a theoretical framework that can explain these data. His point of departure is a sector in which firms engage in monopolistic competition and produce a large assortment of brands of a differentiated product, as in the Helpman–Krugman model. Unlike Helpman–Krugman, however, Melitz assumes that an entrant to the industry faces uncertainty regarding its total factor productivity (TFP). On bearing the entry cost, a firm learns the productivity of its technology, yet before entry, all it knows is the distribution from which its productivity level will be drawn. For this reason, a firm has to form strategies conditional on every conceivable productivity draw to evaluate the profitability of entry: whether it will stay in the industry and bear the fixed cost of production, whether it will serve only the domestic market, or whether in addition to serving the domestic market, it will also export and bear the fixed cost of exporting. In what follows, I focus on a two-country world, so that a firm does not need to choose to which countries to export – only whether to export or not – and it cannot engage in foreign direct investment.[8] After forming these contingent plans, a firm faces a distribution of profits at the entry stage, and it enters only if the expected profits are sufficiently high to cover the entry cost. In a free-entry equilibrium, expected profits just equal the entry cost. This is the economic structure modelled by Melitz (2003).

Firms produce output according to the production function

$$y = \theta h, \tag{3.1}$$

where y is output, θ is productivity – drawn from a known cumulative distribution $G(\theta)$ – and h is labour employment. This production function applies to every variety of the product. Preferences are CES[9] with the elasticity of substitution ε. The fixed production cost is f_d, the fixed export cost is f_x, and the fixed entry cost is f_e.[10] In addition, there are variable trade costs, summarized by the parameter $\tau > 1$; $\tau - 1$ measures the fraction of extra costs, resulting from tariffs or shipment outlays, that an exporter has to bear in order to deliver a product to the foreign country. From this specification it is possible to compute operating profits from serving only the domestic market as a function of productivity, denoted $\pi_d(\theta)$, and the combined profits both from serving the domestic market and from exporting (net of the fixed costs of production and exporting) as a function of productivity, denoted $\pi_{d+x}(\theta)$. As a result, the highest attainable profit level as a function of productivity is $\pi(\theta) = max\{0, \pi_d(\theta), \pi_{d+x}(\theta)\}$, and the free-entry condition is

$$\int_0^\infty \pi(\theta) dG(\theta) = f_e. \tag{3.2}$$

It is clear from this exposition that if the lowest value of θ in the support of $G(\cdot)$ is low enough, then there exists a productivity cut-off θ_d – the domestic cut-off – at which $\pi_d(\theta_d) = 0$, that is, firms with this productivity break even when serving the domestic market only. Firms with productivity above this cut-off have no reason to leave the industry, because they make profits after entry. In addition, whenever $\tau^{\varepsilon - 1} f_x > f_d$, there also exists an export cut-off, θ_x, at which profits from serving the domestic market just equal profits both from serving the domestic market and from exporting, that is, $\pi_d(\theta_x) = \pi_{d+x}(\theta_x)$, such that $\theta_x > \theta_d$. In these circumstances the optimal strategies of firms are represented in Figure 3.1: the lowest productivity firms, with $\theta < \theta_d$, exit the industry, those with productivity $\theta_d < \theta < \theta_x$ stay and serve only the domestic market, and those with $\theta > \theta_x$ stay and serve both the domestic and the foreign market.

This sorting pattern is consistent with the evidence. First, only a fraction of firms export. Second, exporters sell only a portion of their output to foreign customers. Third, exporters are more productive and larger than non-exporters.[11] And finally, the distribution of export sales is skewed toward larger firms. This analysis offers a simple explanation of these patterns in the data, but it does not explain why exporters pay higher wages than non-exporters, because it assumes that the labour market is competitive, and therefore all firms pay the same wages. As a result, there is no wage inequality among workers.

This framework is also useful for understanding episodes of trade liberalization. Bela Balassa (1966, 1967) was the first to note that the formation of the European Common Market did not lead to major reallocations of resources across industries, as would be predicted by traditional Ricardian or Heckscher–Ohlin trade theory, but rather to large

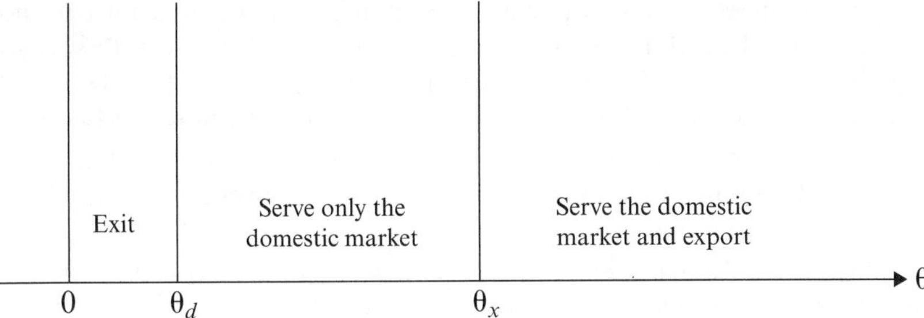

Figure 3.1 Optimal strategies for firms with different productivity levels

reallocations within industries. More recent studies of trade liberalization, which use detailed firm-level data – such as Tybout and Westbrook (1995) for Mexico, Pavcnik (2002) for Chile, and Trefler (2004) for Canada – find large market share reallocations within industries from low- to high-productivity firms, and the exit of low-productivity firms.

To see how the Melitz model can explain these findings, consider a reduction in τ. This raises profits from export sales, which leads to an expansion of output by exporters, and thereby to a shift in market share from firms that do not export to exporters. The expansion of exporting firms raises demand for domestic factors of production and leads to a hike in wages relative to product prices, thereby reducing the profitability of all firms, exporters and non-exporters alike. As a result, the profits of non-exporters decline, and those that are least productive and barely breaking even lose money after trade liberalization and exit the industry. On the other side, while higher input costs reduce the profits of exporters, this reduction is not sufficient to fully offset the initial rise in their profitability as a result of the decline in variable trade costs. Therefore, the final outcome is the exit of the least productive firms and market share reallocation from low-productivity domestic firms to high-productivity exporters. This reallocation of resources within the industry raises the industry's average productivity.

I will use these insights in the analysis of the interdependence of countries with different levels of labour market frictions. But first I discuss the nature of the labour market frictions that will be used in this analysis.

SEARCH AND MATCHING FRICTIONS IN LABOUR MARKETS

To understand the relationship between trade and unemployment, it is necessary to explicitly formulate frictions that lead to unemployment in the first place. For this purpose, Helpman and Itskhoki (2010) and Helpman et al. (2010a, 2010b) use the Diamond–Mortensen–Pissarides search and matching framework for labour markets, which is described in detail in Pissarides (2000). While the Diamond–Mortensen–Pissarides framework is dynamic, it was adapted to static models in the Helpman–Itskhoki–Redding studies. Our static framework, however, represents the steady state of a dynamic model.

Imagine a labour market in which workers match with firms, and the number of successful matches depends on how many workers search for jobs and how many vacancies are posted by firms. The more workers search for jobs or the more vacancies are posted, the larger the number of successful matches. This relationship is represented by a matching function, assumed to take the Cobb–Douglas form

$$H = mV^{\chi}N^{1-\chi},\ 0 < \chi < 1,$$

where H is the number of successful matches, V the number of vacancies, and N the number of workers searching for jobs. The parameter m measures the efficiency of the matching processes, while χ measures the weight of vacancies in the matching function. In this representation, the details of the matching process are not spelled out, yet the matching function is assumed to represent the outcome of this process. This choice of functional form is not arbitrary, however, because it fits the data well.

In the dynamic version of the model, V and N are stocks while H is a flow. As a result, the ratio H/N is a hazard rate, representing the instantaneous probability (per unit time) that a worker finds employment. In the static version of the model to be considered here, H/N simply represents the probability that a worker finds employment, and I treat this probability as a measure of labour market tightness, to be denoted by x. Similarly, the probability that a firm that posts a vacancy finds a worker equals H/V. Therefore, if υ denotes the cost of posting a vacancy, then the expected cost of hiring a worker is $b \equiv \upsilon V/H$, that is, it equals the cost of a vacancy divided by the probability of finding a worker per vacancy posted. b is the cost of hiring, and the matching function implies that it equals

$$b = \tfrac{1}{2}ax^{\alpha},\ \text{where}\ a \equiv \frac{2v}{m^{1+\alpha}}\ \text{and}\ \alpha \equiv (1-\chi)/\chi. \tag{3.3}$$

The derived parameter a summarizes labour market frictions; it rises with the cost of posting vacancies, υ, and declines with the efficiency of the matching process, m. In an economy with multiple sectors, equation (3.3) is sector specific; it represents a relationship between the tightness of the sector's labour market and the sector's cost of hiring.

Workers choose in which sector to search for jobs. Once a worker has committed to a sector, however, his or her chance of being matched with a firm equals the ratio of the number of workers hired in the sector, H, to the number of workers searching for jobs in this sector, N. The probability that a firm fills a posted vacancy equals the sectoral ratio H/V. I allow both the cost of vacancies, υ, and the efficiency of matching, m, to vary across sectors, but – for simplicity – assume that χ is the same in every industry, and therefore so is α. In these circumstances, the measure of labour market frictions, a, also varies across sectors, reflecting differences in the efficiency of matching and vacancy costs.

As described above, a worker chooses in which sector to search for a job, and the probability of finding employment may differ across sectors. In addition, the wage rate may differ across sectors. Therefore, risk-neutral workers choose to search for work in the sector that yields the highest expected wage rate.[12] For now, assume that being matched with a firm secures employment and that all employed workers in a sector are paid the same wage rate (as will be the case in the next section, but not in the one after). Then a worker chooses the sector with the highest value of xw, where x is the sector's labour market tightness and w is the sector's wage rate. In equilibrium, xw obtains the same value in all sectors in which workers search for jobs. In other words, there exists an expected income ω that represents the outside option of a worker who chooses in which sector to search for a job, and in equilibrium

$$xw = \omega \tag{3.4}$$

in every sector with a positive number of workers.[13] After the matching process ends, every firm bargains with its workers over wages.

TRADE AND INTERDEPENDENCE

In this section I describe a number of results on trade and interdependence that are developed in Helpman and Itskhoki (2010). Their model features two countries that are alike except for frictions in their labour markets. There are two sectors, one producing a homogeneous product under constant returns to scale – with one unit of output per worker – the other producing varieties of a differentiated product. Each sector has labour market frictions of the type described in the previous section, with the coefficient a varying across sectors and countries. The countries are indexed by A and B; a_{0j} denotes the coefficient of labour market frictions in the homogeneous sector of country j, and a_j denotes the coefficient of labour market frictions in the differentiated sector of country j. For clarity, it is assumed that $a_A / a_{0A} > a_B / a_{0B}$, so that country B has relatively lower labour market frictions in the differentiated sector. This implies $b_A > b_B$; that is, the cost of hiring in the differentiated sector is larger in country A, as I explain below. The homogeneous sector serves as numeraire, so that the price of the homogeneous product equals 1 and all costs are measured in units of this good.

Every country is populated by a continuum of representative families, with each family having a continuum of members who are workers. A family's preferences are quasi-linear, with the marginal utility of the homogeneous good being constant and equal to one. As a result, families are risk-neutral and each family allocates its workers across sectors to maximize the family's income, which is not random because of the law of large numbers.[14]

In the homogeneous sector, every firm matches with a single worker, and firms enter the industry until the expected profits equal the entry cost, with the latter being the cost of posting a vacancy, υ_0. When a worker and a firm match, they split equally the surplus from the relationship, which equals 1. As a result, the wage rate equals 1/2 in the homogeneous sector and so does the cost of hiring, that is, $w_{0j} = b_{0j} = 1/2$. In these circumstances, the free-entry condition pins down uniquely the level of tightness in the sector's labour market, $x_{0j} = a_{0j}^{-1/\alpha}$, and therefore the outside option of workers searching for jobs in the differentiated sector is $\omega = a_{0j}^{-1/\alpha}/2$. In other words, the higher the frictions in the homogeneous sector's labour market are, the worse is the outside option of workers searching for jobs in the differentiated sector. Using this value of ω, equations (3.3) and (3.4) provide solutions to the hiring cost and market tightness in the differentiated sector. Note that b_j and x_j depend on labour market frictions but not on trade frictions. As a result, both a closed and an open economy have equally tight labour markets, the same hiring costs, and the same wage rates, measured in units of the homogeneous good. Real wages are not the same in a closed and an open economy, however, as argued below.

The differentiated sector is structured in the same way as in the model described in the section on heterogeneous firms within industries, except for the labour market frictions. In particular, firms enter the industry after bearing a fixed entry cost, f_e. On entry, a firm learns its productivity level θ that is drawn from a known distribution, $G(\theta)$. Once it knows its productivity, it has to decide whether to stay in the industry and bear the fixed cost of production, f_d, or exit. Should it decide to stay, it has to choose whether to serve only the domestic market or to serve both the domestic and foreign markets. Exporting requires it to bear the fixed cost, f_x, and the variable trade cost, τ. After deciding on its strategy, which includes the export status, a firm posts vacancies in order to be matched with h workers. The search and matching process in the labour market implies that the cost of being matched with these workers is $b_j h$ in country j. After hiring the workers, a firm engages in multilateral bargaining with them in the manner proposed by Lars Stole and Jeffrey Zwiebel (1996a, 1996b). This bargaining game yields a solution in which the wage rate equals a fixed fraction of revenue per worker, where this fraction depends on the elasticity of substitution between brands of the differentiated product. Anticipating this equilibrium wage structure, a profit-maximizing firm chooses employment h up to the point at which it pays a wage rate equal to the hiring cost, b_j. As a result, similar to the simpler model discussed in the heterogeneous firms section, all firms pay the same wage rate – independently of their productivity or export status – despite the fact that wages are determined in a different manner. The domestic cut-off, θ_d, and the export cut-off, θ_x, are determined in the same way as in the earlier section, and the free-entry condition – that expected profits equal the entry cost, f_e – is also similar (see (3.2)).

Helpman and Itskhoki (2010) use this general equilibrium model of two countries to derive results on the impact of labour market and trade frictions on trade flows, productivity, welfare and unemployment. In this framework country j's unemployment rate equals the weighted average of its sectoral rates of unemployment, $1 - x_0$ and $1 - x$, expressed as

$$u_j = \frac{N_{0j}}{\overline{N}_j}(1 - x_{0j}) + \frac{N_j}{\overline{N}_j}(1 - x_j), \tag{3.5}$$

where N_{0j} is the number of workers searching for jobs in the homogeneous sector, N_j is the number of workers searching for jobs in the differentiated sector, and $\overline{N}_j = N_{0j} + N_j$ is the total number of workers in this country.

First, a larger fraction of differentiated-sector firms export in country B, which has the smaller hiring cost (that is, $b_A > b_B$). Moreover, country B is a net exporter of differentiated products and imports homogeneous goods.[15] In addition, the share of intra-industry trade is smaller the larger the ratio b_A/b_B, that is, the larger the proportional difference in the differentiated sectors' hiring costs.

Second, differentiated-sector total factor productivity is higher in every trade equilibrium than in autarky, as in Melitz (2003). Furthermore, if the productivity θ is distributed Pareto, then TFP is higher in country B's differentiated sector than in A's. Sectoral productivity in the differentiated sector is sensitive to labour market frictions. In particular, a decline in a_j raises this productivity in country j but reduces it in the trade-partner country. In other words, if labour market frictions decline in the differentiated sector of a country, that country enjoys higher total factor productivity, but this generates a negative productivity shock in the trade-partner country.

Third, despite the labour market frictions, both countries gain from trade, but a country's welfare level depends on labour market frictions in its trade-partner country in addition to its own. On the one hand, a reduction in labour market frictions in country j's differentiated sector raises its welfare and reduces the welfare level of its trade partner. This negative transmission is related to the negative transmission of productivity discussed above. On the other hand, a simultaneous proportional reduction in labour market frictions in the differentiated sectors of both countries raises welfare in both of them. This suggests that labour market reforms may turn into beggar-thy-neighbour policies unless they are coordinated across countries. In addition, a reduction in labour market frictions in country j at a common rate in both sectors raises its welfare and does not affect the welfare level of its trade partner. A reduction in trade impediments raises welfare in both countries.

Fourth, in a symmetric world economy in which a_0 and a are the same in both countries, a reduction in labour market frictions in the differentiated sectors at the same rate in both countries reduces aggregate unemployment if and only if a is sufficiently small relative to a_0, and raises unemployment otherwise. In this case, lower frictions reduce the sectoral rates of unemployment (by raising x_0 and x), but they also reallocate labour to the differentiated sector, which raises aggregate unemployment when $a > a_0$ (see (3.5)). The former effect dominates when a is sufficiently small relative to a_0, and unemployment necessarily declines when $a < a_0$. Moreover, a reduction in labour market frictions at a common rate in both sectors and both countries reduces aggregate unemployment. Finally, a reduction in trade impediments – including the opening of trade – raises aggregate unemployment if and only if $a > a_0$, because it reallocates labour toward the differentiated sector, and trade does not impact the sectoral rates of unemployment.

When the countries are not symmetric, richer patterns of unemployment emerge in equilibrium. In particular, the rate of unemployment can be higher in either country A or country B. For example, the rate of unemployment may rise in both countries in response to higher labour market frictions in country A, or it may rise in B and decline in A.

It follows from this analysis that while trade may raise unemployment (which happens when labour market frictions are higher in the differentiated sector), it always raises welfare. Moreover, unemployment does not reflect welfare in the cross section; the country with higher welfare may have higher or lower unemployment. And importantly, uncoordinated reductions in labour market frictions in one country only, while benefiting the reforming country, hurt the trade partner.

The last result has a bearing on the debate about labour market policies in the European Union. In October 1997, the EU amended its governing agreement by the Treaty of Amsterdam, which made employment policies a priority. In November 1997, the extraordinary European Council meeting in Luxembourg launched the European Employment Strategy. Two-and-a-half years later, during the European Council meeting in Lisbon in March 2000, the heads of state launched the Lisbon Agenda, designed for the EU 'to become the most competitive and dynamic knowledge-based economy in the world'. What exactly should the European Union do in order to achieve these objectives? As an example, the UK has been concerned with lack of labour market flexibility in countries such as France and Spain, and it has been promoting labour market reforms. Our results suggest that unilateral labour market reforms in, say, France, may not benefit the UK. But coordinated reductions in labour market frictions can benefit every country.

INEQUALITY

In the previous section wages differ across sectors but not across firms or workers within a sector. Moreover, all firms employ the same composition of workers, who are perfect substitutes for each other. In the data, however, substantial differences exist in workforce composition across firms of different size, there is large variation in wages of workers with the same observed characteristics, larger firms pay higher wages, and exporters pay an export wage premium (that is, they pay a higher wage than a non-exporter with the same productivity would pay). As a result, there is substantial wage inequality within industries, and this inequality varies across sectors. To address these issues, Helpman et al. (2010b) extend the analytical framework from the previous section and provide an analysis of the determinants of both unemployment and wage inequality within industries. In what follows, I report some of their findings, focusing on equilibrium outcomes within a sector for the case of a single type of risk-neutral worker.[16]

Instead of workers being identical, as in the previous section, now assume that workers are perfect substitutes for each other in the homogeneous product sector, but that in the differentiated product sector they are identical ex ante but not ex post. In particular, suppose that when a worker is matched with a firm in the differentiated sector, the quality of the match is random, with a representing the realized ability of the worker on the job in the firm. The ability level, a, is drawn from the Pareto distribution $F(a) = 1 - (a_{min}/a)^k$ for $a \geq a_{min} > 0$, $k > 1$, and these draws are independent across firms and individuals. Importantly, the ability level, a, is observed neither by individual workers nor by their employers. In this event, all firms have the same composition of workers if they do not screen job candidates. Since, however, as will soon become clear, the ability distribution of the workforce impacts a firm's overall productivity, firms have an incentive to screen job candidates. To this end, they have an imperfect screening technology that allows a firm to determine only whether the ability of a worker is above or below a threshold, a_c, but this technology is costly to implement, with the cost being ca_c^δ / δ units of the homogeneous good. In other words, higher ability thresholds are more costly to administer, but the higher the threshold $a_c > a_{min}$, the higher the average ability of the firm's workforce if it retains only workers above the screening threshold.[17]

For the following analysis, also assume that the distribution of a firm's productivity is Pareto, given by $G(\theta) = 1 - (\theta_{min} / \theta)^z$ for $\theta \geq \theta_{min} > 0$ and $z > 1$, and that the production function is

$$y = \theta h^\gamma \bar{a}, 0 < \gamma < 1 \tag{3.6}$$

instead of (3.1), where $\bar{a}$ is the average ability of the firm's workers. In this specification, output is larger the more productive the firm, the higher the average ability of its employees, and the more workers it employs. An important feature of this production function is complementarity between the ability levels of workers: the higher the average ability of the workforce, the higher the marginal product of a worker. Every employee contributes to output both through the employment level, h, and through the average ability, $\bar{a}$. For this reason, adding a worker with below-average ability to the pool of employees raises output through h, but reduces it through $\bar{a}$. For a given pool of potential employees with whom a firm is matched, output rises with the threshold a_c when $\gamma k < 1$. In other words, in this case, dropping the least able workers raises output, because the gain in average ability $\bar{a}$ exceeds the loss in the employment level h. In such circumstances, a firm has an incentive to engage in costly screening.

In this setup, the cost of matching with l workers is bl. After being matched with l workers, a firm chooses a screening threshold $a_c \geq a_{min}$ and hires only workers with ability a above the threshold. The resulting employment level is $h = (a_{min} / a_c)^k l$, and the firm bargains with the h workers over wages. At this stage, the firm knows that every worker has ability above a_c, but it does not know the ability level of each individual worker. This leads to an equilibrium wage that is the same for every worker in the firm. Stole–Zwiebel multilateral bargaining implies that the wage rate is again a fraction of the revenue per worker, except that now this fraction depends both on the elasticity of substitution between brands of the differentiated product and on the parameter γ from the production function (3.6).

As in Melitz (2003), profit-maximizing firms sort into sales strategies by productivity, as described in Figure 3.1: the least productive firms exit, the most productive firms export, and the firms with productivity between θ_d and θ_x serve only the domestic market. Unlike Melitz (2003), however, wages differ across firms. In equilibrium

$$\frac{w(\theta)h(\theta)}{l(\theta)} = b,$$

where $w(\theta)$ is the wage rate in a firm with productivity θ, $l(\theta)$ the number of workers it chooses to match with, and $h(\theta)$ its employment level. Consistent with the data, more productive firms match with more workers, employ more workers, have a better workforce composition (meaning they are more selective in hiring), and pay higher wages, including an export wage premium. Risk-neutral workers are indifferent between being matched with a high- or low-productivity firm, because conditional on being matched, the expected wage is the same in all firms. In other words, workers matched with a firm of productivity θ are hired with probability $h(\theta)/l(\theta)$, and if hired, they receive the wage rate $w(\theta)$, which implies that the expected wage rate equals b.

Now workers can be unemployed for two reasons. First, they may not be matched with a firm. Second, even if matched with a firm, their match-specific ability a may fall below the firm's cut-off a_c, in which case they are not hired. As a result, the sectoral rate of unemployment is not $1 - x$, but rather $1 - \sigma x$, where σ is the industry's average hiring rate $h(\theta)/l(\theta)$.

In this framework, sectoral wage inequality is larger in the open economy than in the closed economy, as long as only a fraction of firms export (that is, as long as $\theta_x > \theta_d$). When all firms export, wage inequality in the open economy is the same as in the closed economy. This implies that rising trade costs may generate non-monotonic responses of wage inequality. In particular, wage inequality within an industry may rise initially with the trade cost and decline with further increases in the trade cost. This is necessarily the case when the fixed export cost f_x rises, but may also be the case when the variable trade cost τ rises.[18]

When ω is invariant to trade (as in the previous section), sectoral unemployment is strictly higher in the open economy than in the closed economy, because exporters are more selective in their hiring than non-exporters.[19] Nevertheless, every worker's ex ante welfare is higher in the open economy than in the closed economy. In other words, workers gain from trade despite the fact that they face more income risk and higher unemployment in the open economy.[20]

Interestingly, trade differentially impacts matches with different abilities a. Helpman et al. (2010a) show that the rate of unemployment of workers with match-specific ability a, $u(a)$, is decreasing in a for all $a \geq a_d$. When an economy opens to trade, unemployment rises for every ability level, but it rises most for medium-ability workers and least for high-ability workers.

The distribution of wages conditional on a, measured in units of the homogeneous good, implies that both average wages and wage inequality are higher for workers with higher ability. Trade, however, affects wage distributions differently for workers with diverse abilities. For low values of a, the conditional wage distribution is the same in autarky and in the trade equilibrium. For high values of a, the conditional wage distribution in the open economy first-order stochastically dominates the conditional wage distribution in the closed economy. For intermediate values of a, the conditional wage distribution in the open economy is first-order stochastically dominated by the wage distribution in the closed economy. It follows that medium-ability workers are the least fortunate when trade opens up, in terms of both wage gains and unemployment. This results from the fact that trade leads to the loss of job opportunities for workers with intermediate ability levels in high-productivity firms, which become exporters. The lowest-productivity workers are not employed by high-productivity firms in the closed as well as open economies, while the highest-productivity workers are employed by high-productivity firms in both the closed and open economies, and therefore the middle range of abilities suffers a relative disadvantage from trade.

The results on the variation in unemployment and wage distributions across workers with different match-specific ability levels imply that average wages and unemployment rates are negatively correlated in the cross section. Figure 3.2 illustrates this relationship in a closed and open economy across quantiles of the wage distribution (with the same number of workers in every quantile). When the economy opens to trade, the largest increase in unemployment takes place among workers with the lowest average wages.

International trade makes trading countries interdependent, which impacts unemployment and inequality. New research that emphasizes firm heterogeneity within industries provides a suitable framework for studying the determinants of trade and foreign direct investment, as well as interdependence across countries in rates of unemployment and income inequality. I have reviewed in this chapter recent research that incorporates

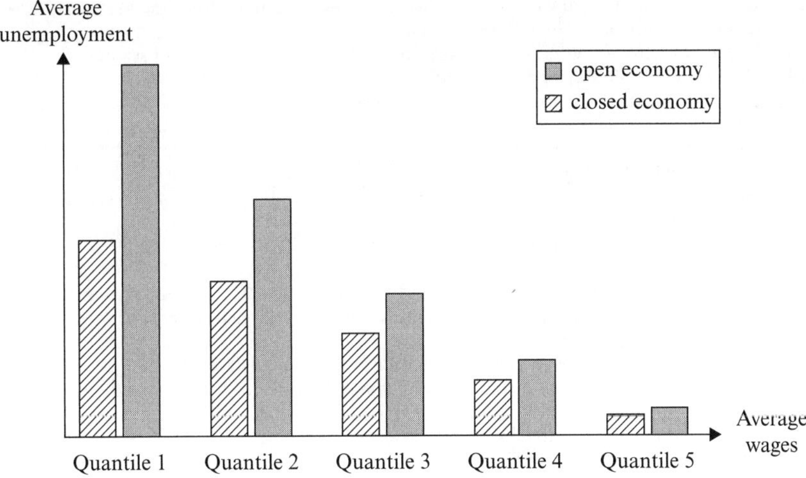

Figure 3.2 Average unemployment across wage quantiles

labour market frictions and worker heterogeneity into this framework in order to address these issues. The new models capture important features of the data and provide a suitable framework for studying trade and labour market policies.

NOTES

1. I thank Oleg Itskhoki and Stephen Redding for comments, Jane Trahan for editorial assistance, and the National Science Foundation for financial support.
2. See Helpman (2006) for a review of this literature.
3. Nunn (2007) in particular finds that the quality of legal institutions is at least as important as human capital in explaining the structure of exports.
4. See Baldwin and Gu (2003) for Canada; Clerides et al. (1998) for Colombia, Mexico and Morocco; Bernard et al. (2003) and Eaton et al. (2004) for France; Delgado et al. (2002) for Spain; and Aw et al. (2000) for Taiwan.
5. See Roberts and Tybout (1997) for Colombia and Bernard and Jensen (2004) for the United States.
6. See Bernard et al. (2007, Table 3) for estimates with industry fixed effects.
7. See Bernard et al. (2007, Table 2).
8. See Helpman et al. (2004) for multiple countries with FDI, and Helpman et al. (2008) for multiple countries and the choice of exporting to only some of them.
9. Constant elasticity of substitution
10. Melitz (2003) analyses a dynamic model, while I use a static version in this chapter. For this reason, I do not distinguish between fixed costs and the sunk cost of entry.
11. They are larger because higher-productivity firms employ more workers, produce more goods, and thus have higher revenue.

12. I focus on risk-neutral workers. See, however, the Appendix in Helpman and Itskhoki (2009) for a formulation with risk-averse individuals.
13. In this equation x and w are sector-specific while ω is the same for all sectors.
14. See, however, the Appendix in Helpman and Itskhoki (2009) for a treatment of risk-averse workers.
15. Davidson et al. (1999) were the first to point out that across-country differences in labour market frictions of the Diamond–Mortensen–Pissarides type can be a source of comparative advantage.
16. Helpman et al. (2010b) also discuss the case of multiple types of workers, risk-averse workers, and general equilibrium interactions.
17. The Pareto distribution implies that the average ability of these workers is $\bar{a} = ka_c / (k - 1)$.
18. It is also possible for wage inequality to be rising in the variable trade cost everywhere when $f_x > f_d$, but wage inequality as a function of the variable trade cost has an inverted-U shape when $f_x < f_d$.
19. I focus here on the case of a constant ω. In many cases, however, ω changes with trade, and then a general equilibrium analysis is required in order to assess the impact of trade on workers' expected income. See Helpman et al. (2010b) for a discussion of such general equilibrium feedbacks.
20. This result also holds when workers are risk averse, but the relative measure of risk aversion is low.

REFERENCES

Aw, Bee-Yan, Sukkyun Chung and Mark J. Roberts (2000), 'Productivity and turnover in the export market: micro-level evidence from the Republic of Korea and Taiwan (China)', *World Bank Economic Review*, **14**, pp. 65–90.

Balassa, Bela (1966), 'Tariff reductions and trade in manufactures among the industrial countries', *American Economic Review*, **56**, pp. 466–73.

Balassa, Bela (1967), *Trade Liberalization Among Industrial Countries*, New York: McGraw-Hill Book Company.

Baldwin, John R. and Wulong Gu (2003), 'Export market participation and productivity performance in Canadian manufacturing', *Canadian Journal of Economics*, **36**, pp. 634–57.

Bernard, Andrew B., Jonathan Eaton, J. Bradford Jensen and Samuel Kortum (2003), 'Plants and productivity in international trade', *American Economic Review*, **93**, pp. 1268–90.

Bernard, Andrew B., J. Bradford Jensen and Robert Z. Lawrence (1995), 'Exporters, jobs, and wages in U.S. manufacturing, 1976–1987', *Brookings Papers on Economic Activity, Microeconomics*, pp. 67–119.

Bernard, Andrew B. and J. Bradford Jensen (1999), 'Exceptional exporter performance: cause, effect, or both?', *Journal of International Economics*, **47**, pp. 1–25.

Bernard, Andrew B. and J. Bradford Jensen (2004), 'Why some firms export', *Review of Economics and Statistics*, **86**, pp. 561–9.

Bernard, Andrew B., J. Bradford Jensen, Stephen J. Redding and Peter K. Schott (2007), 'Firms in international trade', *Journal of Economic Perspectives*, **21**, pp. 105–30.

Clerides, Sofronis K., Saul Lach and James R. Tybout (1998), 'Is learning by exporting important? Micro-dynamic evidence from Colombia, Mexico, and Morocco', *Quarterly Journal of Economics*, **113**, pp. 903–47.

Cuñat, Alejandro and Marc Melitz (2007), 'Volatility, labor market flexibility, and the pattern of comparative advantage', NBER Working Paper No. 13062.

Das, Sanghamitra, Mark J. Roberts and James R. Tybout (2007), 'Market entry costs, producer heterogeneity, and export dynamics', *Econometrica*, **75**, pp. 837–73.

Davidson, Carl, Lawrence Martin and Steven Matusz (1999), 'Trade and search generated unemployment', *Journal of International Economics*, **48**, pp. 271–99.

Delgado, Miguel A., Jose C. Fariñas and Sonia Ruano (2002), 'Firm productivity and export markets: a non-parametric approach', *Journal of International Economics*, **57**, pp. 397–422.

Diamond, Peter A. (1982a), 'Demand management in search equilibrium', *Journal of Political Economy*, **90**, pp. 881–94.

Diamond, Peter A. (1982b), 'Wage determination and efficiency in search equilibrium', *Review of Economic Studies*, **49**, pp. 217–27.

Eaton, Jonathan, Samuel Kortum and Francis Kramarz (2004), 'Dissecting trade: firms, industries, and export destination', *American Economic Review (Papers and Proceedings)*, **94**, pp. 150–54.

Helpman, Elhanan (2006), 'Trade, FDI, and the organization of firms', *Journal of Economic Literature*, **XLIV**, pp. 589–630.

Helpman, Elhanan and Oleg Itskhoki (2010), 'Labor market rigidities, trade and unemployment', *Review of Economic Studies*, **77**, pp. 1100–137.

Helpman, Elhanan, Oleg Itskhoki and Stephen Redding (2010a), 'Unequal effects of trade on workers with different abilities', *Journal of the European Economic Association*, **8**, pp. 456–660.

Helpman, Elhanan, Oleg Itskhoki and Stephen Redding (2010b), 'Inequality and unemployment in a global economy', *Econometrica*, forthcoming.

Helpman, Elhanan, Marc Melitz and Yona Rubinstein (2008), 'Trading partners and trading volumes', *Quarterly Journal of Economics*, **123**, pp. 441–87.

Helpman, Elhanan, Marc J. Melitz and Stephen R. Yeaple (2004), 'Export versus FDI with heterogeneous firms', *American Economic Review*, **94**, pp. 300–316.

Manova, Kalina (2008), 'Credit constraints, equity market liberalizations and international trade', *Journal of International Economics*, **76**, pp. 33–47.

Manova, Kalina (2009), 'Credit constraints, heterogeneous firms and international trade', mimeo, Stanford University, Stanford, CA.

Melitz, Marc J. (2003), 'The impact of trade on intra-industry reallocations and aggregate industry productivity', *Econometrica*, **71**, pp. 1695–725.

Mortensen, Dale T. and Christopher A. Pissarides (1994), 'Job creation and job destruction in the theory of unemployment', *Review of Economic Studies*, **61**, pp. 397–415.

Nunn, Nathan (2007), 'Relationship-specificity, incomplete contracts, and the pattern of trade', *Quarterly Journal of Economics*, **CXXII**, pp. 569–600.

Pavcnik, Nina (2002), 'Trade liberalization, exit, and productivity improvements: evidence from Chilean plants', *Review of Economic Studies*, **69**, pp. 245–76.

Pissarides, Christopher A. (2000), *Equilibrium Unemployment Theory*, 2nd edn, Cambridge, MA: The MIT Press.

Roberts, Mark J. and James R. Tybout (1997), 'The decision to export in Colombia: an empirical model of entry with sunk costs', *American Economic Review*, **87**, pp. 545–64.

Stole, Lars A. and Jeffrey Zwiebel (1996a), 'Organizational design and technology choice under intrafirm bargaining', *American Economic Review*, **86**, pp. 195–222.

Stole, Lars A. and Jeffrey Zwiebel (1996b), 'Intra-firm bargaining under non-binding contracts', *Review of Economic Studies*, **63**, pp. 375–410.

Trefler, Daniel (2004), 'The long and short of the Canada–U.S. free trade agreement', *American Economic Review*, **94**, pp. 870–95.

Tybout, James R. and M. Daniel Westbrook (1995), 'Trade liberalization and the dimensions of efficiency changes in Mexican manufacturing industries', *Journal of International Economics*, **39**, pp. 53–78.

World Trade Organization (2008), *World Trade Report 2008: Transnational Corporations, and the Infrastructure Challenge*, Geneva: World Trade Organization.

4. Exports of knowledge-intensive services and manufactures: the role of ICTs and intersectoral linkages

Valentina Meliciani

INTRODUCTION

The last 20 years have seen deep transformations in the factors affecting countries' international competitiveness. The information and communication technology (ICT) revolution has transformed modes of production and internationalization in both the manufacturing and service sectors. ICT has affected the linkages between manufacturing and service industries by increasing the service content of many manufacturing activities and by facilitating the 'splintering' away of activities once performed inside manufacturing firms. Consequently, the production and export of manufactures and services have become increasingly interrelated, and this is particularly true in knowledge-intensive sectors. Joseph Francis Francois (1990) has highlighted the role of producer services in the linkage, coordination and control of specialized interrelated operations, thus associating their growth with expanded opportunities for trade. Recent studies have also shown that knowledge-intensive services are in high demand as intermediate inputs by high-technology manufacturing industries (Guerrieri and Meliciani, 2005; Francois and Woerz, 2008).

These strong linkages may affect international competitiveness in both manufacturing and service industries. A flourishing literature has shown the role of business services for economic growth and technology diffusion (see among others, Kox and Rubalcaba, 2007), while only a few studies have investigated their impact on international competitiveness in manufacturing industries (Francois and Woerz, 2008; Wolfmayr, 2008) and in service industries (Guerrieri and Meliciani, 2005).

If services and manufactures are not substitutes but complements, specialization in knowledge-intensive services can have a positive impact on international competitiveness in knowledge-intensive manufacturing industries. At the same time, intersectoral linkages between manufacturing and service sectors may affect countries' international competitiveness in services. In fact, a large share of activities in high-tech manufacturing industries may result in a high demand for knowledge-intensive services, thus stimulating their production and export. In other words, there can be a 'home market effect' not based on final demand, but on intermediate demand (supporting evidence for this hypothesis is found in Guerrieri and Meliciani, 2005).

The first novelty of this chapter lies in its study of the role of intersectoral linkages in order to identify the dynamics of export shares in knowledge-intensive manufacturing and services sectors.

The internationalization of knowledge-intensive services has been favoured by the development and diffusion of ICTs. Because of their ample range of applications, these technologies have become central to many industries of the economy and have had a growing impact on the organization of economic activity. While empirical studies on the impact of ICTs on productivity and growth have flourished, there is little research on the relationship between ICTs and international competitiveness.

Recently, Keld Laursen and Valentina Meliciani (2010) found that ICT-related domestic and foreign knowledge flows affect international competitiveness in ICT industries, while only domestic flows have a positive impact on export shares in non-ICT industries. The study by Laursen and Meliciani uses publications in ICT-related scientific fields and attributes them to a particular industry by means of a science-relevance matrix constructed by Keld Laursen and Ammon Salter (2005). Because of data availability, the study considered only manufacturing industries. ICTs may, however, also strongly affect international competitiveness in the services industries not only by increasing their tradability, but also because they have a central role in service firms' innovation activities (see Evangelista, 2000).

The second novelty of this chapter is that it looks at how ICTs affect the dynamics of export market shares in both knowledge-intensive services and manufacturing industries. In particular, I adopt the technology-gap approach to trade (Posner, 1961; Krugman, 1985; Dosi et al., 1990) to study the role of ICTs and intersectoral linkages for the dynamics of sectoral export shares in knowledge-intensive manufacturing and service industries for a sample of 12 countries over the period 1981–2003.

The following section reviews the literature on trade in goods and trade in services and discusses the role of ICTs and intersectoral linkages. The third section presents the empirical model and the econometric methodology, which is followed by a report of the descriptive statistics in the next section. The fifth section gives the results of the estimation, and the last section concludes the chapter.

REVIEW OF THE LITERATURE

The Determinants of Trade in Goods and Trade in Services

Most empirical studies and analyses of international trade have been confined to trade in goods. One reason is that services have been mainly regarded as non-tradable because of their intangibility and the need for simultaneity between production and consumption. Another reason has been the lack of internationally comparable cross-country and cross-industry databases on trade in services. Recently, many studies have emphasized that, as a result of technological developments in telecommunications and information technology, the physical proximity requirement in the delivery of services has been reduced, enhancing their tradability. In fact, empirical evidence suggests that trade in services has grown even faster than trade in goods (WTO, 2008). Moreover, the availability of OECD data on trade in services by industry has stimulated research in this area.

Most of the analyses devoted to explain trade in services have adopted the gravity model also used to explain trade in goods (Grünfeld and Moxnes, 2003; Kimura and Lee, 2004; Mirza and Nicoletti, 2004). In particular, Leo A. Grünfeld and Andreas Moxnes (2003) find that there are strong links between service foreign direct investment (FDI) and trade, since a large proportion of trade is facilitated through foreign affiliate sales, while trade barriers and corruption in the importing country have a strong negative impact on service trade and foreign affiliate sales. Fukunari Kimura and Hyun-Hoon Lee (2004) find that the gravity equation for services trade is as robust as the gravity equation for goods trade, and that geographical distance is more important for services trade than for goods trade. Daniel Mirza and Giuseppe Nicoletti (2004) point out that a unique feature of services trade is that the traded service must use inputs interactively from both the exporting and the importing countries. They find that labour costs and infrastructure supply (in transport and telecommunications) in both countries affect interactively bilateral trade in services. Through using alternative indicators of product market regulation provided by the Organisation for Economic Co-operation and Development (OECD), they also show that restrictive regulations in importing and exporting countries have symmetric negative effects on bilateral services exports.

While empirical studies on trade in services are limited, empirical analyses on the determinants of trade in goods have flourished. A robust result of these studies is that technological factors are at least as important as price factors in explaining countries' international competitiveness.[1] This result is consistent with both new trade theory models (Helpman and Krugman, 1985; Krugman, 1989) and with the 'technology-gap' approach to trade (Posner, 1961; Soete, 1981; Dosi et al., 1990). Moreover, in high-technology sectors competitive advantages in technology appear to be particularly significant (Amable and Verspagen, 1995; Laursen and Meliciani, 2000).

In this chapter, I adopt the technology-gap approach to explain trade in both the knowledge-intensive manufacturing and the services sectors.[2] The main novelty of the chapter – beyond the analysis of trade in services industries – consists of its investigation of the specific role played by ICTs and intersectoral linkages for international competitiveness.

The Role of ICTs and Intersectoral Linkages

Information and communication technologies

Because of the ample range of applications of the technologies, ICTs have become central to many industries of the economy and have had a growing impact on the organization of economic activity. They can thus be considered general purpose technologies (GPTs). GPTs are radical new ideas, or techniques, that have the potential to have important impacts on many industries in an economy (Bresnahan and Trajtenberg, 1995; Helpman, 1998; Aghion et al., 2002). Timothy Bresnahan and Manuel Trajtenberg have identified three key characteristics of GPTs: (1) pervasiveness (they are used as inputs by many downstream industries), (2) technological dynamism (inherent potential for technical improvements), and (3) 'innovational complementarities' with other forms of advancement (meaning that the productivity of research and development (R&D) in downstream industries increases as a consequence of innovation in the GPT).

The recent ICT 'revolution' can be seen as one such GPT, since today, computers and related equipment are used in most industries of the economy, if not directly incorporated into ICT products or non-ICT industries. ICTs have also displayed a substantial level of technological dynamism spurring not only radical improvement in computational capacity (following Moore's Law), but also a successive wave of new technologies (ranging from the semiconductor to the Internet). Moreover, ICTs have facilitated new ways of organizing firms, including decentralized decision making, team production, and so on (Milgrom and Roberts, 1990; Brynjolfsson and Hitt, 2000; Bresnahan et al., 2002). ICTs have thus clearly exhibited innovational complementarities with other forms of advancement.

While the literature has focused on the impact of ICTs on the level (or rate of growth) of total factor productivity (TFP), labour productivity and gross domestic product (GDP) (see for instance, Jorgenson and Stiroh, 2000; Bassanini and Scarpetta, 2002; van Ark and Timmer, 2005), ICTs may also play a fundamental role for international competitiveness.

In particular, ICTs may contribute to increasing a country's exports indirectly by affecting productivity, but also directly by increasing the quality and reliability of the country's goods, and by helping to increase product variety (Laursen and Meliciani, 2010). For services – because of their intangible and information-based nature – the generation and use of ICTs have a central role in firms' innovation activities and performance (Evangelista, 2000). Finally, ICTs allow for the increased transportability of service activities by making it possible for services to be produced in one place and consumed simultaneously in another (Miozzo and Soete, 2001).

Few empirical analyses have looked at the role of ICTs for international competitiveness. At the firm level (for the German service sector), Gunter Ebling and Norbert Janz (1999) show that (firm-level) investment in ICT is a determinant of the magnitude of innovative activities, which in turn is a central determinant of firms' export performance. At the country level, Paolo Guerrieri and Valentina Meliciani (2005) find that investment in ICT has a positive impact on export market shares in producer services. Also at the aggregate level, Meliciani (2002) shows that national specialization in fast-growing technological fields (where ICTs – measured by patent statistics – are *the* fastest growing technologies) is positively associated with the rate of growth of export shares and negatively associated with the rate of growth of import shares. Finally, at the sectoral level, Laursen and Meliciani (2010) find that domestic and foreign ICT-related scientific knowledge flows have a positive and significant impact on export market shares in ICT manufacturing industries, while only domestic flows positively affect export shares in non-ICT manufacturing industries.

Thanks to the availability of a sectoral database (the EU-KLEMS database) containing data on ICT investment and ICT capital stock, I will now investigate the importance of sectoral and aggregate ICT for the dynamics of export shares in knowledge-intensive manufacturing and service sectors.

Intersectoral linkages

The growing complexity in the organization of manufacturing production and distribution resulting from the application and use of new technologies has increased the interdependence between manufacturing and services (Miozzo and Soete, 2001). Moreover, the 'splintering' away of service activities once performed inside manufacturing firms has led to a growing demand for services by those firms.

The availability of business services has, therefore, become an important factor of competitiveness, and several empirical analyses have looked at the role of domestic and imported services on productivity. Paul Windrum and Mark Tomlinson (1999), for example, find that knowledge-intensive services increase output and productivity especially in those countries where the degree of integration between services and other economic activities is high. Daniela Di Cagno and Valentina Meliciani (2005) find that technology-intensive services increase labour productivity for the whole manufacturing sector while, distinguishing among Pavitt's categories, imported services have a significant impact only in specialized supplier types of industries and domestic services in scale-intensive industries.

Few studies have looked at the role of services for international competitiveness. Yvonne Anna Wolfmayr (2008) finds that the interconnectivity between the manufacturing sectors and the service sectors (measured as the amount of service deliveries to the manufacturing sector calculated from input–output tables) has a positive and highly significant impact on export market shares in high-skilled, technology-driven industries. Joseph Francis Francois and Julia Maria Woerz (2008) show how business services are highly demanded, especially by knowledge-intensive industries. They find that there are significant and strong positive effects from increased business service openness on exports of industries such as machinery, motor vehicles, chemicals and electric equipment, supporting the notion that off-shoring of business services may promote the competitiveness of the most skill-and-technology-intensive industries in the OECD.

While only a few studies have looked at the role of services, and in particular of knowledge-intensive services, for the export of manufacturing goods, the impact of the composition of the manufacturing sector on countries' ability to export knowledge-intensive services has been even more overlooked.

Several studies have argued that the rise of services, particularly of producer services, in the last 30 years is mostly the result of an increase in the demand for services as intermediate goods (Francois, 1990; Rowthorn and Ramaswamy, 1999; Klodt, 2000). Therefore, intersectoral linkages should play an important role in affecting the rise of business services via intermediate demand. Moreover, these services (and in particular the subgroup of knowledge-intensive business services, KIBS) are typically supplied to business through strong supplier–user interactions (Muller and Zenker, 2001). As a consequence, the presence of industrial sectors that are high users of business services is expected to favour the production of these services. If this is the case, in the presence of transport costs, the composition of the manufacturing sector should also affect countries' ability to export business services, in other words, there can be a 'home market effect' not based on final demand, but on intermediate demand. Guerrieri and Meliciani (2005) find empirical support for this prediction. In fact they find that absolute and comparative advantage in some producer services (financial, communication and business services) is positively affected by a composition of the manufacturing sector towards industries that are high users of producer services.

EMPIRICAL SPECIFICATION AND ECONOMETRIC METHODOLOGY

The main purpose of this chapter is to study the role of intersectoral linkages and ICT for international competitiveness in knowledge-intensive manufacturing and services sectors. Since ICT is a GPT, and since there can be important spillover effects, I have considered both the sectoral and the aggregate level of this variable. In particular, I have made export share equations depend on the sectoral and aggregate level of the ICT capital stock per employee.

In order to study the impact of intersectoral linkages, I make export shares in high-tech manufacturing industries depend on value-added specialization in knowledge-intensive services, and export shares in knowledge-intensive services depend on valued-added specialization in manufacturing and service industries that are high users of these services. The choice of the sectors to include is based on the results emerging from the use of input–output analysis (see the next section).

Together with these variables – as is standard in technology-based theories of trade – I explain export market shares with price and technology variables. In particular, I use the stock of R&D per employee and the stock of non-ICT physical capital per employee as proxies of technological differences across countries, while I use unit labour costs corrected for the exchange rate as proxies of price factors. Finally, in order to capture several cumulative mechanisms that reinforce the competitiveness of firms in international markets, I estimate a dynamic model with an autoregressive structure in the dependent variable (as in Amendola et al., 1993; Greenaway et al., 1998; Laursen and Meliciani, 2000, 2002; Santos-Paulino and Thirlwall, 2004).

Adopting the autoregressive representation on the variables, I thus obtain:

$$EXP_{ijt} = \alpha_0 + \alpha_1 EXP_{ij,t-1} + \alpha_2 ULC_{ijt} + \alpha_3 KICT_{ijt} + \alpha_4 KNICT_{ijt} + \alpha_5 KRD_{ijt} + \alpha_6 LINK_{ijt} + \mu_j + \mu_t + v_{ijt} \quad (4.1)$$

where EXP_{ijt} is exports in current prices and dollar exchange rates of country j in industry i at time t; *ULC* is unit labour costs (wages per worker in current prices, divided by labour productivity and multiplied by the dollar exchange rate);[3] *KICT* is the ICT capital stock per employee, *KNICT* the non-ICT capital stock per employee, *KRD* the R&D capital stock per employee, *LINK* the value-added share of knowledge intensive services when the equation is estimated for manufacturing, and the share of value added in industries (both manufacturing and services) that are high users of knowledge intensive services (those above average in Table 4.1, next section)[4] when the equation is estimated for services; $\mu_j + \mu_t + v_{ijt}$ is the error term where μ_j and μ_t are the country and time specific residuals respectively. All variables are divided by the average value for all countries in the sample (for each industry and time period) and are expressed in logarithms. The analysis is based on a panel of 12 countries (Austria, Denmark, Finland, Germany, Italy, Japan, Korea, the Netherlands, Portugal, Sweden, the United Kingdom and the United States)[5] over the period 1981–2003 for manufacturing and 1985–2003 for services (because of data availability). Data on trade for manufacturing industries are taken from the OECD STAN database, while data for trade in the services industries are taken from the OECD Trade in Services database. Data on labour compensation, value added, employment, R&D stocks, capital stocks (both ICT and non-ICT) are taken from the EU-KLEMS database.[6]

As is standard in the literature, I expect unit labour costs to have a negative impact on export share dynamics, although this effect could be null considering that the dependent variable is expressed in current prices and I am focusing on knowledge-intensive industries.

The originality of this chapter lies in its introduction of ICT capital stock and intersectoral linkages as explanatory variables of export share dynamics. As explained in the previous section, I expect the ICT capital stock to positively affect international competitiveness in knowledge-intensive industries by increasing the quality of produced goods and services and, in the case of services, by also increasing their tradability. ICT may affect export shares also via a decrease in prices, and this effect should be captured by my unit labour cost variable. It can also be noted that for manufacturing industries, I capture 'additionality effects' with the ICT capital stock variables by controlling for 'own-industry innovative activities' using the sectoral R&D stock. For the services sectors, on the contrary, ICT is the sole technology indicator because of the lack of data on R&D stocks at the sectoral level.[7] Since the literature on productivity has found important spillover effects from ICT, I have also included the total economy ICT capital stock.

Rather than assuming constant impacts for all industries, it may be important to distinguish groups of industries. That is because the impact of ICT on the higher reliability of the country's goods, new features or through an increased product variety and a higher tradability of services produced within the country should be expected to be much higher for firms in industries that produce ICTs, rather than primarily using them. In other words, ICT capital is expected to affect competitiveness much more strongly in ICT industries than in other industries (see also Laursen and Meliciani, 2010).

In order to define ICT industries, I adopt the OECD classification.[8] Since, however, the OECD classification is based on a more detailed level of disaggregation (four digit ISIC Rev. 3) than the one used in this chapter, I define an industry as being ICT when it includes mainly sub-industries classified by the OECD as being ICT. Therefore, of the knowledge-intensive (or high-tech) manufacturing industries included in the analysis ('chemicals and chemical products'; 'office, accounting and computing machinery'; 'electrical machinery'; 'radio, television and communication equipment' and 'medical, precision and optical instruments'), I define as manufacturing ICT the following industries: 'office, accounting and computing machinery'; 'radio, television and communication equipment' and 'medical, precision and optical instruments'.

Knowledge-intensive service industries are defined according to the EUROSTAT classification. Also in this case, since the classification is based on a more detailed level of disaggregation (four digit ISIC Rev. 3) than the one used here, I define an industry as being knowledge intensive when it includes mainly sub-industries that are classified by the EUROSTAT as being knowledge intensive. These include: 'post and telecommunications'; 'financial intermediation'; 'computer and related activities' and 'other business services'. Of these service industries, 'post and telecommunications' and 'computer and related activities', again on the basis of the OECD classification, are defined as ICT services.

In equation (4.1), since EXP_{ijt} is a function of μ_j, so is $EXP_{ij,\,t-1}$, and this renders the ordinary least squares (OLS) estimator biased and inconsistent. The fixed effects (FE) estimator eliminates μ_j, but will be biased for the short time series since $EXP_{ij,\,t-1}$ will be correlated with the FE-transformed residual by construction. Because of the short time series of my sample, I adopt the Blundell–Bond (BB) generalized method of moments (GMM) estimator, which gives consistent estimates provided that there is no second-order serial correlation among the errors, and I report tests for first and second order autocorrelation. This GMM specification is preferred to the original Arellano–Bond estimator because of the high persistence in the series (see Blundell and Bond, 1998).

I estimate a robust version of BB with heteroscedastic errors, and I assume, as is standard in this literature, exogeneity of all explanatory variables. The exogeneity of relative prices is a common hypothesis in estimating export equations and is based on the idea that the export supply price elasticities facing any individual country are infinite. Technology variables are assumed to be exogenous since they should capture structural characteristics that may respond only very slowly to changes in export shares. Moreover, I consider stocks of these variables.

DESCRIPTIVE STATISTICS

Intersectoral Linkages between Knowledge-Intensive Manufacturing and Service Industries

In order to better identify the pattern and the significance of intersectoral linkages, in what follows I test whether there are important regularities across countries in the industries that are high/low users of knowledge-intensive services. In particular, I perform an analysis of variance focused on the importance of industry effects in explaining the share of knowledge-intensive services on the output of manufacturing and service industries using the Eurostat symmetric input–output tables for the year 2000 across a sample of European countries.[9]

The analysis of variance indicates that there are significant industry effects that explain the use of knowledge-intensive services ($R^2 = 0.87$, $F = 53.19$ significant at 1 per cent) as also found in Guerrieri and Meliciani (2005). Table 4.1 reports the coefficients in the regression of the share of knowledge-intensive services in total output on industry dummies, distinguishing between manufacturing and service sectors. It can be observed that among the manufacturing industries that make considerable use of knowledge-intensive services, there are (with the exception of tobacco products) high-technology industries (radio, television and communication equipment and apparatus; printed matter and recorded media; chemicals and chemical products; office machinery and computers; medical, precision and optical instruments, watches and clocks), while labour- and scale-intensive industries appear, on average, to be low or medium users of knowledge-intensive services (see Table 4.1).

At the same time, one can observe that, of the service sectors, as expected, the highest users are the same knowledge-intensive sectors (financial intermediation services; computer and related services; post and telecommunication services; other business services and R&D services) while the lowest shares are found in 'transport services', 'hotel and restaurants', and several other non-market services.

Overall, these results suggest that the structure of the economy (in

Table 4.1 Share of knowledge-intensive services in total industry output

Above-average manufacturing	**Share (%)**	**Above-average service industries**	**Share (%)**
Radio, television and communication	12.09	Financial intermediation services, except insurance and pension funding services	25.66
Tobacco products	10.69	Computer and related services	23.58
Printed matter and recorded media	10.23	Post and telecommunications services	22.39
Chemicals and chemical products	10.16	Other business services	20.92
Office machinery and computers	9.08	Services auxiliary to financial intermediation	19.30
Medical, precision and optical instruments	8.54	Research and development services	18.51
Average manufacturing	**Share (%)**	**Average service industries**	**Share (%)**
Electrical machinery and apparatus n.e.c.*	7.20	Insurance and pension funding services, except compulsory social security services	15.26
Machinery and equipment n.e.c.	7.20	Membership organization services n.e.c.	14.40
Rubber and plastic products	6.70	Sewage and refuse disposal services, sanitation and similar services	13.22
Other transport equipment	6.70	Renting of machinery and equipment without operator and of personal and household goods	11.74
Food products and beverages	6.32	Recreational, cultural and sporting services	11.55

Table 4.1 (continued)

Average manufacturing	**Share (%)**	**Average service industries**	**Share (%)**
Furniture; other manufactured goods n.e.c.	6.26	Wholesale trade and commission trade, except of motor vehicles and motorcycles	11.25
Other non-metallic mineral products	6.13	Supporting and auxiliary transport services; travel agency services	10.58
		Retail trade services, except of motor vehicles and motorcycles; repair services of personal and household goods	10.03
Below-average manufacturing	**Share (%)**	**Below-average service industries**	**Share (%)**
Fabricated metal products, except machinery and equipment	5.58	Public administration and defence services; compulsory social security services	8.61
Motor vehicles, trailers and semi-trailers	5.40	Air transport services	8.11
Pulp, paper and paper products	5.38	Other services	8.05
Leather and leather products	5.16	Water transport services	7.29
Clothing apparel; furs	5.15	Land transport; transport via pipeline services	6.75
Textiles	5.12	Real estate services	6.65
Basic metals	4.28	Hotel and restaurant services	6.60
Wood and products of wood and cork (except furniture); articles of straw and plaiting materials	4.00	Health and social work services	4.55

Table 4.1 (continued)

Below-average manufacturing	**Share (%)**	**Below-average service industries**	**Share (%)**
Coke, refined petroleum products and nuclear fuels	2.77	Education services	4.03
		Public administration and defence services; compulsory social security services	8.61
		Air transport services	8.11
Average	*6.82*	*Average*	*12.43*
Standard deviation	*2.39*	*Standard deviation*	*6.25*

Notes: Industries are defined as above (below) average when the share is higher (lower) than the average plus (minus) (1/2)*standard deviation.
* Not elsewhere classified.

particular its sectoral composition) can condition the rise of knowledge-intensive services. In fact, one expects countries with a large share of activities in high-technology manufacturing industries and in knowledge-intensive services to experience a higher demand for these services and, therefore, to be more likely to develop and export these activities. At the same time, one also expects that international competitiveness in high-technology manufacturing industries can be positively affected by the size of countries' activities in knowledge-intensive services since they are important intermediate inputs for these industries.

Summary Statistics

Table 4.2 reports summary statistics by country for the last available year[10] for the variables used in the estimation distinguishing between knowledge-intensive manufacturing (KIM) and knowledge-intensive service (KIS) industries.

From the table, one can observe that countries specialized in knowledge-intensive manufacturing sectors are the Netherlands, Korea, Japan, the United States and Germany, while countries specialized in knowledge-intensive services are the United Kingdom, Sweden, and again the Netherlands and the United States. Italy and Portugal have very low levels of specialization in both groups of industries, while Japan and Korea perform much better in manufacturing than in services.

Table 4.2 Descriptive statistics

Country	Comparative advantage		Export share		ICT capital per employee ($ 000)		Non-ICT capital per employee ($ 000)		R&D capital per employee ($ 000)	Total economy ICT capital per employee ($ 000)	Value-added specialization in KIS	Value-added specialization in high users of KIS
	KIM	*KIS*	*KIM*	*KIS*	*KIM*	*KIS*	*KIM*	*KIS*	*KIM*			
Austria	0.65	0.81	0.02	0.03	14.05	82.34	114.70	93.93	na	16.60	0.85	0.83
Denmark	0.82	0.93	0.02	0.02	30.71	75.65	102.86	101.43	89.38	28.77	0.90	0.88
Finland	0.94	0.84	0.01	0.01	19.41	45.44	83.84	63.98	160.69	14.15	0.71	0.89
Germany	1.03	0.79	0.19	0.16	10.38	48.06	100.23	126.03	84.10	12.90	1.03	1.04
Italy	0.58	0.62	0.05	0.06	16.87	36.02	128.47	406.61	36.41	11.69	0.93	0.86
Japan	1.47	0.37	0.18	0.05	32.65	99.24	303.98	245.19	202.23	16.96	0.90	0.95
Korea	1.48	0.21	0.07	0.01	8.21	27.85	129.84	155.90	29.15	4.54	0.89	1.13
Netherlands	1.49	1.26	0.10	0.10	28.73	54.17	140.76	107.03	129.15	17.92	1.27	1.17
Portugal	0.57	0.74	0.01	0.01	18.29	63.34	84.78	86.30	na	9.25	0.92	0.81
Sweden	0.81	1.38	0.02	0.04	16.75	47.92	104.75	136.89	212.16	12.03	0.95	1.00
UK	0.96	2.81	0.09	0.27	29.02	85.54	100.51	68.14	90.29	20.90	1.38	1.25
USA	1.21	1.23	0.24	0.25	36.68	92.35	137.54	100.11	168.79	22.96	1.26	1.19

Sources: Own elaborations on OECD STAN and Trade in Services database and EU-KLEMS.

Looking at market shares, the USA, Germany and the Netherlands are in the first four positions in both manufacturing and services, while Japan is in the first four positions only in manufacturing, and the UK only in services (it ranks first with a market share of 27 per cent).

When looking at the ICT indicator, one finds that the USA, Japan, Denmark and the UK are in first position both in manufacturing and in services, while the Netherlands and Finland perform better in manufacturing. Looking at capital stocks in non-ICT industries, Japan and Korea are in the top position in both manufacturing and services, while the Netherlands and the USA have high values in manufacturing, and Italy and Sweden in services. Sweden, Japan, the USA and Finland have the highest R&D expenditure in high-tech manufacturing. Finally, the UK, the USA, the Netherlands, Korea and Germany are specialized in industries that are high users of producer services, while the same countries, with the exception of Korea, are also specialized in knowledge-intensive service industries.

Looking at correlation coefficients across countries and years (Tables 4.3 and 4.4), one finds that high market shares in knowledge-intensive manufacturing sectors are positively correlated to all variables considered, with particularly high values for the correlation coefficient with value-added specialization in KIS (0.55). It is also worth noting that the correlation coefficient is higher with the total economy ICT stock (0.43) than with the sectoral one (0.37).

In the case of knowledge-intensive services, one also observes a positive correlation with all variables with the exception of the non-ICT capital stock per employee (−0.14). Moreover, the higher correlation coefficient

Table 4.3 Correlation coefficients in knowledge-intensive manufacturing industries

Knowledge-intensive manufacturing	EXP	KICT	KICTT	LINK	R&D
Export share (EXP)	1.00				
ICT capital per employee (KICT)	0.37	1.00			
Total economy ICT capital per employee (KICTT)	0.43	0.74	1.00		
Non-ICT capital per employee (KNICT)	0.52	0.49	0.60	1.00	
Value-added specialization in KIS (LINK)	0.55	0.22	0.30	0.18	1.00
R&D stock per employee (RD)	0.31	0.21	0.36	0.39	0.31

Table 4.4 Correlation coefficients in knowledge-intensive service industries

Knowledge-intensive services	EXP	KICT	KICTT	LINK
Export share (EXP)	1.00			
ICT capital per employee (KICT)	0.13	1.00		
Total economy ICT capital per employee (KICTT)	0.50	0.50	1.00	
Non-ICT capital per employee (KNICT)	−0.14	0.20	0.24	1.00
Value-added specialization in high users of KIS (LINK)	0.56	0.05	0.26	−0.14

is also found with specialization in the high users sectors (0.56) in this case. One identifies once more that the correlation coefficient with the total ICT capital stock is higher (0.50) than the one with the sectoral ICT stock (0.13).

ESTIMATION RESULTS

Tables 4.5 and 4.6 report the results of the estimation of equation (4.1) respectively for manufacturing and service industries. As stated above, I distinguish between manufacturing and services sectors and between 'ICT industries' and 'non-ICT industries', reporting both the short- and long-run coefficients. Moreover, I report results for a specification including only the 'own industry ICT capital stock' and for one equation including also the total economy's ICT capital stock.

From the tables, one can see that when looking at the group of high-tech manufacturing industries (including both ICT and non-ICT industries), the ICT capital stock and the index of specialization in knowledge-intensive services have a positive and significant impact on export market share dynamics. Moreover, 'own industry R&D' also has a significant positive impact while costs do not matter. When distinguishing, however, between ICT and non-ICT industries, the ICT capital stock is significant only in ICT industries, while intersectoral linkages matter in the other high-tech industries, where the non-ICT capital stock also has a positive impact on export market shares. Moreover, in the ICT industries, relative costs adjusted for the exchange rate show up with a positive significant sign. This result may depend on the low price elasticity of demand in these sectors.

Table 4.5 Regression results for knowledge-intensive (KI) manufacturing industries

	Manufact. KI			ICT			Non-ICT			Manufact. KI			ICT			Non-ICT		
	Coef.	Prob.	*z*-value	Coef.	Prob.	*z*-value	Coef.	Prob.	*z*-value	Coef.	Prob.	*z*-value	Coef.	Prob.	*z*-value	Coef.	Prob.	*z*-value
Lagged exports	0.78	0.00	16.66	0.81	0.00	15.74	0.73	0.00	12.23	0.74	0.00	17.52	0.77	0.00	16.27	0.72	0.00	15.20
Unit labour costs																		
Short-run	0.02	0.20	1.28	0.05	0.02	2.31	−0.01	0.84	−0.20	0.01	0.51	0.65	0.05	0.03	2.18	−0.01	0.68	−0.42
Long-run	0.11	0.19	1.29	0.28	0.02	2.26	−0.02	0.84	−0.20	0.05	0.51	0.65	0.22	0.02	2.26	−0.04	0.69	−0.40
ICT capital stock																		
Short-run	0.11	0.02	2.25	0.16	0.01	2.62	0.03	0.69	0.40	−0.06	0.40	−0.83	0.00	0.97	0.03	−0.04	0.58	−0.55
Long-run	0.51	0.08	1.78	0.82	0.05	1.95	0.10	0.71	0.37	−0.24	0.41	−0.83	0.01	0.97	0.03	−0.14	0.58	−0.55
ICT total capital stock																		
Short-run										0.34	0.00	2.99	0.26	0.04	2.06	0.15	0.31	1.02
Long-run										1.27	0.01	2.46	1.11	0.08	1.77	0.52	0.34	0.95
Non-ICT capital stock																		
Short-run	0.19	0.12	1.55	0.12	0.47	0.72	0.26	0.02	2.31	0.22	0.09	1.69	0.13	0.46	0.73	0.25	0.02	2.30
Long-run	0.89	0.13	1.52	0.60	0.46	0.73	0.98	0.00	2.91	0.83	0.10	1.66	0.54	0.46	0.74	0.88	0.00	2.96
R&D stock																		
Short-run	0.17	0.02	2.26	0.15	0.13	1.52	0.13	0.06	1.90	0.08	0.38	0.37	0.10	0.39	0.86	0.09	0.30	1.04
Long-run	0.81	0.03	2.22	0.76	0.16	1.39	0.48	0.04	2.01	0.32	0.38	0.38	0.41	0.40	0.84	0.32	0.29	1.05

Table 4.5 (continued)

	Manufact. KI			ICT			Non-ICT			Manufact. KI			ICT			Non-ICT		
	Coef.	Prob.	*z*-value	Coef.	Prob.	*z*-value	Coef.	Prob.	*z*-value	Coef.	Prob.	*z*-value	Coef.	Prob.	*z*-value	Coef.	Prob.	*z*-value
Linkages																		
Short-run	0.48	0.03	2.22	0.31	0.30	1.05	0.67	0.01	2.50	0.52	0.02	2.33	0.34	0.26	1.13	0.67	0.01	2.54
Long-run	2.22	0.02	2.50	1.59	0.22	1.23	2.51	0.01	3.63	1.98	0.01	2.50	1.48	0.20	1.28	2.36	0.00	3.37
Number of observations	934			560			374			934			560			374		
AR(1)	−4.01	0.00		−3.04	0.00		−3.26	0.00		−3.95	0.00		−3.06	0.00		−3.27	0.00	
AR(2)	1.19	0.23		0.72	0.47		1.61	0.11		0.91	0.36		0.58	0.55		1.57	0.12	

Notes: Time dummies included but coefficients not reported. The *z*-values are based on heteroscedasticity consistent standard errors (using White's method). AR(1) and AR(2) are Arellano–Bond tests of the hypothesis that average autocovariance in residuals (of respectively order 1 and 2) is zero.

Table 4.6 Regression results for knowledge-intensive (KI) service industries

	KIS			ICT			Non-ICT			KIS			ICT			Non-ICT		
	Coef.	Prob.	z-value	Coef.	Prob.	z-value	Coef	Prob.	z-value	Coef.	Prob.	z-value	Coef.	Prob.	z-value	Coef.	Prob.	z-value
Lagged exports	0.44	0.02	2.37	0.73	0.00	21.32	0.29	0.19	1.32	0.43	0.02	2.41	0.71	0.00	15.12	0.29	0.20	1.29
Unit labour costs																		
Short-run	0.03	0.61	0.52	0.02	0.58	0.55	0.15	0.01	2.47	−0.00	1.00	−0.00	−0.05	0.34	−0.95	0.15	0.05	1.99
Long-run	0.06	0.57	0.56	0.06	0.58	0.56	0.21	0.01	2.77	−0.00	1.00	−0.00	−0.15	0.31	−1.00	0.21	0.01	2.54
ICT capital stock																		
Short-run	0.02	0.87	0.16	0.11	0.13	1.52	−0.08	0.63	−0.49	−0.18	0.32	−1.00	−0.18	0.35	−0.94	−0.04	0.86	−0.18
Long-run	0.04	0.87	0.16	0.40	0.15	1.43	−0.12	0.63	−0.48	−0.31	0.36	−0.91	−0.63	0.30	−1.04	−0.05	0.86	−0.18
ICT total capital stock																		
Short-run										0.43	0.27	1.10	0.60	0.07	1.83	−0.11	0.78	−0.28
Long-run										0.76	0.34	0.95	2.05	0.02	2.28	−0.15	0.76	−0.30
Non-ICT capital stock																		
Short-run	0.09	0.74	0.34	−0.08	0.41	−0.82	0.42	0.04	2.06	0.05	0.84	0.20	−0.16	0.16	−1.42	0.43	0.06	1.88
Long-run	0.15	0.73	0.35	−0.29	0.41	−0.83	0.58	0.02	2.27	0.09	0.84	0.21	−0.54	0.12	−1.55	0.60	0.02	2.25
Linkages																		
Short-run	1.37	0.27	1.10	0.44	0.59	0.55	2.67	0.03	2.11	1.20	0.34	0.95	0.01	1.00	0.01	2.70	0.05	2.01
Long-run	2.43	0.24	1.17	1.64	0.60	0.53	3.74	0.00	2.83	2.12	0.31	1.01	0.02	0.99	0.01	3.78	0.00	2.80
Number of observations	667			329			338			667			329			338		
AR(1)	−2.09	0.04		−3.10	0.00		−1.72	0.08		−2.05	0.04		−3.26	0.00		−1.74	0.08	
AR(2)	1.54	0.12		1.02	0.30		1.58	0.11		1.52	0.13		1.04	0.30		1.59	0.11	

Notes: Time dummies included but coefficients not reported. The z-values are based on heteroscedasticity consistent standard errors (using White's method). AR(1) and AR(2) are Arellano–Bond tests of the hypothesis that average autocovariance in residuals (of respectively order 1 and 2) is zero.

Another interesting result is that, when the total economy ICT capital stock is also introduced into the regression, it shows up with a positive sign and is highly significant, while the 'own industry ICT capital stock' loses significance. This may be interpreted as giving support to theories that emphasize the fact that ICTs are GPTs and, therefore, their indirect impact on competitiveness is greater than their direct impact.

Turning to services, one finds that, in order to have significant effects, it is essential to distinguish ICT services from other knowledge-intensive services. In fact, it is only in the ICT services that one finds that the ICT capital stock has a positive and significant impact on the dynamics of export shares, while in non-ICT knowledge-intensive services the intersectoral linkages and the non-ICT capital stock show up with a positive and significant coefficient. As in the case of manufacturing, as well as of services, the total economy ICT capital stock matters more than the sectoral one.

The results for manufacturing industries can be compared with those found by Laursen and Meliciani (2010). Different from the conclusions of this chapter, they find that knowledge flows from a domestic ICT science base appear to be important not only for ICT manufacturing industries but also for other manufacturing industries. The different results may depend on the ICT indicators (capital stock rather than knowledge flows). In fact, knowledge, being immaterial, may generate more spillovers than the capital stock. This explanation is not consistent, however, with the fact that the total economy's ICT capital stock affects international competitiveness in ICT sectors. An alternative explanation could be the different coverage of non-ICT sectors, since in this analysis they include only 'chemicals and chemical products' and 'electrical machinery', where investment in communication might not be particularly relevant for innovation. In fact, when I restrict the analysis only to IT capital, it shows up with a positive and significant sign (see Appendix).

As for the role of interindustry linkages, the results give support to the view that knowledge-intensive services are a strategic input for high-tech manufacturing industries, thus fostering their international competitiveness. On the other hand, the positive role played by intermediate demand in fostering competitiveness of knowledge-intensive services is found only for non-ICT services. This result may depend on the fact that ICT services can be more easily traded and, therefore, local demand may matter less than in other business services.

Overall, an important result to emphasize is that, consistently with the heterogeneity of services, factors of competitiveness are even more sector-specific for services than for manufacturing. In addition, it appears more difficult to explain export shares in services than in manufacturing. This may give support to previous research emphasizing that traded services must use inputs from both the exporting and importing countries interactively (Mirza and Nicoletti, 2004). Therefore an increase in, say, the ICT capital stock in both the exporting and the importing country would result in higher services trade, but not in higher market shares.

CONCLUSIONS

This chapter has investigated the factors affecting export market shares in knowledge-intensive manufacturing and services industries, with particular attention to the role played by ICTs and by intersectoral linkages. I have argued that ICTs may affect international competitiveness indirectly by affecting productivity and prices, and directly by leading to increased variety and quality of products. ICTs can contribute to increasing the tradability of services. In addition, because of the intangible and information-based nature of services, the generation and use of ICTs may have a central role in services' innovation activities. The empirical analysis has given support to these hypotheses. In fact, I have found that ICTs have a positive impact on export shares in ICT manufacturing and services industries. Moreover, it is the total economy's stock of ICT capital that matters more than the 'own industry stock'. This result is consistent with the view of ICTs as general purpose technologies.

Different, however, from the results of previous studies on ICT-related knowledge flows, I have not found that the sectoral or the total economy's ICT capital stocks have a significant impact on the non-ICT sectors. This is somewhat surprising again considering the wide range of applications of these technologies.

In the case of manufacturing, one explanation might be the fact that, by having confined the analysis only to knowledge-intensive sectors, the non-ICT sectors included only 'chemical and chemical products' and 'electrical machinery', where 'communication investment' might not be particularly relevant. In fact, when I used the IT rather than the ICT capital stock, it also had a positive impact on export market share in non-ICT manufacturing sectors.

In the case of non-ICT services, the ICT capital stock was expected to affect export shares by affecting the tradability and innovation of services. Much of the trade in these industries (which includes 'financial services' and 'other business services') involves what the World Trade Organization's (WTO) General Agreement on Trade in Services (GATS) defines as the 'mode 3 of services' trade', that is, firms establishing a foreign affiliate. While ICTs may contribute to this type of trade, this is not captured by services' exports, but by FDI. Future research is therefore needed to shed more light on the impact of ICTs on trade in these service industries, requiring internationally comparable data on FDI at the sectoral level.

In this chapter, I have also argued that ICTs have contributed to making manufacturing and service activities increasingly interrelated. Since knowledge-intensive sectors are highly demanded as intermediate inputs by high-technology manufacturing industries, I have demonstrated, on the one hand, that international competitiveness in high-tech manufacturing industries may be positively affected by the availability of knowledge-intensive services that are used as intermediate inputs. On the other hand, I have maintained that competitiveness in knowledge-intensive services may be positively affected by specialization in manufacturing and service sectors that use knowledge-intensive services via a larger intermediate demand. The chapter has found support for the importance of such linkages for the dynamics of export market shares in high-tech manufacturing sectors and in non-ICT knowledge-intensive services.

The complementarity between knowledge-intensive manufacturing and service activities has important implications, since it suggests that a country's ability to develop an efficient and dynamic service economy is linked to the structure of its manufacturing sector. At the same time, the availability of knowledge-intensive services also contributes to increasing international competitiveness in knowledge-intensive manufacturing industries.

I have considered only domestic services here, while future research could also assess the role played by imported services on manufacturing exports (some evidence suggests a positive role, see Wolfmayr, 2008). Finally, further analyses are needed to investigate whether there are heterogeneities across countries, over time and across different sub-sectors in the role played by ICTs and intersectoral linkages.

NOTES

1. See, for example, Fagerberg (1988), Amendola et al. (1993), Magnier and Toujas-Bernate (1994), Amable and Verspagen (1995), Verspagen and Wakelin (1997), Montobbio (2003), Laursen and Meliciani (2000, 2002, 2010).
2. The term 'knowledge-intensive' has been extensively applied to services. In the case of manufacturing, I use the same term to refer to what are more commonly known as 'high-technology' sectors.
3. Data on labour compensation, value added, employment and the value-added deflator at the sectoral level are taken from the EU-KLEMS database.
4. When data were not available at the level of disaggregation shown in Table 4.1, I

included the more aggregate sector only when the majority of sub-sectors were included in Table 4.1. This led me to consider the following sectors: radio, TV and communication equipment; printing, publishing and reproduction; chemicals and chemical products; office, accounting and computing machinery; medical, precision and optical instruments; financial intermediation; computer and related activities; R&D; and other business services.

5. Austria and Portugal are not included in regressions that include R&D because of lack of data for this variable.
6. EU-KLEMS Database, March 2008, see Timmer et al. (2008).
7. I also tried with some proxies of sectoral human capital (the share of skilled labour hours worked over total hours worked and the share of skilled labour remuneration over total remuneration), but I did not get any significant results.
8. In 1998, OECD member countries agreed on a common definition of the ICT sector; see OECD (2002).
9. Knowledge-intensive services are defined on the basis of the Eurostat classification and include: post and telecommunications; financial services; computer and related services; R&D; other business services. The countries on which I perform the analysis of variance are the European ones included in the estimation of markct shares (see next section). These include: Austria, Denmark, Finland, Germany, Italy, the Netherlands, Portugal, Sweden and the United Kingdom.
10. This is 2005 for all variables except comparative advantage, export shares and R&D stock, which are from 2003.

REFERENCES

Aghion, P., P. Howitt and G.L. Violante (2002), 'General purpose technology and wage inequality', *Journal of Economic Growth*, **7**, pp. 315–45.

Amable, B. and B. Verspagen (1995), 'The role of technology in market shares dynamics', *Applied Economics*, **27**, pp. 197–204.

Amendola, G., G. Dosi and E. Papagni (1993), 'The dynamics of international competitiveness', *Weltwirtschaftliches Archiv*, **129**, pp. 451–71.

Bassanini, A. and S. Scarpetta (2002), 'Growth, technological change, and ICT diffusion: recent evidence from OECD countries', *Oxford Review of Economic Policy*, **18**, pp. 324–44.

Blundell, R. and S. Bond (1998), 'Initial conditions and moment restrictions in dynamic panel data models', *Journal of Econometrics*, **87**, pp. 115–43.

Bresnahan, T., E. Brynjolfsson and L.M. Hitt (2002), 'Information technology, workplace organization, and the demand for skilled labor: firm-level evidence', *Quarterly Journal of Economics*, **117**, pp. 339–76.

Bresnahan, T. and M. Trajtenberg (1995), 'General purpose technologies: engines of growth', *Journal of Econometrics*, **65**, pp. 83–108.

Brynjolfsson, E. and L.M. Hitt (2000), 'Beyond computation: information technology, organizational transformation and business performance', *Journal of Economic Perspectives*, **14**, pp. 23–48.

Di Cagno, D. and V. Meliciani (2005), 'Do inter-sectoral flows of services matter for productivity growth? An input/output analysis of OECD countries', *Economics of Innovation and New Technology*, **14**, pp. 149–71.

Dosi G., K. Pavitt and L. Soete (1990), *The Economics of Technical Change and International Trade*, London: Harvester Wheatsheaf.

Ebling, G. and N. Janz (1999), 'Export and innovation activities in the German service sector: empirical evidence at the firm level' (99–53), Mannheim: Center for European Economic Research (ZEW).

Evangelista, R. (2000), 'Sectoral patterns of technological change in services', *Economics of Innovation and New Technology*, **9**, pp. 183–221.

Fagerberg, J. (1988), 'International competitiveness', *Economic Journal*, **98**, pp. 355–74.

Francois, J.F. (1990), 'Producer services, scale, and the division of labor', *Oxford Economic Papers*, **42**, pp. 715–29.

Francois, J.F. and J. Woerz (2008), 'Producer services, manufacturing linkages, and trade', *Journal of Industry, Competition and Trade*, **8**, pp. 199–229.

Greenaway, D., W. Morgan and P. Wright (1998), 'Trade reform, adjustment and growth: what does the evidence tell us?', *Economic Journal*, **108**, pp. 1547–61.

Grünfeld, L.A. and A. Moxnes (2003), 'The intangible globalization: explaining the patterns of international trade and foreign direct investment in services', Norwegian Institute of International Affairs, mimeo.

Guerrieri, P. and V. Meliciani (2005), 'Technology and international competitiveness: the interdependence between manufacturing and producer services', *Structural Change and Economic Dynamics*, **16**, pp. 489–502.

Helpman, E. (ed.) (1998), *General Purpose Technologies and Economic Growth*, Cambridge, MA: MIT Press.

Helpman, E. and P. Krugman (1985), *Market Structure and Foreign Trade*, Cambridge, MA: MIT Press.

Jorgenson, D.W. and K.J. Stiroh (2000), 'Raising the speed limit: U.S. economic growth in the information age', *Brookings Papers on Economic Activity*, **1**, pp. 125–211.

Kimura, F. and H.-H. Lee (2004), 'The gravity equation in international trade in services', Paper presented at the European Trade Study Group Conference, University of Nottingham, 9–11 September.

Klodt, H. (2000), 'Structural change towards services: the German experience', University of Birmingham IGS Discussion Paper, July.

Kox, H. and L. Rubalcaba (2007), *Business Services in European Economic Growth*, London: Macmillan.

Krugman, P. (1985), 'A "technology gap" model of international trade', in K. Jungenfelt and D. Hague (eds), *Structural Adjustment in Advanced Economies*, London: Macmillan, pp. 39–45.

Krugman, P. (1989), 'Differences in income elasticities and trends in real exchange rates', *European Economic Review*, **33**, pp. 1031–54.

Laursen, K. and V. Meliciani (2000), 'The importance of technology-based intersectoral linkages for market share dynamics', *Weltwirtschaftliches Archiv*, **136**, pp. 702–23.

Laursen, K. and V. Meliciani (2002), 'The relative importance of international vis-à-vis national technological spillovers for market share dynamics', *Industrial and Corporate Change*, **11**, pp. 875–94.

Laursen, K. and V. Meliciani (2010), 'The role of ICT knowledge flows for international market share dynamics', *Research Policy*, **39**, pp. 687–97.

Laursen, K. and A. Salter (2005), 'The fruits of intellectual production: economic and scientific specialisation among OECD countries', *Cambridge Journal of Economics*, **29**, pp. 289–308.

Magnier, A. and J. Toujas-Bernate (1994), 'Technology and trade: empirical

evidence for the major five industrialized countries', *Weltwirtshaftliches Archiv*, **130**, pp. 494–520.
Meliciani, V. (2002), 'The impact of technological specialisation on national performance in a balance-of-payments-constrained growth model', *Structural Change and Economic Dynamics*, **13**, pp. 101–18.
Milgrom, P. and J. Roberts (1990), 'The economics of modern manufacturing technology, strategy and organization', *American Economic Review*, **80**, pp. 511–28.
Miozzo, M. and L. Soete (2001), 'Internationalization of services: a technological perspective', *Technological Forecasting and Social Change*, **67**, pp. 159–85.
Mirza, P. and G. Nicoletti (2004), 'What is so special about trade in services', Research Paper, February, Nottingham: University of Nottingham.
Montobbio, F. (2003), 'Sectoral patterns of technological activity and export market share dynamics', *Cambridge Journal of Economics*, **27**, pp. 523–45.
Muller, E. and A. Zenker (2001), 'Business services as actors of knowledge transformation: the role of KIBS in regional and national innovation systems', *Research Policy*, **30**, pp. 1501–16.
OECD (2002), *Measuring the Information Economy*, Paris: OECD.
Pavitt, K. (1984), 'Sectoral patterns of technical change: towards a taxonomy and a theory', *Research Policy*, **13**, 343–73.
Posner, M.V. (1961), 'International trade and technical change', *Oxford Economic Papers*, **13**, pp. 323–41.
Rowthorn, R. and R. Ramaswamy (1999), 'Growth, trade and deindustrialisation', *IMF Staff Papers*, **46**, pp. 18–41.
Santos-Paulino, A. and A.P. Thirlwall (2004), 'The impact of trade liberalisation on exports, imports and the balance of payments of developing countries', *Economic Journal*, **114**, pp. 50–72.
Soete, L.L.G. (1981), 'A general test of the technological gap trade theory', *Weltwirtschaftliches Archiv*, **117**, pp. 638–66.
Timmer, M., M. O'Mahony and B. van Ark (2008), 'The EU KLEMS growth and productivity accounts: an overview', University of Groningen and University of Birmingham; available to download at: www.euklems.net.
van Ark, B. and M. Timmer (2005), 'Does information and communication technology drive EU–US productivity growth differentials?', *Oxford Economic Papers*, **57**, pp. 693–716.
Verspagen, B. and K. Wakelin (1997), 'Trade and technology from a Schumpeterian perspective', *International Review of Applied Economics*, **11**, pp. 181–94.
Windrum, P. and M. Tomlinson (1999), 'Knowledge-intensive services and international competitiveness: a four country comparison', *Technology Analysis and Strategic Management*, **11**, pp. 391–408.
Wolfmayr, Y. (2008), 'Producer services and competitiveness of manufacturing exports', *FIW Research Report* (009), June.
WTO (2008), *International Trade Statistics*, Geneva: World Trade Organization.

APPENDIX: REGRESSION RESULTS FOR MANUFACTURING INDUSTRIES WITH IT CAPITAL

	ICT			Non-ICT		
	Coef.	Prob.	*z*-value	Coef	Prob.	*z*-value
Lagged exports	0.77	0.00	16.66	0.74	0.00	15.55
Unit labour costs	0.06	0.02	2.38	0.02	0.55	0.59
IT capital stock	0.13	0.00	2.92	0.07	0.06	1.88
Non-IT capital stock	0.18	0.24	1.18	0.19	0.04	2.08
R&D stock	0.21	0.09	1.71	0.20	0.01	2.58
Linkages	0.41	0.13	1.51	0.54	0.04	2.06
Number of observations	554			370		
AR(1)	−2.88	0.00		−3.19	0.00	
AR(2)	0.51	0.61		1.52	0.13	

Notes: Time dummies included but coefficients not reported. The *z*-values are based on heteroscedasticity consistent standard errors (using White's method). AR(1) and AR(2) are Arellano–Bond tests of the hypothesis that average autocovariance in residuals (of respectively order 1 and 2) is zero.

5. How integrated are Chinese and Indian labour into the world economy?

Richard N. Cooper

Wages of the median and of unskilled workers have stagnated during the past decade in many rich countries, including the United States, even while economic growth remained robust until 2008. At the same time, corporate profits excelled. An explanation for these widespread phenomena is that the effective world labour supply was greatly increased by the integration of China and India – the world's two most populous countries – into the global economy as a result of changes in policy in both of those countries, giving encouragement to greater engagement with the rest of the world. Between them, China and India are said to have added over a billion workers to world labour supply, without a corresponding increase in the capital stock. Simple neoclassical economics would suggest a rise in returns to capital and a fall in wages of unskilled workers in the rest of the world. (To these two countries could be added the former Soviet Union, Eastern Europe and Vietnam, but the numbers of potential workers there are less dramatic, and skill levels higher; the focus here will be on China and India.)

China and India are similar in many ways. Both are populous, physically large, socially diversified, economically poor countries. In 1978 they had roughly the same per capita GDP in terms of purchasing power parity (Maddison, 2001, p. 304). Their labour forces have very different characteristics, however. A significantly higher fraction of China's population is in economic employment; China is much more urbanized; less of China's labour force is in agriculture; and in rural areas, a substantially higher fraction of rural employment is non-agricultural. Population growth in both countries has declined significantly in recent decades, but the decline has been markedly sharper in China. India has had far greater protection against imports than China, although it has lowered non-agricultural tariffs in recent years. India has been less hospitable to foreign direct investment (FDI) than China, and is more dependent on official foreign assistance. By 2000, India's real per capita GDP had doubled from 1978; China's had nearly quadrupled. These differences, and others, influence the degree of integration of these economies into the world economy, and in particular the role that their labour forces play in the world economy.

I start with a description of key population and employment characteristics of China and India. The next section describes their policies, and outcomes, with respect to foreign trade and foreign investment. The third section offers theoretical considerations about how a poor country, and in particular its labour force, might be integrated into the world economy. The fourth section discusses emigration from China and India in recent years. The fifth section then pulls together the empirical and theoretical material and offers some judgements about current and future integration of the two countries into the world economy.

POPULATION AND EMPLOYMENT

Table 5.1 presents the populations of China and India from 1980 to 2005, and US Census Bureau projections to 2050, along with estimates of the number of people in the age bracket 15–64, roughly those who could be in the labour force. Several features are noteworthy. First, population growth has been slowing in both China and India, and is expected to continue to do so. China's population grew by 1.5 per cent a year in the decade 1980–90, declined to 0.6 per cent a year in 2000–05, and population is expected to peak in 2032, declining thereafter. India's population grew by 2.0 per cent from 1980–90, declined to 1.4 per cent in 2000–05, and growth is expected to continue to decline to 0.7 per cent a year between 2030 and 2040. These declines reflect significant decreases in birth rates – indeed to below the reproduction rate in China's case – with implications for the age structure of the population. Those aged 15–64 accounted for 66 per cent of China's population in 1990, rising to 71 per cent in 2005, and the proportion is expected to decline to 67 per cent in 2030 and 63 per cent in 2040 as the population ages, and as new entrants to the labour force decline. (China's median age rose from 25 years in 1990, to 32 in 2005, and will rise to over 41 in 2030.) The corresponding percentages for India are 59 per cent in 1991, 64 per cent in 2005, and 68 per cent in 2030. In China, the important 20–24 age group – those receiving advanced education and generally the most flexible component of the labour force – is already declining from year to year, and is expected to decline at an annual rate of 3 per cent in the period 2020–25. That age group in India continues to grow in the near future, but reaches a peak in 2020. In the subsequent five years, it will also be declining, albeit at a much more modest 0.1 per cent a year.

Table 5.1 Total and working-age population, China and India (in millions)

Year	Total		Age 15–64	
	China	India	China	India
1980	985	687	NA	NA
1990	1148	842	757	504*
2000	1269	1003	858	620
2005	1306	1080	928	690
2010	1348	1155	973	757
2020	1431	1297	987	874
2030	1462	1421	977	962
2040	1455	1522	911	1022
2050	1424	1601	864	1048

Note: *1991.

Source: US Census Bureau.

In short, the potential labour force has grown more rapidly than the population in both countries, producing the so-called 'demographic dividend' as birth rates decline and young adults increase more rapidly than dependent children – and before dependent elders become quantitatively significant. This process has about run its course in China, but will continue on a moderate scale in India for some decades, resulting (on this account) in some slowdown in China's future growth, but permitting somewhat faster growth in India.

Of course, translating the demographic dividend into actual growth depends also on labour force participation rates, and on actually employing potential workers productively. Participation rates in the two countries differ significantly. Fifty-seven per cent of China's population were employed in 2000, compared with 37 per cent in India.[1] Part of the difference can be explained by the difference in age structure, with 68 per cent of China's population being between 15 and 64 in 2000, compared with 63 per cent in India in 2001. In addition, participation rates among women were far lower in India. This may be explained in part by the higher rural and agricultural population in India, where women in fact work hard at home but are not considered employed in the conventional sense. There is also a stronger tradition, encouraged by the Communist Party, for women to enter the labour force in China, whereas in India some religious groups actively discourage it. There is also the Hindu tradition that Brahmins, as priests, do not work; this tradition is breached in urban areas, but not in all rural areas.

Even if persons are in the labour force (that is, they are working or looking for work), they may not be employed productively. Official figures on unemployment have been low in both countries – in the order of 3 per cent of the urban labour force. But these low figures certainly understate the involuntary idleness among workers in both countries. Angang Hu (2007) reckons that real urban unemployment in China was nearly thrice the official figure in 2000: 17 million rather than the official 6 million. The official figure had risen to 8.3 million by 2007, 4.0 per cent of the urban labour force. In India the official unemployment rate was 2.8 per cent in 2000, but Ajit Ghose (2004) explains why the very concept of 'unemployment' is not very meaningful in a country like India, where most of the labour force is in the informal or unorganized sectors of the economy, in which jobs available to individual workers may be highly sporadic, averaging only a few days a month. Such people are not unemployed by conventional definitions, but they are not fully or productively employed either. Thus, argues Ghose, true underemployment in India (against a baseline assumption of six days a week of work) is in the order of 13 per cent of all employed persons, more than four times the official rate.

China, on the other hand, has moved people out of agriculture considerably more rapidly than India. While the two countries were similar in the share of agricultural employment in 1980, at 69 per cent of total employment, by 2001 China had created many more non-agricultural jobs in rural areas; 33 per cent of rural employment was non-farm and half of the income in rural areas was generated by non-agricultural activity (Li et al., 2003, pp. 101, 104). In 2000, 59 per cent of employment in India was in agriculture. By 2000, China's agricultural employment had fallen to 50 per cent of the labour force, and to 42 per cent in 2007. In 2000, industry (including construction) accounted for 16 per cent of India's employment (manufacturing for 11 per cent), up from 14 per cent in 1981, compared with 22 per cent in China, up from 18 per cent in 1980. In short, both countries increased industrial employment as a share of total employment, implying significantly more jobs considering the growth in the total labour force. The increase in share, while larger for China, was nevertheless modest in both countries.

The 'organized' sector in India, to which labour market laws and regulations apply, in principle covers all organizations that employ more than ten persons. But it accounts for a remarkably small share – 9 per cent in 1996 – of total employment; and more than two-thirds of the organized sector comprises government or quasi-governmental organizations. Regular wage and salary workers – those with regular employment paying a regular wage – accounted for about 40 per cent of employment in urban areas in 1999–2000 (Sundaram and Tenduklar, 2004, Table 12).

In 1981, China and India had about the same degree of urbanization: 23 per cent of the population in India, 21 per cent in China. During the subsequent two decades, China urbanized much more rapidly, such that by 2000, 36 per cent of the population lived in urban areas. The rural population remained essentially unchanged in numbers, while 245 million (equivalent to nearly all the population growth) urbanized. By 2007, the urban share had risen further to 45 per cent, resulting in a decline in the rural population by 80 million (some of the change resulted from reclassification of rural to urban). India, in contrast, urbanized much more slowly, and more slowly than had been forecast by Indian authorities, such that by 2001 only 28 per cent of the population were urbanized. The rural population increased by 218 million over the period 1981–2001, while the urban population increased by 125 million, mostly from births to urban families.

Trends in manufacturing employment have also been very different in the two countries. Because of severe labour regulations applying to firms of over ten employees, private manufacturing employment in India's 'organized' (that is, closely regulated) sector is astonishingly low and actually declined slightly over the period 1981–91 to 4.5 million (another 1.9 million were employed in state-owned manufacturing enterprises). This figure rose by a modest 2.9 per cent a year over the 1990s, but remained under 6 million, compared with a 9.0 per cent annual growth in output (Banga, 2005, Table 3). According to India's 1991 census, a total of 28.7 million persons worked in 'industry' in that year, organized and unorganized, including the more than 800 manufacturing activities that were reserved to the household sector (which accounted for 6.8 million persons). This was up modestly from the 25.1 million thus engaged in 1981. By 2000, the total had grown to perhaps 40 million.

Timothy Besley and Robin Burgess (2004) have examined employment in 16 Indian states over the period 1958–92. They found that those states that passed pro-worker legislation (within the framework established by union legislation in 1947) experienced lower growth in manufacturing output, lower growth in employment in registered manufacturing firms, and increases in urban poverty compared with those states that passed pro-employer legislation or none at all. These findings suggest that over-regulation of the labour market goes some way toward explaining the small size of the private organized sector.

In 1980, China had 77.1 million persons in the 'secondary sector', which covers manufacturing but also mining, utilities and construction. This rose steadily to 166 million in 1998, then declined for four years before increasing again to 169 million in 2004, but almost all the recent increase has been in construction. Employment in urban state-owned enterprises (SOEs) declined by 49 million between 1995 and 2007, so jobs in the private sector absorbed the equivalent of those laid off.

China's industrial labour market was highly regimented in 1980, with both wages and employment of individuals being determined by the state. These regulations were gradually relaxed, and in 1995, a labour contract system was introduced, such that by 2001, 72 per cent of SOEs determined their wages, as did 81 per cent of non-SOEs (Li et al., 2003, p. 103). Enterprises are 'entitled to employ or lay-off labour on the basis of the labour contract and in accordance with the market conditions and the performance of the enterprise' (Li et al., 2003, p. 109). By 2005, it could fairly be said that China's urban labour market was largely free, subject only to some remaining restrictions on internal migration within China, restrictions that were routinely violated, and are in the process of being formally relaxed (Li, 2006).

Internal migration in China seems to be more substantial than it is in India. Li et al. (2003, p. 107) report that 60 million Chinese, nearly 5 per cent of the population, lived outside their province of origin in 2000, and that half the migrants are women, representing a large increase from 1990 and earlier, when the authorities seriously limited rural-to-urban migration. Migrants from the countryside typically have less formal education and fewer technical skills than urban workers; they tend to concentrate in construction, transportation, cleaning, household services and other jobs that mainly require manual labour. As noted above, nearly all the growth in China's population over the period 1980–2000 has become urban, leaving the rural population virtually unchanged, and its share down by 16 percentage points (and a further 9 percentage points in 2000–07).

Rural–urban migration is also occurring in India, but the share of urban population has grown by only 4.5 percentage points over the two decades 1981–2001, to 28 per cent, compared with 36 per cent in China. In contrast with China, India's rural population grew by 218 million over two decades, by 42 per cent. These figures are of course influenced by the more rapid population growth in India, by 1.9 per cent a year compared with China's 1.3 per cent over the two decades. Nonetheless, India's urbanization increased by only 3 percentage points of total population, which was much less than Indian authorities expected in the mid-1980s. Most of the increase in urban population over the period occurred through natural increase (and some re-classification); only 13 million persons (net) – 1.8 per cent of the total population – migrated from rural to urban areas during the decade 1981–91, and the number cannot have been much greater during the 1990s, since the rate of urbanization did not accelerate.

Most of the interstate migration in India is male, and the men are largely between the ages of 15 and 44. Rural women often migrate, but typically through marriage to men in neighbouring villages. Tripathy and Dash (1997), on the basis of interviews of over 500 families in eight Orissa villages in 1993–94, report that most male migration is to towns or cities in other states. They find that migration widens knowledge, experience and tolerance, and opens people to new ideas. Families with migrants are notably better off than those without: they are more able to pay off their debts to money lenders, the bane of landless workers constantly in hock; buy more food and better clothes; build better houses; and buy more or better agricultural inputs, such as seeds, fertilizer and pumps. Migration also lowers the birth rate (since males are away for long periods) and introduces new attitudes and new ideas. Remittances are very important to the families of migrants and improve rural well-being. Broadly similar findings for internal migrants result from a survey of over 400 village households in southern China (OECD, 2005[2]).

Basic educational attainment is notably higher in China than in India, although both have made significant advances in the last two decades. Adult literacy was 84 per cent in China in 2000, and 57 per cent in India. Youth literacy (age 15–24) was 98 per cent in China, and 73 per cent in India, up from 93 per cent and 60 per cent respectively in 1985. Secondary school enrolment rates were 50 and 39 per cent, respectively, in 1998 (UNDP, 2002, pp. 183–4). India historically placed less emphasis on primary education than did China, especially in rural areas, and more on university education. By 2005, India had 2.5 million new university-level graduates, 10 per cent in engineering (*The Economist*, 17 December 2005, p. 58).

China undertook a major expansion of university-level education during the decade 1995–2007, nearly doubling the number of institutions to 1908, almost tripling the number of faculty to 1.17 million, more than sextupling the number of students to 18.8 million, and quintupling the number of graduating students to 4.5 million, including 312000 graduate degrees. By 2007, over a quarter of the relevant age cohort was entering tertiary education.

OPENNESS TO THE WORLD ECONOMY

Both China and India had essentially closed economies 30 years ago. While both traded with the world, trade – and indeed economic activity generally – was highly controlled by their governments, and much trade was through bilateral barter agreements with other countries. Both have moved significantly toward more open economies since 1980, although communist China started earlier and proceeded more aggressively than did democratic India. Liberalization of the domestic economy began in China in 1978, and in India in the early 1980s. Liberalization of foreign trade and investment soon followed in China, but it was not until after the 1990–91 financial crisis that it began in earnest in India. Both countries have accepted Article VIII of the International Monetary Fund (IMF), requiring currency convertibility for current account transactions: India in August 1994, China in December 1996. (India joined the IMF on independence in 1947, but invoked a transition clause for nearly half a century; China joined the IMF in 1980.) Both countries maintain controls on capital movements, particularly outward movement of resident capital. Both officially encourage the inflow of foreign direct investment, but India does so more hesitatingly and with more restrictions on foreign ownership than does China. Both have reduced import barriers significantly, but China has gone much further, partly as a result of its accession to the World Trade Organization (WTO) in 2001. Even after its reductions, India, until recently, remained one of the most protected markets in the world, with average tariffs of 33 per cent in 2003–04 (47 per cent on agricultural goods), compared with China's 16 per cent in 2000 (Dahlman and Utz, 2005, p. 28). Among developing countries, India was exceeded only by Egypt and a few small African countries in its restrictiveness in 2002, according to the United Nations Industrial Development Organization's (UNIDO) index of inward openness (UNIDO, 2005, p. 159). India, in 2008, reduced its maximum import tariff on many non-agricultural goods to 10 per cent, but that does not include the supplemental import duties that India sometimes imposes, nor the extensive use of anti-dumping duties.

Actual interactions with the rest of the world reflect these policies, as well as continuing (although declining) hostility to foreign goods and investment among Indian intellectuals. Remarkably, even in 1980 China's exports were more than twice India's exports of $8 billion. China ran a small trade surplus; India ran a large trade deficit – imports were nearly $14 billion, financed in large part by foreign aid, including food aid. By 1990, China's exports had grown to $52 billion, India's to $18 billion. By 2002, the two figures were $326 billion and $51 billion, respectively, and by 2007 they were $1218 billion and $187 billion. Imports into both countries rose in tandem, China maintaining its modest trade surplus (which grew dramatically, however, after 2004) and India its trade deficit. Thus, India's exports increased a respectable 8.9 per cent a year – 5.5-fold – over the two decades ending in 2002, but China's increased a startling 14.7 per cent a year – fifteen-fold – over the same 20 years. India's export growth accelerated over the period, but China's export growth stayed ahead of it, reaching 6.5 per cent of world exports. India has received much attention in recent years for outsourcing by US and European firms, especially in computer software and back-office work. But even India's exports of services lag those of China, reaching $25 billion in 2002, compared to China's $39 billion, although $19 billion of India's exports were in communications and software, compared to China's $13 billion (travel was much more important to China) (Dahlman and Utz, 2005, p. 30).

In 2003, the ratio of exports to GDP reached 35 per cent in China, while that ratio was 15 per cent for India, up from 6 per cent in 1982. (In December 2005, China revised upward its estimate of GDP for 2004 by 17 per cent, mostly correcting for under-reporting of domestic services, so this adjustment would lower China's recent export-to-GDP ratio to 30 per cent.)

A similar story to merchandise exports can be told about FDI, where foreign firms hold equity and have a voice in management – sometimes the controlling voice – in local firms. India experienced some disinvestment by foreign firms in the mid-1970s (as IBM and Coca-Cola withdrew because of unacceptable impositions), and then recorded *no* inward FDI until 1991, from which point it rose steadily, reaching an estimated $5.8 billion in 2004. Net FDI inflows into India had cumulated to $28 billion over the period 1991–2003.

China recorded $440 million of inward FDI in 1982 (the first year of balance-of-payments records), growing steadily over the years, first exceeding $2 billion in 1987, $20 billion in 1993, and reaching an extraordinary $138 billion in 2007, never having dropped below $35 billion a year – more than India's cumulative FDI in 2003 – since 1995. Relative to gross domestic product (GDP), China's FDI has been around 5 per cent, India's barely 1 per cent. In addition to formal restrictions on foreign ownership, India maintains numerous non-discriminatory barriers to private business. In international comparison, the procedures to start a business are complex, and the time and cost involved are high; it is extremely difficult, and costly, to fire workers; the time and cost of enforcing contracts are high; and closing a business on average takes ten years, with an exceptionally low financial recovery rate (Dahlman and Utz, 2005, Appendix 8).

Both countries have experienced foreign purchases of equity – not involving management – in roughly equal measure in recent years: net inflows into India of $31 billion over the period 1996–2004, compared with $37 billion into China (World Bank, 2005a, p. 146).

Care must be taken in interpreting these figures. It has been said that as much as one-third of the inward FDI into China is actually resident capital, run through a foreign shell (often based in Hong Kong, a separate economic entity, or in the British Virgin Islands), entering China under the guise of FDI to take advantage of the tax and other privileges that the

Chinese government accords to FDI. Perhaps another third comes from persons of Chinese origin living in Hong Kong, Taiwan, or Singapore. But India also has a large diaspora, which has only more recently begun to invest in India on any scale.

Similarly, the rapid growth of Chinese exports needs to allow for the fact that exports are recorded at invoice value, and that China has become a processing and assembly location for imports from many other economies, especially Korea, Taiwan and Southeast Asia. Thus, the domestic value-added in many Chinese exports is relatively low, in the order of 20–30 per cent. As we have seen, China's employment in manufacturing has actually declined in recent years, in sharp contrast to the extraordinary growth in exports of manufactures. A high fraction of the exports – perhaps 60 per cent – arises from foreign-invested firms in China, whether FDI or joint ventures, where productivity (and wages) are notably higher than in domestic firms. Nonetheless, manufacturing value-added in China experienced a significant increase, from \$116 billion (in 1995 dollars) in 1990 to \$460 billion in 2002, or 12 per cent a year (calculated from UNIDO, 2005, p. 157). The manufacturing share of GDP rose from 33.1 per cent in 1990 to 34.5 per cent in 2002. In India, in contrast, manufacturing value-added rose from \$41 billion to \$81 billion over the same period, or 'only' 6 per cent a year; the share of manufacturing in GDP fell from 16.6 per cent to 15.8 per cent – as indeed it did in most rich countries of the world, and in many other developing countries.

CONCEPTUAL AND THEORETICAL CONSIDERATIONS

It is useful to distinguish among three concepts of a country's economic relations to the rest of the world, or to other countries: engagement, integration, and influence. 'Engagement' occurs whenever a country's factors of production (for example, labour) produce for sale in another country, either through migration to that country or through exports. 'Integration' occurs when product or factor markets are so closely linked that prices move together. Complete integration is rare, being approximated most closely by some commodity markets and by short-term financial markets in rich countries. But a key indicator of integration is how closely prices move together. It is noteworthy that, in principle, integration can be high even with low levels of international transactions, so long as markets are open and linked; for example, the price of domestically produced oil is determined by world oil prices. Thus, we may want to say that factors are 'engaged' in the world economy even if their production is sold into the domestic market, so long as the relevant market is integrated into the world market. That is a question of semantic taste.

Markets may not be integrated and labour and capital may not be engaged and still there could be a significant international 'influence' on the domestic economy, for example, through foreign assistance, or through inward transfer of technology, or through changes in the terms of trade. Thus, the rise in world oil prices in the 1970s influenced both India (an oil importer) and China (an oil exporter) by affecting their budget constraints even though domestic prices were insulated from world price changes. The green revolution was made possible in India by importing technology, even though domestic food prices were insulated from world price developments.

Economic integration implies that when economic agents try to improve their economic well-being by responding to incentives for higher income, they succeed, even when the opportunities are in different sectors or in different geographic areas. Global integration occurs when such success spans many different countries. An important part of this process is the movement of workers, especially from rural to urban areas within countries, or from poor to rich countries internationally, or at least to where better economic opportunities exist. International migration is discussed in the next section. Suffice it to say here that there are major policy obstacles to international migration – few countries welcome non-homogeneous immigrants – as well as the usual human obstacles of cost, risk, language and cultural alienation.

Up to a point, international trade can be a functional substitute for migration, while avoiding some of the costs. Workers can make products in excess of domestic needs and sell them abroad, thereby earning a better livelihood at home. Economists have an elegant theory of comparative advantage based on relative factor endowments – conjectured by the Swedish economic historian Eli Heckscher, developed further by his student Bertil Ohlin, and formalized by Paul Samuelson – now known as H–O or HOS theory. The key point is that under free trade, countries will specialize in products that use intensively factors that they have in relative abundance. This is obvious in the case of natural resources or agriculturally productive land, which are not evenly distributed among countries, but it also applies in principle to labour and capital. For example, countries with a relative abundance of unskilled labour (compared with land, capital and skilled labour) will export products that require a relatively high amount of unskilled labour in their production, for example, apparel. When certain demanding conditions are met, such specialization can even result in equalization of factor prices across countries, through trade alone, without migration. This remarkable result has fascinated economists ever since Samuelson first propounded the theorem in 1948; but the conditions for equalization are extremely severe (including competitive product and factor markets, homogeneous factors of production, a menu of identical technologies available to all countries, unique factor-intensity in production of each product, and the relevant countries producing a list of commodities in common that is large enough to cover all factors). They are not observed in practice.

Indeed, there is some question about the applicability of the HOS theory to a world of rapid, but uneven, technical change and factors that are not, and cannot be, homogeneous except in the very long run. Concretely, in the short to medium run, both skilled labour and capital are specialized for the industries in which they work, resulting in a large number of specialized, not homogeneous, factors of production. Over the long run, capital can be redeployed (as old capital depreciates), and labour can be retrained or replaced with new members of the labour force, trained differently. But over this same long run – measured sometimes in decades rather than years – the technology of production will also have changed significantly, and differentially by country, despite growing international diffusion of technology.

Nonetheless, a weak version of the insight propounded originally by Heckscher may be thought to have some applicability, particularly where unskilled labour can be found in abundance, as in China and India. Thus, we should see such countries exporting goods and services that require relatively high amounts of unskilled labour. This specialization on the world scene would put downward pressure on unskilled labour markets in countries where unskilled labour was less abundant, reducing wages and/or employment of such labour. It should also raise the wages of unskilled workers in countries where it is in relative abundance, compared with a situation in which trade is not allowed or is seriously inhibited. I discuss below the extent to which such phenomena can be observed.

EMIGRATION

As noted above, international migration is one mechanism through which integration of factor markets might take place. Globally, migration has taken place on a large scale. In 2000, an estimated 175 million people lived outside their countries of origin – about 4 per cent of the world's population over age 14. Both China and India are countries of substantial net emigration, with an estimated 1.95 million persons a year having left China during 1995–2000 and an estimated 1.4 million persons having left India (World Bank, 2005b, Table 6.13). The outstanding stock is unknown, but 20 million Indians were estimated to be living outside India in 2000,[3] with Burma at 2.9 million having the most numerous Indian population, followed by the United States at 1.6 million. (The US Census of 2000 records 1.02 million persons born in India living permanently in the United States, and 0.99 million born in China, third and fourth after Mexico and the Philippines, respectively.)

The stock of emigrants from China must be at least as great, since an estimated 16 million Chinese emigrated in the decade 1990–2000. These large numbers represent a small fraction, roughly 2 per cent, of their respective populations. They would, however, represent a significantly larger fraction of the urban labour force, assuming they were predominantly working-age persons from urban areas, and they would represent a still larger fraction of the highly educated population. For example, 48 per cent of Chinese living in OECD countries had a tertiary education, and 60 per cent of Indians, compared with 2 and 5 per cent of the home populations, respectively (Doquier and Marfouk, 2004, reported in Kapur and McHale, 2005, p. 149). The United States issues H1B visas allowing foreigners with special talents or skills to work in the United States for three years (renewable for three years). About 134 000 such visas were issued for initial employment (excluding renewals) in 1999; about half of the petitions (which must be made by US employers) granted in 1999–2001 were for Indians, largely in information technology, followed distantly by Chinese, Canadians and British. Indians accounted for 70 per cent of the 100 000 decline in visa petitions granted between 2001 and 2002, after the 'dot.com' bubble burst (Mann, 2006, Chapter 3.3).

Not all emigrants, however, are highly educated. Many moderately educated Chinese from Fujian province were allegedly smuggled abroad, especially into the United States (Kwong, 1997), and many low-educated Indians work in the oil-rich Gulf states, the former being illegal under US law, and the latter on temporary work permits.

There is a complex set of potential economic relations between an emigrating population and those that remain. Concerns expressed decades ago about a 'brain drain' from developing to rich countries have not disappeared, but they have become much more nuanced in recent years, especially for China and India where an extensive overseas diaspora is playing a significant and increasing role in their home countries – through remittances, returnees, venture capital, entrepreneurship, and marketing access abroad. In a world endowed only with homogeneous workers and capital, emigrants drawn from the average population, taking their capital with them, under competitive conditions would leave those behind neither better nor worse off than before, except insofar as publicly financed education was paid for by borrowing from future income. Allowance for productive land, which cannot migrate, would leave those behind somewhat better off. But such statements in practice need to be heavily qualified in a number of ways, especially if the migrants are educated better than average. On the other hand, the possibility of emigration may create an incentive for more people to become better educated than otherwise, even though many of the hopefuls do not actually emigrate.[4]

GREATER INTEGRATION?

One measure of integration between two markets is what happens to wages (and other factor prices), especially wages of unskilled workers. According to HOS theory, integration of labour-abundant economies into the world economy should increase the real wage of unskilled workers, as more products that use unskilled labour intensively are exported from those countries. The test is not decisive, since wages can change for many reasons, especially when an economy is growing rapidly. The impact on wages in China and India is complicated by the fact that both have millions of workers in low-productivity agriculture. While the numbers have declined in relative terms, and in China in absolute terms, a large reservoir of agricultural labour remains, putting downward pressure on the domestic wages of unskilled workers. Further difficulties arise from the inadequacy of data. To quote the *Indian Economy Yearbook of Statistics* (1998, p. 97): 'Data relating to earnings of workers are scanty and disorganized'.

India experienced a significant amount of inflation during the 1970s and 1980s (although modest compared with many other developing countries), and the money earnings did not keep up, so 'the trends [to 1996] in real earnings of the workers engaged in factories show a steep decline since the early seventies' (*Indian Economy Yearbook of Statistics*, 1998, p. 9). The real earnings of casual rural workers increased, however, by 2.8 per cent a year in 1981–95. Surjit Bhalla (2002, p. 124), arguing that these are the most poorly paid of Indian workers, also suggests a rise of about 3 per cent a year between 1983 and 1999. This growth in real wages is puzzling given the increase in the person–land ratio as India's rural population and labour force increased, but that was apparently more than compensated by increased irrigation, technical improvements in agriculture, and increased use of agricultural inputs such as fertilizer. There has been too little rural-to-urban migration in India to make much difference, although cases can be found (for example, in Orissa) where land has gone idle both because the workers have migrated and the land-owning Brahmins cannot till their land because of inadequate farming skills and because it would be beneath their priestly dignity.

In the urban 'organized' sector, wage determination is heavily influenced by the governments (which taken together account for two-thirds of organized employment), so these wages are not really determined by competitive market forces (Banga, 2005). This marks a sharp contrast with China today, where wages and other conditions of employment are determined by enterprises, paying what is necessary to get the labour they need (see Li et al., 2003, Chapter 3). It is ironic that both the European Union and the United States officially consider China a non-market economy, implying that in assessing anti-dumping duties, surrogate economies are used to calculate costs, and the surrogate sometimes used is India!

Given the structure of the Indian economy, labour regulations, trade policy and religious practice (where in rural areas the occupation-determining caste system is very much alive), it is difficult to conclude that the Indian labour force, taken as a whole, is integrated into the world economy at all, or even well integrated across India. An exception is the much-publicized IT and business back-office activities, where perhaps one million workers are employed in ways that plug them into the rest of the world, and where earnings are influenced by that connection. This, however, is a small and relatively well-educated portion of India's labour force. Although India produces many engineers annually, most are unsuitable for working abroad (as engineers) or in foreign firms in India. McKinsey (2005, p. 32), on the basis of surveys of human resource managers in dozens of firms, concluded that only about 25 per cent of Indian graduate engineers would qualify (and only 10 per cent of the Chinese graduates), and many of those graduates would be inaccessible because of their unwillingness to move near a major airport. Devesh Kapur and John McHale (2005, p. 98) also discuss the large number of faculty vacancies, the large classes, and the generally poor teaching in Indian universities. In practice, India remains largely a closed economy.

China is markedly different. Again, the data are limited, but we do have average monthly earnings of employees in town-and-village enterprises (TVEs), which in terms of employment are overwhelmingly (94 per cent) in rural areas and draw on largely unskilled rural workers. Real earnings rose 81 per cent in 1978–95, or 3.5 per cent a year on average, and 240 per cent (4.8 per cent a year) over the period 1978–2004, reaching 9814 yuan ($1185) by 2004. These earnings were significantly below average earnings in SOEs (16 729 yuan a year) and less than half average earnings of 20 440 yuan in foreign enterprises. 'Foreign' enterprises exclude those whose owners are from Hong Kong, Macao and Taiwan, where average earnings at 15 727 yuan were less than earnings in SOEs, although 60 per cent more than in TVEs. (Real earnings are calculated by deflating money earnings by a consumer price index. This procedure may give inadequate allowance for the fact that urban Chinese must these days purchase many items, such as housing, health care, and even education, that were once provided in kind.)

Although there are many casual workers in China, especially in agriculture and recent migrants into the cities, regular employment is much more common than in India. The rapid growth in wages pulled people out of agriculture, and indeed whole families sometimes migrated to the vicinity of cities, where older migrants look after children and work the farms vacated by villagers who now work in factories, while young adult migrants are also employed in factories.

There is much regional variation in earnings in China. Within TVEs (largely unskilled labour), average earnings by province in 2004 varied from a low (in Heilongjiang) of 6473 yuan to a high (in Shanghai) of 20, 127 yuan, a ratio of 3 to 1. (For comparison, average earnings of workers covered by unemployment insurance by state in the United States – a much less homogeneous group – varied only by 1.7 across states in 1996.)

There is nonetheless a problem with interpretation of the dramatic increase in wages that has taken place in China. As we have seen, China's employment in manufacturing has fallen, not risen, despite a sharp increase in exports of manufactured goods. Wage increases reflect not merely integration into the world economy – manifested in increased exports, especially from foreign enterprises or joint ventures – but also a significant restructuring of the economy, including the entire manufacturing sector. This restructuring was no doubt facilitated by the opening of China's economy, and especially by the growth in exports, but it differs from the process characterized by HOS theory, which assumes that the demand for unskilled labour would have risen.

Furthermore, wage differentials for well-educated Chinese have risen, not fallen as strict HOS theory would require. Differential earnings for those with tertiary education over those with primary education rose from about 25 per cent in 1988 to 75 per cent in 1999; differentials of high school graduates over primary school graduates rose from 12 per cent to 35 per cent over the same period of time (Hu, 2007). Indeed, China is increasingly able to recruit back to China students who have been educated in US or European universities.

The high rate of investment in China has raised capital–labour ratios dramatically (from admittedly low levels two decades ago), by nearly 11 per cent a year in 1995–2001. Labour productivity has risen correspondingly, by over 7 per cent a year over the period 1978–2001. Capital productivity, however, has fallen since 1995, pulling down the growth in total factor productivity to less than half its 1978–95 rate during the period 1995–2001 (Hu, 2007). It no doubt fell further during the investment boom of 2003–04.

In conclusion, the past two decades have seen increasing *engagement* by portions of China's labour force with the world economy; this has been much less the case for India. Although it is much greater than 20 years ago, *integration* with the world economy remains highly incomplete, again especially for India, where it can be said that it has hardly taken place at all, with the partial exceptions of the IT sector and parts of the automobile and apparel sectors. Nonetheless, the world economy has had an increasing *influence* on both countries through introduction of foreign technologies, changes in terms of trade brought about by rising prices for raw materials (especially oil), and sensitivity of some sectors to changes in demand in the world economy. Finally, there seems to have been some *convergence* in real incomes, in that real wages of the least-skilled members of the labour forces in both countries have risen more rapidly than the wages of low-skill workers in the United States and Europe. Moreover, skill differentials have widened, as elsewhere in the world, suggesting that wages of high-skill workers have also risen faster than those in the United States and Europe.

CONJECTURES ABOUT THE FUTURE

China still has much potential for moving unskilled workers out of agriculture into more productive economic activities, and has a demonstrated capacity to do it. Therefore, China will continue to grow the service sector and the production and assembly of light manufactures, with an increasing ratio of domestic value added (thus reducing China's dependence on imported components). China, however, is now the largest exporting country in the world, and thus Chinese products will meet increasing market resistance compared with when China was smaller for two quite different reasons. First, China's market share is now high in many products, and it will be more difficult to pry customers away from favoured suppliers. Second, China will encounter increasing protectionist resistance from competitors determined to hold onto their markets, especially (now that China is entitled to non-discriminatory treatment under its WTO membership, except for transitional provisions against import surges from China) in the form of anti-dumping cases, the current and grossly misused favourite form of protection in the European Union, the United States, and indeed a growing number of countries. India already has the largest number of anti-dumping duties against Chinese firms.

As educational attainment rises in China, it will gradually increase production of more sophisticated products, just as Japan, Korea and Taiwan did earlier. Nevertheless, the impact on the composition of China's trade will be limited, at least for some years, by the demands of China's military modernization for the higher skills, including production of military equipment, and especially by its abundance of unskilled labour, which will keep China's international comparative advantage in products that use the unskilled labour.

India is much less well positioned than China. Internal mobility, both geographic and occupational, is very much lower, and India has been much less successful in creating new non-agricultural jobs for unskilled labour in the tradable sectors. India no doubt will continue to excel at aspects of information technology and outsourced back-office work, but even that will be limited by the availability of suitably skilled labour. Exports of manufactured goods will continue to develop further, particularly selected apparel, auto parts, and perhaps motorcycles, bicycles and similar light manufactures, as well as some engineering goods. India's exports have a much higher ratio of domestic valued-added than do China's. India will, nevertheless, be subject to stiff competition from China, Indonesia, Vietnam and Bangladesh in less sophisticated manufactured goods, and from Eastern Europe (especially in European markets), Brazil, China and perhaps Indonesia for more sophisticated products. India's belated adoption of special economic zones may increase both foreign direct investment and exports from India, but at this stage it is too early to tell both how 'streamlined' the bureaucratic requirements will actually be and whether the required infrastructure improvements will be made.

Some of the most skilled Indians will continue to emigrate, at least temporarily, to rich countries – especially English-speaking countries, but also to Germany and the Netherlands. They will meet competition from Eastern Europeans, including Russians, where technical education is as good or better. Even after extensive liberalization (compared with India's starting point, but not compared with other important emerging markets), the Indian economy remains remarkably self-absorbed and inward oriented. This inward orientation is undoubtedly changing, but the pace of change in the coming decade is still open to question. Moreover, if Indian exports do grow dramatically, following the lead of China 15 years ago, they too will encounter some protectionist resistance, India's management of its economy will come under greater scrutiny, and many allegedly 'unfair' practices will no doubt be found (for example, electricity prices below cost).

Emigration from both China and India, particularly those who study abroad and then settle there, will undoubtedly continue to enrich the economies of the host countries, especially the United States, Britain, Australia and Canada, which have a demonstrated capacity to absorb such immigrants, and their children, into mainstream society. Increasing returnees will also enrich the home countries with their education and experience abroad, including their experience in business. The numbers are likely to remain small relative to national populations, but significant on certain margins, for example, engineers in the United States.

The future of India may be different if trade is increasingly liberalized and more inward FDI occurs. India's merchandise exports in 2002 were $51 billion, about the same as China's in 1990, and exports of services were $19 billion. They grew rapidly in the following six years, as did foreign investment in India, both direct and portfolio. The next decade could see a dramatic rise in the integration of part of India's labour force into the world economy. Despite the great surge of exports of apparel by China following the expiration of the Multifiber Agreement in 2005, India also experienced a sharp increase in exports to the United States. The basis for China's exports is high volume/low cost. India seems to have done much better in the upscale, lower volume, higher mark-up market, from an industry still based on the skills of master tailors rather than mass production (Tewari, 2005). Thus, India may succeed in finding a special role in the world market for apparel.

Cutting in the other direction, however, are attempts by governments – state as well as union – to incorporate the IT sector increasingly into the 'organized' sector, that is, to subject it to heavy labour market regulation by closing the loopholes that have permitted it to function more flexibly to date. For an upbeat assessment of India's economic future, without ignoring the challenges and unfinished reforms, see Nilekani (2009).

A discussion of the future of manufacturing in the United States goes well beyond the scope of this chapter. Suffice it to say that public discussion of the issue has unhelpfully confused trends in manufacturing employment and output. Manufacturing is likely to proceed as agriculture did before it, with continued declines in employment (in absolute as well as relative terms) combined with continued increases in output, as productivity continues to rise at a faster rate than output and routine jobs are increasingly mechanized. US manufacturing employment reached its all-time peak in 1979 at 19 million workers; by 2007, manufacturing employment had fallen below 14 million (some of the decline resulting from reclassification of jobs that were outsourced by manufacturing firms to domestic service providers), while real manufacturing output had nearly doubled. This long-term trend will continue, and is only marginally sensitive to imports from countries such as China and India.

NOTES

1. Unless otherwise specified, data for China come from the *China Statistical Abstract* for 2005 and 2008; those for India come from Ghose (2004), *Indian Economy Yearbook of Statistics 1998*, and Mohan and Dasgupta (2004).
2. Zhang et al. (2003), cited in Appendix A by the Food and Agriculture Organization of the United Nations (FAO; OECD, 2005).
3. High-level Committee on the Indian Diaspora, 2001, cited by Sidel in Geithner et al., 2004, p. 217; this probably included second- and third-generation Indians. See Martin et al. (2006, p. 198).
4. See Kapur and McHale (2005) for an up-to-date discussion of the impact of emigrants on those remaining behind; see also *Global Economic Prospects* (World Bank, 2006).

REFERENCES

Banga, Rashmi (2005), 'Impact of liberalisation on wages and employment in Indian manufacturing industries', Working Paper No. 153, February, New Delhi: Indian Council for Research on International Economic Relations.

Besley, Timothy and Robin Burgess (2004), 'Can labor regulations hinder economic performance? Evidence from India', *Quarterly Journal of Economics*, **CXIX**, February, pp. 91–134.

Bhalla, Surjit S. (2002), *Imagine There's No Country*, Washington, DC: Institute for International Economics.

China Statistical Abstract [in Chinese] (2005 and 2008), Beijing: China Statistics Press.

Dahlman, Carl and Anuja Utz (2005), *India and the Knowledge Economy*, Washington, DC: World Bank.

Geithner, Peter F., Paula D. Johnson and Lincoln Chen (eds) (2004), *Diaspora Philanthropy and Equitable Development in China and India*, Cambridge, MA: Harvard University Press for Asia Center.

Ghose, Ajit K. (2004), 'The employment challenge in India', *Economic and Political Weekly*, **27** (November), pp. 5106–16.

Hu, Angang (2007), *Economic and Social Transformation in China: Challenges and Opportunities*, New York: Routledge.

Indian Economy Yearbook of Statistics 1998 (1998), New Dehli: National Publishing House.

Kapur, Devesh and John McHale (2005), *Give Us Your Best and Brightest: The Global Hunt for Talent and its Impact on the Developing World*, Washington, DC: Center for Global Development.

Kwong, Peter (1997), *Forbidden Workers, Illegal Chinese Immigrants and American Labor*, New York: The New Press.

Li, Xiaoxi (ed.) (2006), *Assessing the Extent of China's Marketization*, Aldershot: Ashgate.

Li, Xiaoxi et al. (2003), *A Report on the Development of China's Market Economy 2003*, Beijing: China Foreign Economic Relations and Trade Publishing House.

Maddison, Angus (2001), *The World Economy: A Millennial Perspective*, Paris: OECD Development Centre.

Mann, Catherine L. (2006), *Accelerating the Globalization of America: The Role of Information Technology*, Washington, DC: Institute for International Economics.

Martin, Philip, Manolo Abella and Christiane Kuptsch (2006), *Managing Labor Migration in the Twenty-first Century*, New Haven, CT: Yale University Press.

McKinsey Global Institute (2005), 'The emerging global labor market', Report, June, San Francisco.

Mohan, Rakesh and Shubhagato Dasgupta (2004), 'Urban development in India in the twenty-first century: policies for accelerating urban growth', June, Mumbai: Reserve Bank of India.

Nilekani, Nandan (2009), *Imagining India: The Idea of a Renewed Nation*, New York: Penguin Press.

Organisation for Economic Co-operation and Development (2005), *Review of Agricultural Policies: China*, Paris: OECD.

Sundaram, K. and Suresh D. Tendulkar (2004), 'The poor in the Indian labour forcc', *Economic and Political Weekly*, **27**, November, pp. 5125–32.

Tewari, Meenu (2005), 'Post-MFA adjustments in India's textile and apparel industry: emerging issues and trends', Working Paper No. 167, July, New Delhi: Indian Council for Research on International Economic Relations.

Tripathy, S.N. and C.R. Dash (1997), *Migrant Labour in India*, New Delhi: Discovery Publishing House.

United Nations Development Program (2002), *Human Development Report*, New York: UNDP.

United Nations Industrial Development Organization (2005), *Industrial Development Report 2005: Capability Building for Catching Up*, Vienna: UNIDO.

World Bank (2005a), *Global Development Finance*, Washington, DC: World Bank.

World Bank (2005b), *World Development Indicators*, Washington, DC: International Bank for Reconstruction and Development/World Bank.

World Bank (2006), *Global Economic Prospects*, Washington, DC: World Bank.

6. The changing sexual division of labour*

Shelly Lundberg

Man may work from sun to sun, But woman's work is never done.
(Saying)

In the United States, considerable media attention has been focused on the possibility that, as employment continued to fall in the autumn of 2009, the proportion of non-farm payroll jobs held by women could exceed 50 per cent. If this reversal of male–female employment patterns occurs, it will be a transitory one. Women's employment has been less sensitive to the business cycle than men's, and the current recession has had a particularly devastating impact on male-dominated industries such as manufacturing and construction.[1] A female majority in the US workforce is unlikely, therefore, to survive an economic recovery but, all the same, a milestone in the gender division of labour in the market will have been reached. The economic lives of men and women are converging – more slowly in some countries than in others, but inexorably.

In almost all societies, from hunter-gatherer communities to post-industrial economies, task assignment is gender specialized. The early care and nourishment of children are always in the women's sphere, and there has been considerable controversy in the social sciences as to how much of the sexual division of labour is determined by reproductive biology rather than social or cultural processes. A number of economists have constructed models that show how sex differences, including initial maternal investments in children and differential fecundity, can interact with constraints in the market and the household to produce distinct economic roles for men and women. Though sexual biology is stable, changes in technology and the development of markets have altered the comparative advantage of men and women in ways that have dramatically changed their allocation of time. Historically, increases in the return to human capital have set in motion a number of endogenous and interconnected processes that have reduced gender specialization: increases in women's education, changes in fertility and marriage patterns, and the marketization of household production.

As economies develop and production shifts from agriculture to industry to services, the organization of work also changes and alters the relationship between men's work and women's work. Farming as a joint family enterprise gives way to the 'separate spheres' of home and work in industrialized economies and then to the dense markets and shrinking households of wealthy post-industrial societies. Households have become smaller and less stable, and this has hastened the movement of economic activity from the family system to the market. In turn, the shrinking economic role of the family has reinforced the erosion of traditional family structures and changed the selection of individuals into marriage and parenthood.

Falling fertility and the increasing market returns to brains rather than brawn have reduced the economic significance of biological differences between men and women. This development raises the question of whether the sexual division of labour, and the gender wage gap that emerges from it, can ever be completely eliminated. The attention of researchers in many fields has been focused on measuring cognitive/behavioural differences in the capabilities of the sexes that could prevent this from happening – Are boys handicapped in early learning? Are women too averse to competition? The findings to date are limited, and distinguishing innate differences from the consequences of early socialization is difficult, but new insights about gender differences are likely to emerge over the next few years.

With the movement of women's work out of the orbit of the family enterprise has also come a shift in property rights. The distribution of the returns to family production depends on family governance structures; control of market resources empowers the individual within the family, and increased employment has empowered women. Beyond increased gender equality in distribution both within and across families, the implications of this change in control for economic development are unclear. Many believe that women's empowerment should be good news for children and for the growth of human capital; in particular, evolutionary models suggest that females have a greater interest in making investments in their offspring than do males. Changes in the economic roles of men and women have been accompanied, however, by changes in family structure that separate many children from their biological fathers. This implies that the well-being of children and investments in the next generation will depend both on the resources that women control, and on the contributions that men continue to make to their progeny – either individually or through some collective process.

MEN'S WORK AND WOMEN'S WORK

How Much Work? The Path to Equality

It is a common belief that modern women, with their double burden of market work and household responsibilities, must work more hours than men do. Michael Burda and colleagues (2008) report that a small majority of surveyed economists (and a somewhat larger majority of sociologists) believe that American women work at least 5 per cent more than men, if home work is added to market work. They go on to examine recent time diary data from 27 countries, and find that per capita income is positively related to gender equality in total work hours (Figure 6.1) and that women work substantially more than men on average in the low- and middle-income countries in their sample. Women also work more than men in several European countries, including Italy, Slovenia and Spain. Burda et al. emphasize, however, what they call the 'iso-work' phenomenon: the gender difference in the sum of market and household work hours is small and insignificant in rich, non-Catholic countries, including the United States. In most high-income countries, the additional hours that men

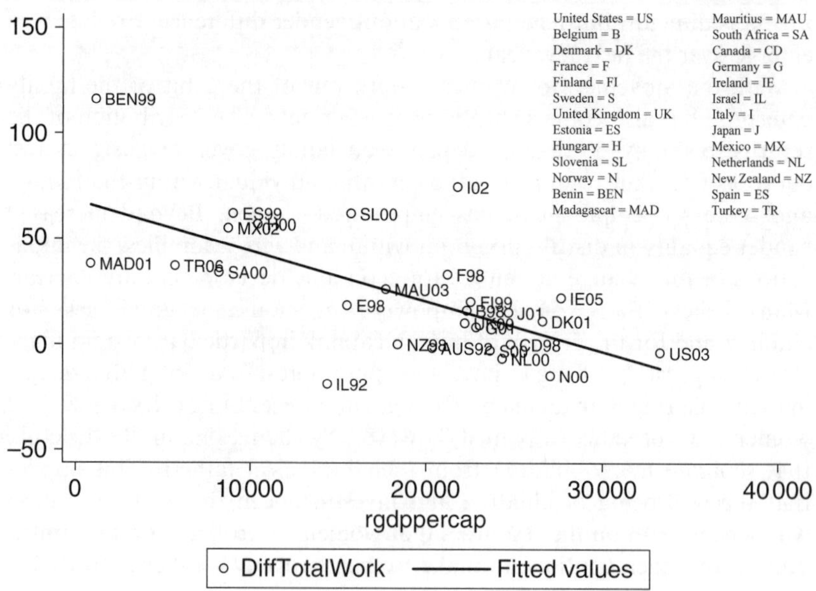

Figure 6.1 Female total work minus male total work compared to real GDP per capita, 27 countries (Fig. 2 in Burda et al., 2008)

supply to market jobs are completely offset on average by the excess work that women perform at home.[2]

Though historical data on time use is limited, it is tempting to conclude from this sort of cross-sectional evidence that economic development tends to promote gender equality in work effort. Time diary data from poor agricultural countries indicate that women work 20–40 per cent more hours than men on average,[3] and Burda et al. find excess female work of 10 per cent or more in middle-income countries such as South Africa, Mexico and Turkey. Western European countries that do not conform to the 'iso-work' pattern are those that report more traditional attitudes to gender roles, and have maintained a more unequal division of domestic labour even as women's education levels and labour force participation rates have risen. It seems reasonable to expect that one important dimension of the changing sexual division of labour in the coming decades will be decreasing hours of work for women throughout much of the world, towards equality with men's hours.

Most of this trend towards equality will come from a decrease in women's domestic labour. The gender realignment of domestic work in the USA and in Europe has been limited; women still provide most of the housework and childcare hours (twice as much care time and 56 per cent more time in 'household activities', according to the latest American Time Use Survey data).[4] Noted less frequently is that the total amount of work being done at home has decreased sharply as fertility rates decline and home-produced goods and services are replaced by market-purchased substitutes. Since 1965, adult men's non-market work in the United States has increased by nearly four hours per week, but women's weekly hours have fallen by more than 12, more than offsetting a seven-hour increase in women's market work.[5]

Looking at men's and women's work using standard data sources that are available over long periods of time and for a large sample of countries, work at home is essentially invisible, and the focus must be on measures of labour supply that reflect participation in market activities. Claudia Goldin has estimated a U-shaped relationship between women's labour force participation and income, both over time in the United States (Goldin, 1990) and for a cross-section of countries (Goldin, 1995). She explains the initial decrease in women's market work as incomes rise as a result of industrialization and the expansion of cities. The physical separation of home and work makes combining family care and remunerative labour infeasible, and leads to declining labour force participation by mothers. Figure 6.2 plots women's labour force participation and per capita income for a large sample of countries in 2005, and a quadratic regression shows a distinct U-shape. Women in many poor African countries have high market

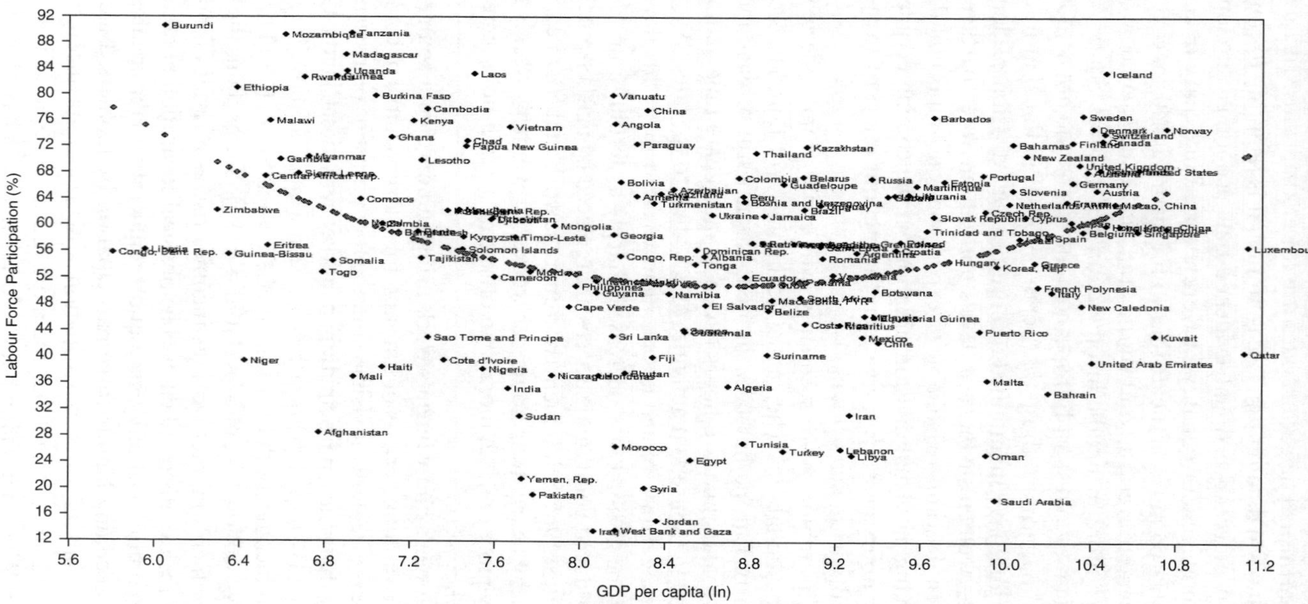

Figure 6.2 Women's labour force participation rate and per capita income, 2005 (data from Gapminder, 2008)

participation rates; in middle income countries – such as those in Latin America – women's participation rates are lower than those in Europe, North America and Oceania.

The source of much of this variation in labour force participation, of course, is not how much women work, but where they work. The role of institutional changes as the formal sector of the labour market grows with economic development can be shown by disaggregating the workforce by sector. The proportion of the labour force that is accounted for by 'family workers' is decreasing in per capita income, while the prevalence of salaried workers is sharply increasing in income.[6] Figure 6.2 also demonstrates the influence of political and cultural factors – communist countries such as China and Vietnam have more employed women than their income level would predict, and Muslim countries in the Middle East with many sequestered women drag down the centre of the 'U'.

What Kind of Work? Comparative Advantage and Gender Task Segregation

In most societies, men and women do very different kinds of work. The care of young children (and most of the care of older children, the sick, and the elderly as well) is women's work. Some activities requiring great physical strength are restricted to men, though women perform a great deal of strenuous physical labour, particularly in agriculture. In market employment, there is substantial occupational segregation, with women's jobs often related in function and skill requirements to domestic work and offering lower pay than men's jobs. The extent to which this division of labour is the outcome of biological differences between men and women, rather than of social organization and cultural constraints, has been a continuing subject of controversy in the social sciences. Economists have generally focused on the interaction between biological differences and market incentives as the source of sex-biased comparative advantage and the division of labour between men and women.

The economics of the household and of the sexual division of labour date from the late 1950s and early 1960s, and are firmly rooted in American family life in that period. In 1960, the labour force participation rate of women in the USA was less than 40 per cent – well down in the U of Figure 6.2 – and married couple families accounted for three-quarters of all households. In the 'new home economics' of the 1960s,[7] the specialization of married men and women in market work and household production, respectively, was explained as an efficient allocation of family effort that maximized total output and family welfare. The fundamental basis of men's comparative advantage in the market, and thus the sexual division of labour, was the reproductive role of women. Gary Becker (1981) emphasizes women's 'heavy biological commitment to the production and feeding of children' (p. 37) because of lengthy periods of gestation and lactation. He argues that it is easier to combine the care of older children with the production of new ones than market activities. Over time, men become more productive in the market, and women become more productive at home, so that their divergent roles are further reinforced. With sector-specific investments in skills, a small initial difference in capabilities becomes a large productivity gap between men and women in equilibrium.

More recently, Aloysius Siow (1998) focuses on a different aspect of sexual biology – the fact that women are fecund for a shorter period of their lives than men – and its impact on labour market incentives. In a marriage market that allows for divorce and remarriage, women who are able to bear children are scarce, and older men have the opportunity to compete with younger men for them in the remarriage market. If their first marriage fails, men are more likely to remarry if their second period wage, which depends on their first period labour supply, is higher. Siow shows that young married men will work more in the market than young married women because of the option value of remarriage, which is not available to older (and non-fecund) women by assumption.

Economic approaches to occupational segregation by sex acknowledged differences in physical capabilities – women's manual dexterity, men's height and strength – but they too have emphasized the constraints imposed by maternity. Working mothers (or women who expect to be mothers) may choose employment that is compatible with childrearing and other domestic responsibilities. Expecting their labour force attachment to be relatively short and intermittent because of child-related withdrawals from employment, women will have an incentive to self-select into occupations that do not impose heavy penalties on such intermittency, that is occupations in which the depreciation rate of occupation-specific human capital is low.[8] These job separations will also cause losses in firm-specific human capital and lead to a shorter work-life with a lower expected return to any investment in skills. This implies that women, and their employers, will invest less in their human capital, resulting in lower wages and lower returns to tenure. Women's concentration in occupations involving personal service or care was also considered to reflect their comparative advantage, in terms of both preferences and capabilities, in activities related to mothering.[9]

Of course, men and women are heterogeneous, and individuals of either sex may have skills and preferences that would predispose them to market or domestic tasks. If optimal specialization within marriage requires that one spouse specialize in market work and the other in household production, and if sector-specific skill investments are made prior to marriage, a coordination problem arises. Individuals will be better off if they marry someone with complementary skills, but they do not know who they will marry, other than that it will be someone of the opposite sex.[10] Sex-specific early training can solve this problem, and investments in sector-specific skills can overwhelm within-gender heterogeneity in innate tendencies towards one sector or the other. Such training also provides a mechanism for the development of social norms and preferences that rationalize and support specialized roles for men and women. Such a social coordination mechanism can generate a sexual division of labour that is independent of biological differences – the assignment of genders to roles is arbitrary.[11] The structural functionalist approach to the family, exemplified by sociologist Talcott Parsons' characterization of the 'instrumental' roles played by men and the 'expressive' roles played by women, captures some aspects of these economic models of the family fairly well.

Anthropologists have reflected more broadly, both in space and time, on the sexual division of labour and possess an analytical framework that shares with economics an emphasis on the interaction of environment, production technology and human capital. This literature is instructive for economists: it provides an analysis of male–female production complementarities under different resource conditions, conceptual links between the division of labour in the nuclear family and the community, and an evolutionary context. Researchers have concluded that gender-based task segregation is nearly ubiquitous, but highly variable and contingent on resources and technology. Most pre-industrial societies distinguish between men's tasks and women's tasks, but there are many departures from the familiar men hunt–women gather dichotomy. In a classic study, Rhoda Halperin (1980) uses five case studies from subsistence foraging societies to show how the environment affects the allocation of tasks. In some societies, only men hunt; in others, both men and women hunt and fish but in many cases use different technologies to do so. Halperin emphasizes the production complementarities between men's and women's tasks and their mutual dependence in subsistence communities. Nevertheless, geographical and seasonal variation in the abundance of resources changes the extent and type of gender specialization, with scarcity associated with greater specialization in cooperative procurement.

Women's work in all societies includes the production of and early investments in children. Pregnancy and childcare responsibilities limit women's ability to participate in large game hunting in most (but not all) hunter-gatherer societies. Douglas White and colleagues (1977) analyse the joint production processes that lie behind the varying sexual division of labour across societies: they assert that production economies arise from combining tasks that are adjacent in the production process and 'clusters based on physical location and temporal sequences of the tasks'; reproductive diseconomies arise from exposing adult females and infants to danger.

Two forces are seen in this literature as driving the development of extreme specialization in male and female activities. First, technological advances in the technology of food acquisition and processing required that individuals learn to perform more complex tasks. Gender segregation provides both a learning environment and a coordination mechanism for such skill acquisition. Second, the transition from hunter-gatherer to sedentism and the adoption of animal husbandry appears to change the extent to which women move independently and acquire resources. Patricia Draper (1975) studies the division of labour between men and women in two groups of !Kung – one a traditional hunter-gatherer group and the other sedentary at a permanent water source.[12] The first group is relatively egalitarian, with women travelling long distances to forage and contributing 60–80 per cent of the family's food. In the second group, the women are mostly homebound while the men travel and accumulate wealth by cultivating crops and accumulating stock.[13]

More recently, researchers in human behavioural ecology (a field of anthropology that takes an evolutionary approach to the study of economic and demographic behaviour) have applied contrasting optimizing models to explain the sexual division of labour. In many societies, men pursue high-variance foraging strategies, such as hunting large game, with the output of a successful hunt treated as a public good and shared widely across households. Women, in contrast, provide for children and close kin by gathering and hunting small, more predictable game. This pattern can be explained as the optimal foraging strategy of a couple with complementary skills. Women's tasks are more childcare compatible; the sharing of game among men creates reciprocal obligations within the community that have insurance benefits for the household, and the diversity of sources provides a nutrient-rich diet. Alternatively, men's hunting can be treated as a form of competitive signalling of male prowess that can yield private returns in social status or improved mating opportunities.[14] In a study of foraging strategies in an Australian Aboriginal community, Rebecca Bliege Bird and Douglas Bird (2008) argue that Martu women hunt lizards to reliably feed their children and maintain cooperative relationships with other women, while men hunt kangaroo and 'trade off reliable consumption benefits to the hunter's family for more unpredictable benefits in social standing for the individual hunter' (p. 655). Men hunt to impress potential in-laws, build their reputation as hunters, and make contributions to the collective good that help them rise in social status.

This signalling model of the household division of labour adds another dimension to the anthropological focus on the efficient allocation of human resources – sexual conflict based on the divergent reproductive interests of men and women. In general, men and women choose to invest resources in two alternative activities that contribute to reproductive fitness: providing for current children or acquiring additional ones. Parental certainty and limited fecundity push women to more intensive parenting investments in the children they have; men have more mating opportunities and pursue a strategy that emphasizes mating effort and the acquisition of more children. These differences imply a conflict of interest between men and women: their distinct foraging efforts reflect their inconsistent foraging goals. Michael Gurven and Kim Hill (2009) point out, however, that the sexual conflict implied by the 'hunting as signalling' model may be over-stated. Since family members can benefit indirectly from men's social status and the claims on group reciprocity that a good hunter acquires, the cooperative provisioning model may be robust to evidence that risky hunting yields signalling benefits.

The analysis of foraging strategies in hunter-gatherer societies shows that biology can be an important ingredient in explaining the sexual division of labour, but that the way biological incentives and constraints affect behaviour depends on the social and material environment. In modern economies, the sexual division of labour is determined in two arenas: the market and the family. The convergence in men's and women's economic lives over the past century – increases in women's market employment, a decreasing gender wage gap, and falling occupational segregation – has two principal drivers, demand and supply. Changes in production technology and capital accumulation have increased the relative demand for female labour, while demographic changes have reduced the domestic demands on women and increased their market labour supply.

TECHNOLOGY AND RELATIVE WAGES

The history of women's employment in industrialized economies has received considerable attention from economists, and the role of changing technology in increasing both the demand for and supply of female labour has been an important theme in that work. Technological advances that increased the relative productivity of women pulled them into market jobs. In many countries, the introduction of manufacturing processes that increased the returns to worker manual dexterity have been accompanied by increases in the employment and relative wages of women and children. Goldin (1990) has documented the role of the new information technologies introduced in the early twentieth century in the increased demand for office and clerical workers – many of them female graduates of the new US high schools. On the home front, labour-saving innovations freed women from many hours of domestic drudgery. The electrification of households led to the development of new domestic appliances, such as washing machines and refrigerators, which substantially increased the productivity of women's time at home and reduced the opportunity cost of market work. The prices of major domestic appliances fell steadily as production volume rose, technology improved, and competition increased, but over the twentieth century investment in household appliances as a proportion of GDP tripled.[15]

More recently, increasing returns to education and rising inequality in the wage and earnings distributions of many countries have been interpreted as the consequence of skill-biased changes in production techniques, such as computerization. Though in general low-wage workers – such as those with low levels of education – have fared relatively poorly in recent decades, the gender wage gap has been declining. Francine Blau and Lawrence Kahn (1997) characterize the rising relative wages of American women during the 1980s as 'swimming upstream' despite changes in the wage structure unfavourable to low-wage workers. They find that women's pay rose because of relative improvements in their occupational distribution (and work experience) and a decrease in the 'unexplained' portion of the gender wage gap.

One explanation is that men and women, conditional on observed factors such as education and experience, bring different skill vectors to the market and that the demand structure for those skills is changing. Oded Galor and David Weil (1996) investigate the gender gap in a simple growth model with three factors of production – physical capital, physical labour and mental labour. Male and female workers have equal mental abilities, but only men supply physical labour. Capital is assumed to increase the marginal product of mental labour proportionately more than it raises the marginal product of physical labour, so that capital is more complementary with women's labour input than with men's. This implies that an increase in the amount of capital per worker increases the relative wages of women.

A more disaggregated approach to examining the role of changing returns to skills in reducing the gender wage gap has been taken by a number of recent empirical studies. These studies have used measures of the specific tasks performed or skills required in jobs to estimate the returns to these skills, how they have changed over time, and what impact those changes have had on the wages of men and women. In general, they have found that changes in the returns to specific job skills in industrial countries have systematically benefited women. Marigee Bacolod and Bernardo Blum (2010) use the *Dictionary of Occupational Titles* (DOT) data linking worker skills to 12000 occupational titles to estimate the wage returns to cognitive, motor, and 'people' skills and to physical strength in the US labour market between 1968 and 1990. They find that the returns to cognitive and people skills more than doubled during this period, and that these changing skill prices differentially benefited women. With job assignment and worker qualifications held constant, rising prices for cognitive and people skills explain about 20 per cent of the narrowing of the gender wage gap during the 1980s. The gender wage gap was also reduced by increases in the relative education and experience levels of female workers, and by changes in the job assignments of men and women. Bacolod and Blum show that, at all education levels, women moved more rapidly than men into cognitive skill-intensive and people skill-intensive jobs. Lex Borghans and colleagues (2006) also find that the returns to people ('soft') skills has increased in Germany and the UK, and that these price changes explain part of the rise in relative female wages in these countries as well.

Using worker self-reports of routine and non-routine tasks performed on the job, Sandra Black and Alexandra Spitz-Oener (2007) find that changes in task prices do not play a role in the narrowing of the gender gap in Germany between 1979 and 1999. Instead, they find that much of the relative improvement in women's wages during this period was accounted for by changes in the tasks performed, that much of this change occurred within occupations and industries, and that tasks changed most dramatically in association with computerization. Female workers experienced large relative increases in the non-routine interactive and analytical tasks they performed. Female workers also reported a substantial reduction in the performance of routine tasks, but male workers did not.

It seems reasonable to conclude that changes in production technology and in the structure of demand since 1980 have benefited female workers more than male workers. Women's jobs have been upgraded, both in terms of the skill requirements of the tasks performed, and in terms of the relative compensation for those skills. What these studies cannot answer is why this job reassignment has occurred – whether female workers have a comparative advantage in working with new technologies or whether pre-existing occupational barriers have been lifted.

DEMOGRAPHIC TRANSITIONS AND THE TRANSFORMATION OF WOMEN'S WORK

Increasing returns to female labour in the market have led to dramatic changes in domestic life. Children have become more expensive as the price of a primary input – mother's time – has increased, and births have been delayed to accommodate extended periods of education for women. In turn, falling fertility and the outsourcing of much household work have reduced the potential returns to marriage as a production-based (and gender-specialized) partnership. The surplus from modern marriage and cohabitation is increasingly based on consumption – of household public goods and companionship – and this has influenced marital stability and selection into marriage. Emerging patterns of marriage and fertility thus both reflect and help to determine the work that men and women do.

Fertility

The large declines in fertility that began in the late nineteenth century in Western Europe were preceded by decreases in mortality. Decreasing death rates, particularly declines in infant mortality, dramatically increased the reproductive productivity of women and drove rapid population growth during the early stages of the first demographic transition. Fertility declines, however, did not only offset the increasing probability of child survival. Birth rates continued to fall for more than 100 years, reducing the number of surviving children continuously through the twentieth century except for the brief interlude of the post-war baby boom. The implications of this large reduction in family size, which has now occurred in most parts of the world, are profound for the sexual division of labour. With increased expected life-spans from reduced maternal mortality and less time spent in pregnancy and lactation, women's time allocation is no longer sharply constrained by maternity. Of course, more time can be invested in each child in these smaller families, but some of that investment can also be delegated or outsourced.

Galor and Weil (1999) argue that the fundamental cause of the demographic transition was not a decrease in infant and child mortality (an outcome of the Agricultural Revolution that increased the food supply) or a rise in per capita income, but rather an acceleration in the rate of technological progress that increased the demand for human capital. An increase in the return to human capital as part of the second phase of the Industrial Revolution caused parents to reallocate their resources towards child quality and away from child quantity, triggering declining fertility across a set of countries with very different levels of income (England, Germany and Finland). The increasing demand for human capital also increased the wage differential between adult (skilled) and child (unskilled) labour, and prompted support for educational reforms and for laws restricting child labour. In earlier work, Galor and Weil (1996) suggest a reinforcing mechanism that ties the demographic transition to technological progress and capital accumulation – the complementarity of capital with mental-intensive tasks, and therefore with female labour. Industrial development, as we have seen, increases the relative demand for women's labour, shrinks the gender wage gap, and also increases the cost of children.

The trade-off between women's childrearing time and market work is not always obvious in the cross-section. Suzanne Bianchi (2000) shows that maternal employment has remarkably little impact on mothers' time with children in the United States, and Jonathan Guryan and colleagues (2008) document a strong positive relationship between parental education and time with children in a sample of 14 countries, although more educated parents also spend more time at work. During the past couple of decades, what had been a negative correlation between fertility and women's labour force participation across European countries has become a positive correlation as women's market work has increased in all countries. Countries with very high rates of female employment, such as the Nordic countries and the United States, have been able to maintain (or even increase) fertility rates, while many countries with relatively low female participation, such as Italy, Greece and Japan, have experienced substantial drops in fertility to extremely low (sub-replacement) rates. Explanations for the low-fertility, low-market work outcome have included limited public support for working mothers and underdeveloped childcare markets (Del Boca and Vuri, 2007). Low marriage and fertility rates are also correlated, however, with survey reports of traditional gender norms and excess female work. Almudena Sevilla-Sanz (2005) suggests that, although efficient marital arrangements in these countries would involve a more egalitarian division of labour as women's wages rise, persistent social norms prevent a young couple from making a credible marital contract that supports that more equal division.

Marriage

One consequence of the marketization of domestic labour has been a decline in the returns to marriage and other co-residing family arrangements. Economies of scale in the production of household goods, once achieved in the kitchens and nurseries of large families, can be bested by canned soup factories and daycare centres. Many of the gains to specialization and exchange that were generated within households are provided by low-cost market goods. Household production complementarities between men and women have decreased in importance as sources of marital surplus, and the relative role of consumption complementarities has necessarily increased. Joint consumption of household public goods and the enjoyment of leisure time together generate the returns to a modern companionate marriage.

This change in the sources of marital surplus has implications for how individuals choose among different family arrangements, and for patterns of assortative mating. The value of household production is maximized by marriages of men and women with very different capabilities and preferences for household tasks and market work – by negative assortative mating. Gains from the joint consumption of public goods, on the other hand, imply positive assortative mating on the preferences for these goods (Lam, 1988). The observed increase in the degree of positive assortative mating on education is consistent with a shift in the source of marital surplus from production to consumption (Schwartz and Mare, 2005).

New sources of data worldwide provide opportunities to examine marital sorting and marital homogamy on determinants of individual capability and preferences beyond education and religion. Although large longitudinal surveys in both developed and developing countries now collect data on a wide range of individual attributes, including preferences and psychological and physical characteristics, their role in family formation and their implications for the changing division of labour in households have been little studied. One piece of evidence comes from the German Socio-economic Panel Study, which in recent years has collected measures of personality and other psychological characteristics from a representative sample of the German population.

Personality traits may be reflective of both individual capabilities (and therefore inputs into household production) and individual preferences (including preferences for household public goods). Someone who is conscientious, for example, will both do a good job of coordinating the family's finances and prefer an orderly household environment, while someone who is highly open to experience will perform well at tasks that require creativity and be bored by a quiet, orderly family life. This implies that it matters, in predicting how personality types select into marriage, whether the gains from marriage come primarily from production complementarities or from the joint consumption of public goods. If specialization and exchange are important determinants of marital surplus, then we expect to see that different personality profiles will be associated with selection into marriage for men and women. If marital surplus is generated by the joint consumption of household public goods and the mutual enjoyment of leisure activities, then we would expect to see that the same traits predict marital status for both men and women.

David Lam (1988) shows, in a model in which the gains from marriage depend only on a household public good and potential spouses vary only in wealth, that there will be positive assortative mating on wealth. In this case, there are returns from spouses having similar demands for the public good. Similarly, there will be returns from spouses having similar tastes for public goods consumption, and we expect to see that individuals with stronger preferences for marital public goods are more likely to marry. On the other hand, if marital public goods are produced in the household and if men and women supply different inputs to that production process, then potential marital surplus and the probability of marriage will depend on different traits for men than for women.

If the sources of the gains to marriage are changing as women spend more time in market work, fertility rates fall, and gender specialization decreases, then this should be reflected in changing patterns of selection into marriage. Using longitudinal data to construct the marriage histories of several cohorts of German men and women, I find that the characteristics that predict marriage by age 35 and the probability of divorce are indeed distinctly different for cohorts born between 1946 and 1959 and later cohorts born between 1960 and 1969 (Lundberg, 2009), and in ways that suggest a change from production- to consumption-based marriage.[16]

Among the older cohorts, the determinants of marriage are very different for men than for women: women who score high on the personality traits 'agreeableness' and 'neuroticism' are significantly more likely to marry than women who do not, and men who are 'antagonistic' (the converse of agreeable) and 'conscientious' are more likely to marry. Thus, women who are emotional and place a high value on harmonious relations select into marriage, as do men who possess personality characteristics that many studies have found to be predictive of labour market success. 'Agreeableness' also reduces the probability of divorce for women, as does 'conscientiousness' for men. These patterns are consistent with gender-specialized contributions to marital surplus, with men providing stable material support and women providing nurturance.

In contrast, the determinants of selection into marriage for younger cohorts[17] are essentially identical for men and women – 'conscientiousness' increases the probability of marriage for both, and 'openness to experience' decreases the probability of marriage. These results are less consistent with specialization as a source of marital surplus, but rather with common preferences for marital public goods. Since 'conscientiousness' includes a willingness to comply with conventional norms, and low 'openness to experience' implies a low demand for variety and novelty, these selection patterns may provide a rather discouraging view of marriage and cohabitation in Germany, but the increase in gender homogeneity across cohorts is striking. These results strongly suggest that a gendered division of labour within families is no longer an important determinant of marriage patterns and that, in Germany, this change has occurred among recent cohorts.

HUMAN CAPITAL: WHAT'S WRONG WITH MEN? WHAT'S WRONG WITH WOMEN?

The convergence in wages, time use and patterns of selection into marriage between men and women in post-industrial, low-fertility economies suggests that the sexual division of labour may eventually disappear altogether. Other research in human development and behavioural economics, however, continues to document persistent differences in the abilities and behaviour of males and females that raise doubts about an economically gender-neutral future.

Women's levels of human capital have been catching up with men's around the globe, and in many countries the educational credentials of young cohorts of women exceed those of men. Women represent 54 per cent of new entrants to tertiary education in OECD countries.[18] The post-war gender gap in college enrolments in the United States had disappeared by 1980, and nearly 60 per cent of current college students are women. A reduction in male advantage in educational attainments can be explained by women's rising expectations of future employment and lower fertility, but the widening gap in favour of women throughout much of the world requires some explanation, since neither wages nor employment rates have reached parity.

Claudia Goldin and colleagues (2006) argue that, once the barriers to women's educational access and job opportunities were reduced ('a more level and wider playing field for girls. . .'), women began to invest more in college education than men because their economic returns are higher and their effort costs of college preparation and completion are lower. They note that women's college wage premium is higher than men's, though a complete accounting of the returns to education would also include the returns from increased work hours and from lifetime gains in the marriage market. The risk of divorce and the need to provide continued support for children has increased women's demand for general human capital. Goldin et al. note that women have consistently outperformed men in secondary education in terms of both completion and achievement, and that many of the factors contributing to that earlier success – lower rates of behavioural problems and learning disabilities and more homework – may provide the key to women's relative success in higher education as well.

Differences in social and behavioural skills between boys and girls arise early and have a significant impact on gender differences in school performance. Thomas DiPrete and Jennifer Jennings (2009) find that an index of skills including self-control and interpersonal skills has a substantive impact on a range of academic outcomes from kindergarten to fifth grade, including reading and maths scores, teacher assessments and grade retention. Boys and girls receive approximately the same return to these skills, but girls enter school with more advanced skills, and their advantage grows over time. A debate persists as to whether these differences are a result of biologically determined maturation processes, cultural practices such as family socialization, or an interaction between the two, such as school environments that are poorly designed to meet the developmental needs of boys. The apparent male disadvantage in academic success and its source in social and behavioural factors may explain recent changes in the relative skill endowment of men's and women's jobs mentioned above, with women benefiting more from the rising returns to cognitive and people skills.

Women's lack of success in highly demanding fields, such as the upper echelons of business (and the economics profession) has led to a search for more subtle sex differences in the laboratory. A substantial body of recent experimental evidence in both psychology and economics indicates systematic differences in the preferences of men and women that could contribute to sex segregation in economic activities.[19] In choices among both real and hypothetical lotteries in a lab setting, women are more risk averse than men, and this is consistent with studies showing that women make more conservative decisions in allocating their own assets. Explanations for this difference include different emotional responses to outcomes (women are more likely to experience fear in the face of losses, while men are more likely to feel anger, and this affects their assessment of the riskiness of a gamble), a greater degree of mens' overconfidence of success in uncertain situations, and gender differences in the interpretation of a risky situation as a threat or a challenge. Women are more reluctant to enter a competition, such as a tournament or an auction, and in a competitive environment, men's actual performance improves relative to women's. Muriel Niederle and Lise Vesterlund (2007) allow men and women to choose between a tournament or a piece-rate compensation scheme for a task in which there is no gender difference in performance: most of the men choose the competition and most women choose the piece-rate system. The results of these studies indicate that the gender differences in compensation systems are the consequence of both male overconfidence and actual preference for competition. Both laboratory studies and surveys show that women are less likely to initiate or to participate in a negotiation.

The question that underlies the recent prevalence and intense interest in these studies appears to be: Can the division of labour in modern societies ever be gender neutral? The inevitable discussion of the role of nature vs. nurture in producing differences in male and female competitiveness can call on a number of interesting studies. If women learn to avoid competitive situations, perhaps because they expect to be punished for assertive behaviour, then we would expect gender differences to develop as children age, and perhaps to vary across societies. William T. Harbaugh and colleagues (2002) find that gender differences in experimental play emerge during childhood, with younger children (between second and fifth grade) playing identically, but older boys and girls (ninth to twelfth grade) playing differently. Uri Gneezy et al. (2009) find that men in a patriarchal society (the Maasi in Tanzania) are twice as likely to choose to compete than women, while women in a matriarchal society (the Khasi in India) are more likely to choose competition than men, suggesting that social structure and culture are important determinants of individual experimental play. On the other hand, literature that links hormones such as testosterone and cortisol to aggression and competitive behaviour supports a biological origin for some part of the observed sexual differences in behaviour, even if they are accentuated by socialization. The jury is still out on the extent to which innate differences explain sex differences in experimental measures of risk aversion and competitiveness.

POWER, PROPERTY RIGHTS AND GROWTH

Given that the time use and market roles of men and women are rapidly becoming more equal in much of the world, what are the implications for long-term outcomes, such as economic growth? Apart from the implications of changing gender roles for population growth, the answer depends on differences in the allocation choices of men and women, and the way that decisions emerge from multi-agent households. Economic models of the family now include both cooperative and non-cooperative bargaining models, most focusing on the decisions of married couples.[20] In a standard cooperative model, the two players – husband and wife – agree on an allocation that depends on their individual preferences, their collective resources and their threat points. In marital bargaining, the threat point is usually specified as the best outcome for each spouse outside the marriage – in other words, a divorce threat. Alternatively, the threat point can be a non-cooperative outcome that does not end the marriage, though the deadlock is likely to be inefficient (Lundberg and Pollak, 1993). In either case, the partner with greater control over resources will have a more attractive fall-back position, more power in the marriage and the ability to get (closer to) what they want. These resources can be economic or social, but control over income is the standard metric of household power. The changing division of labour that moves women's work out of the family orbit and into the market can be expected to increase women's ability to affect the allocation of household resources, as can legal changes that increase women's control over their own income and property. The question then is: Will this change in control have any effect on the allocation of resources in the economy as a whole?

Variation in policies, institutions and labour market conditions that can alter the extra-marital options facing men and women, or the control of resources within the household, have been the subject of a number of empirical studies of intra-household distribution. In general, improvements in women's ability to control reproduction,[21] acquire title to land,[22] divorce and receive alimony payments,[23] and earn a living[24] have been shown to have positive effects on outcomes for women in partnerships, including fertility control, leisure and physical security. A World Bank report reviewed the literature and asserted that 'the evidence on determinants of intra-household resource allocation and investments makes a strong case for targeting interventions by gender – to promote gender equality and more effective development' (World Bank, 2001, p. 163).

Why should specialization in household production, rather than market work, necessarily reduce women's bargaining power within marriage? Both partners have contributed to the well-being of a joint household and invested in a set of productive skills, and the withdrawal of domestic services can provide an effective threat, as does the withdrawal of income. Home skills are not likely to support the same kind of threat point as market skills, however. One source of asymmetry lies in the degree to which market and domestic skills are valuable both inside and outside the marriage (Baker and Jacobsen, 2007). The return on investments in an individual's market earning power is not generally conditional on domestic arrangements,[25] while some part of domestic skill is likely to be marriage specific, and therefore of no value in single life or in subsequent relationships. To the extent that parents value biological children more than step-children, investments in children are also relationship specific.

Women's economic and political rights tend to increase with economic development and are strongly correlated with income per capita (Doepke and Tertilt, 2009). As recently as the early nineteenth century in the United States and England, women had no independent legal status and were essentially the property of their husbands or fathers. Women ceded control of their property and earnings to husbands when they married, and had no right to enter into contracts without consent or to retain custody of their children in the event of divorce. Reforms beginning in mid-century in both countries granted significant property rights to married women before they attained the right to vote. For economists, the rapid and comprehensive empowerment of women is explained, not as the outcome of evolving cultural and political forces, but as a reflection of the changing self-interest of male voters. The centrepiece of economic models of women's liberation is the trade-off that men face between voting for the extension of rights that will augment the bargaining power of their own wives vs. increasing the bargaining power of the wives of other men – including their own daughters. A man would prefer to preserve patriarchal power in his own marriage, but cares about the well-being of his daughters and the success of his grandchildren. His daughters will benefit directly from reform (though sons will be harmed) and, if women invest more of the resources they control in children than men do, all of his grandchildren will benefit as well. A change in the balance over time between these costs and benefits can occur in a number of ways: falling fertility increases the cost of the disparity in well-being of sons and daughters in the 'no rights' regime,[26] or technological change that increases the returns to investments in education makes increasing mothers' weight in family decisions more important for future generations.[27]

If power within the family is driven by individual control of income and other resources, then government policies, laws and social institutions that influence the economic and political positions of men and women can also affect their relative well-being in households. If men and women have systematically different preferences over how to utilize the resources they command – if women, for example, care more about children – then changing the balance of power in the household can affect society's investment in human resources and the pace of economic development. The connection between female empowerment and child well-being relies both on mothers' traditional role in childcare and on evolutionary arguments that women have an incentive to invest more in fewer children because of limited fecundity and are more certain about maternity than fathers can be about paternity. Advocates of the empowerment of women in developing countries have linked male dominance to adverse outcomes ranging from child mortality and malnutrition to political extremism and terrorism. The rationale for increasing women's access to education and property rights where this access is currently limited rests in part on the prospects for improving child well-being and the human capital of the next generation of workers.

Is it true that women will invest more in children? Many studies have found a significant relationship between women's control of income and child health and spending on children, but not all do so.[28] One interesting aspect of time use trends in the United States is that, despite declining fertility, increased preschool enrolment and growing maternal employment, the number of hours devoted to childcare by both men and women increased between 1965 and 2003. Increased childcare by fathers has occurred as part of the juggling in dual-earner households, but the maintenance of mothers' time with children as their participation in the paid workforce increased has been somewhat of a surprise. In part, this is because working women appear to have protected their time with children, and in part because stay-at-home mothers in earlier decades spent little time in direct childcare, as opposed to other household work.[29]

One substantial challenge to the proposition that increasing the market power of women will improve the well-being of children comes from evidence of increasing inequality in the resources devoted to children in the United States, as parental time and incomes decline in the single-parent households at the bottom of the income distribution (McLanahan, 2004). This is in part the consequence of the very modest social welfare support provided to low-income families in the USA. It suggests, however, that with the changes in family structure that have accompanied the changes in the sexual division of labour, increases in child investments will require not only an increase in women's control over resources, but also a mechanism for maintaining paternal investments in their progeny, either individually or through some collective process.

NOTES

* I would like to thank Dick Startz and Meredith Startz for comments, and Kelvin Wong for research assistance.

1. Mulligan (2009).
2. Burda et al. argue that this convergence in hours as incomes rise is best explained by a model in which leisure consumption is driven by strong social cluster norms. As incomes rise, men and women move from gender-specific to gender-neutral reference groups, and their leisure hours converge. It is not clear why gender-specific reference groups should necessarily result in less leisure for women, however.
3. Juster and Stafford (1991) summarize data from rural Botswana and Nepalese villages that show substantially higher work hours for women. Among the candidate explanations they give for the unequal allocation of leisure time in these societies are measurement issues – that the apparent 'free time' of men includes planning and organizing activities – and the possibility that male free time serves as a contingency resource that communities can draw on in case of emergency.
4. Bureau of Labor Statistics, American Time Use Survey Tables, http://www.bls.gov/tus/tables/a1_2008.pdf, 7 April.
5. Aguiar and Hurst (2006). These differences do not control for changes in demographics,

such as marital status and number of children, which the data reported in the published version of these authors' paper (Aguiar and Hurst, 2007) do.

6. The data and graphic tools provided by Gapminder can easily be used to show this.
7. Grossbard-Schechtman (2001) provides an intellectual history of the development of the new home economics at Chicago and Columbia.
8. This argument is developed in Polachek (1981).
9. England et al. (2002) document a wage penalty for both men and women working in occupations involving care work.
10. Same-sex partnerships provide an obvious exception. If we take sexual orientation as exogenous, however, this does not alter the basic point.
11. Echevarria and Merlo (1999), Engineer and Welling (1999), and Hadfield (1999) present interesting variations on such a model. Engineer and Welling show that with heterogeneous aptitudes for home and market work, there exist equilibria in which aptitude, rather than gender, determines training even if marital matching is random (that is, on the basis of 'true love').
12. This could be considered an early version of the natural experiment.
13. This association of traditional agriculture with extreme gender specialization and female disadvantage is supported by the Food and Agriculture Organization's characterization of the division of labour between men and women in agricultural societies (FAO, 2009): '. . .men tend to do the work of large-scale cash cropping, especially when it is highly mechanized, while women take care of household food production and small-scale cultivation of cash crops, requiring low levels of technology. This pattern is particularly pronounced in sub-Saharan Africa, where men and women customarily farm separate plots. Men tend to grow cash crops and keep the income, while women use their land primarily for subsistence crops to feed their family'.
14. See Smith et al. (2003), and the review and references cited in Winterhalder and Smith (2000).
15. Greenwood et al. (2005). It would be a mistake to treat the labour-saving improvements in domestic technology as a purely exogenous technology shock. The development of a mass market for electric appliances reflects the rising value of women's time.
16. Since personality traits are quite stable through adult life, personality measures in 2005 are a good indicator of personality at marriage.
17. Cohabitation is not distinguished from legal marriage in the GSOEP marital histories, so the increase in cohabitation between the cohorts is not likely to be a contributing factor to the different patterns.
18. There are substantial variations across countries (OECD, 2009). Switzerland and Turkey are the only OECD countries in which fewer than 50 per cent of upper secondary graduates are female.
19. A recent and extensive survey of this literature is provided by Croson and Gneezy (2009).
20. See McElroy and Horney (1981), Manser and Brown (1980), Lundberg and Pollak (1994).
21. Pezzini (2005).
22. Field (2003), Panda and Agarwal (2005).
23. Chiappori et al. (2002), Rangel (2006).
24. Aizer (2009).
25. Though married men consistently earn more than single men (Korenman and Neumark, 1991) and the career prospects of men in the 1950s could be affected by a superior's perception of the supportiveness and stability of their domestic arrangements.
26. Fernàndez (2009) finds that property rights reforms occurred earlier in US states with lower levels of survival fertility (by age 10).
27. Doepke and Tertilt (2009) take a theoretical approach, but note that the historical debates on women's rights showed increasing concern for the education and welfare of children over the nineteenth century. Geddes and Lueck (2002) outline a different path to women's rights in which the increasing returns to human capital made it more

advantageous to give women control over their own earnings and the incentive to increase them.

28. See Duflo (2005), Lundberg and Pollak (2008).
29. See also Bianchi (2000).

REFERENCES

Aguiar, Mark and Erik Hurst (2006), 'Measuring trends in leisure: the allocation of time over five decades', NBER Working Paper No. 12082.

Aguiar, Mark and Erik Hurst (2007), 'Measuring trends in leisure: the allocation of time over five decades', *Quarterly Journal of Economics*, **122** (3), pp. 969–1006.

Aizer, Anna (2009), 'Poverty, violence, and health', Providence, RI: Brown University.

Bacolod, Marigee and Bernardo Blum (2010), 'Two sides of the same coin: U.S. "residual" inequality and the gender gap', *Journal of Human Resources*, **45** (1), pp. 197–242.

Baker, Matthew J. and Joyce P. Jacobsen (2007), 'Marriage, specialization, and the gender division of labor,' *Journal of Labor Economics*, **25**, pp. 763–93.

Becker, Gary S. (1981), *Treatise on the Family*, Cambridge, MA: Harvard University Press. (Enlarged edition, 1991.)

Bianchi, Suzanne M. (2000), 'Maternal employment and time with children: dramatic change or surprising continuity?', *Demography*, **37** (4), pp. 401–14.

Black, Sandra E. and Alexandra Spitz-Oener (2007), 'Explaining women's success: technological change and the skill content of women's work', NBER Working Paper 12116.

Blau, Francine D. and Lawrence M. Kahn (1997), 'Swimming upstream: trends in the gender wage differential in the 1980s', *Journal of Labor Economics*, **15** (1: 1), pp. 1–42.

Bliege Bird, Rebecca and Douglas W. Bird (2008), 'Why women hunt: risk and contemporary foraging in a western desert aboriginal community', *Current Anthropology*, **49** (4), pp. 655–90.

Borghans, Lex, Bas ter Weel and Bruce Weinberg (2006), 'People people: social capital and the labor-market outcomes of underrepresented groups', NBER Working Paper 11985.

Burda, Michael, Daniel S. Hamermesh and Philippe Weil (2008), 'Total work, gender, and social norms', available at: https://webspace.utexas.edu/hamermes/www/IsoWork120407.pdf.

Chiappori, Pierre-André, Bernard Fortin and Guy Lacroix (2002), 'Marriage market, divorce legislation, and household labor supply', *The Journal of Political Economy*, **110** (1), pp. 37–72.

Croson, Rachel and Uri Gneezy (2009), 'Gender differences in preferences', *Journal of Economic Literature*, **47** (2), pp. 448–74.

Del Boca, Daniela and Daniela Vuri (2007), 'The mismatch between employment and child care in Italy: the impact of rationing', *Journal of Population Economics*, **20** (4), pp. 805–32.

DiPrete, Thomas and Jennifer Jennings (2009), 'Social/behavioral skills and the gender gap in early educational achievement', Working Paper, Columbia University.

Doepke, Matthias and Michèle Tertilt (2009), 'Women's liberation: what's in it for men?', *Quarterly Journal of Economics*, **124** (4), pp. 1541–91.

Draper, Patricia (1975), '!Kung women: contrasts in sexual egalitarianism in foraging and sedentary contexts', in R.R. Reiter (ed.), *Toward an Anthropology of Women*, New York: Monthly Review Press, pp. 77–109.

Duflo, Esther (2005), 'Gender equality in development', BREAD Policy Paper No. 001.

Echevarria, Cristina and Antonio Merlo (1999), 'Gender differences in education in a dynamic household bargaining model', *International Economic Review*, **40** (2), pp. 265–86.

Engineer, Merwan and Linda Welling (1999), 'Human capital, true love, and gender roles: is sex destiny?', *Journal of Economic Behavior and Organization*, **40** (2), pp. 155–78.

England, Paula, Michelle Budig and Nancy Folbre (2002), 'Wages of virtue: the relative pay of care work', *Social Problems*, **49** (4), pp. 455–73.

Fernández, Raquel (2009), 'Women's rights and development', Working Paper, New York University.

Field, Erica (2003), 'Fertility responses to land titling: the roles of ownership security and the distribution of household assets', Cambridge, MA: Harvard University.

Food and Agriculture Organization (2009), 'Gender and food security', available at: http://www.fao.org/gender/en/lab-e.htm (accessed, November 2009).

Galor, Oded and David N. Weil (1996), 'The gender gap, fertility, and growth', *American Economic Review*, **86** (3), pp. 374–87.

Galor, Oded and David N. Weil (1999), 'From Malthusian stagnation to modern growth', *American Economic Review*, **89**, pp. 150–54.

Gapminder World (2008), Available at: http://www.gapminder.org/ (accessed 28 January 2010).

Geddes, Rick and Dean Lueck (2002), 'The gains from self-ownership and the expansion of women's rights', *American Economic Review*, **92** (4), pp. 1079–92.

Gneezy, Uri, Kenneth L. Leonard and John A. List (2009), 'Gender differences in competition: evidence from a matrilineal and a patriarchal society', *Econometrica*, **77** (5), pp. 1637–64.

Goldin, Claudia (1990), *Understanding the Gender Gap: An Economic History of American Women*, Oxford: Oxford University Press.

Goldin, Claudia (1995), 'The U-shaped female labor force function in economic development and economic history', in T. Paul Schultz (ed.), *Investment in Women's Human Capital and Economic Development*, Chicago: University of Chicago Press, pp. 61–90.

Goldin, Claudia, Lawrence Katz and Ilyana Kuziemko (2006), 'The homecoming of American college women: the reversal of the college gender gap,' *Journal of Economic Perspectives*, **20** (4), pp. 133–56.

Greenwood, Jeremy, Ananth Seshadri and Mehmet Yorukoglu (2005), 'Engines of liberation', *The Review of Economic Studies*, **72** (1), pp. 109–33.

Grossbard-Shechtman, Shoshana (2001), 'The new home economics at Columbia and Chicago', *Feminist Economics*, **7** (3), pp. 103–30.

Gurven, Michael and Kim Hill (2009), 'Why do men hunt? A reevaluation of "man the hunter" and the sexual division of labor', *Current Anthropology*, **50** (1), pp. 51–74.

Guryan, Jonathan, Erik Hurst and Melissa Kearney (2008), 'Parental education and parental time with children', *Journal of Economic Perspectives*, **22** (3), pp. 23–46.

Hadfield, Gillian K. (1999), 'A coordination model of the sexual division of labor', *Journal of Economic Behavior and Organization*, **40** (2), pp. 125–54.

Halperin, Rhoda H. (1980), 'Ecology and mode of production: seasonal variation and the division of labor by sex among hunter-gatherers', *Journal of Anthropological Research*, **36**, pp. 379–99.

Harbaugh, William T., Kate Krause and Steven G. Liday (2002), 'Bargaining by children', University of Oregon Economics Department Working Paper 2002-4.

Juster, F. Thomas and Frank P. Stafford (1991), 'The allocation of time: empirical findings, behavioral models, and problems of measurement', *Journal of Economic Literature*, **29**, pp. 471–522.

Korenman, Sanders and David Neumark (1991), 'Does marriage really make men more productive?', *Journal of Human Resources*, **26** (2), pp. 282–307.

Lam, David A. (1988), 'Marriage markets and assortative mating with household public goods', *Journal of Human Resources*, **23** (4), pp. 462–87.

Lundberg, Shelly (2009), 'Personality and marital surplus', University of Washington.

Lundberg, Shelly and Robert A. Pollak (1993), 'Separate spheres bargaining and the marriage market', *The Journal of Political Economy*, **101** (6), pp. 988–1010.

Lundberg, Shelly and Robert A. Pollak (1994), 'Noncooperative bargaining models of marriage', *American Economic Review*, **84** (2), pp. 132–7.

Lundberg, Shelly and Robert A. Pollak (2008), 'Family decisionmaking', in S.N. Durlauf and L.E. Blume (eds), *The New Palgrave Dictionary of Economics*, New York: Palgrave Macmillan.

Manser, Marilyn and Murray Brown (1980), 'Marriage and household decision-making: a bargaining analysis', *International Economic Review*, **21** (1), pp. 31–44.

McElroy, Marjorie and Mary Horney (1981), 'Nash-bargained decisions: toward a generalization of the theory of demand', *International Economic Review*, **22**, pp. 333–49.

McLanahan, Sara (2004), 'Diverging destinies: how children are faring under the second demographic transition', *Demography*, **41** (4), pp. 607–27.

Mulligan, Casey (2009), 'A milestone for women workers', *The New York Times*, 14 January, http://economix.blogs.nytimes.com/2009/01/14/a-milestone-for-women-workers/.

Niederle, Muriel and Lise Vesterlund (2007), 'Do women shy away from competition? Do men compete too much?', *Quarterly Journal of Economics*, **122** (3), 1067–101.

OECD (2009), *Education at a Glance 2009: OECD Indicators*, available at: www.oecd.org/edu/eag2009.

Panda, Pradeep and Bina Agarwal (2005), 'Marital violence, human development, and women's property status in India', *World Development*, **33** (5), pp. 823–50.

Pezzini, Silvia (2005), 'The effect of women's rights on women's welfare: evidence from a natural experiment', *Economic Journal*, **115** (502), pp. C208–C227.

Polachek, Solomon William (1981), 'Occupational self-selection: a human capital approach to sex differences in occupational structure', *The Review of Economics and Statistics*, **63** (1), pp. 60–69.

Rangel, Marcos (2006), 'Alimony rights and intrahousehold allocation of resources: evidence from Brazil', *The Economic Journal*, **116** (513), pp. 627–58.
Schwartz, Christine R. and Robert D. Mare (2005), 'Trends in educational assortative marriage. From 1940 to 2003', *Demography*, **42**, pp. 621–46.
Sevilla-Sanz, Almudena (2005), 'Social effects, household time allocation, and the decline in union formation', Washington, DC: Congressional Budget Office.
Siow, Aloysius (1998), 'Differential fecundity, markets, and gender roles', *Journal of Political Economy*, **106** (2), pp. 334–54.
Smith, Eric Alden, Rebecca Bliege Bird and Douglas W. Bird (2003), 'The benefits of costly signaling: Meriam turtle hunters and spearfishers', *Behavioral Ecology*, **14**, pp. 116–26.
White, Douglas R., Michael L. Burton and Lilyan A. Brudner (1977), 'Entailment theory and method: a cross-cultural analysis of the sexual division of labor', *Behavior Science Research*, **12** (1), pp. 1–24.
Winterhalder, Bruce and Eric Alden Smith (2000), 'Analyzing adaptive strategies: human behavioral ecology at twenty-five', *Evolutionary Anthropology*, **9** (2), pp. 51–72.
World Bank (2001), 'Engendering development: through gender equality in rights, resources, and voice', *World Bank Policy Research Report*.

7. Round table discussion: how do nations adapt to changes in the division of labour?

Bina Agarwal, Martin Baily, Jean-Louis Beffa and Robert M. Solow

Robert M. Solow (MIT) You have, here, three strong characters and one mouse – so it is very hard to know what will occur! A very complicated bargaining procedure originated by John Nash in 1950-something helped us decide that the first speaker would be Martin Baily, who is now at the Brookings Institution in Washington, DC, after a long and distinguished career including a term as chairman of the Council of Economic Advisers in the United States, and a period during which he and I worked together over a series of interesting studies of economic performance and productivity. But I knew him as a very young man writing, as part of his PhD thesis, what I think may have been the first, and was certainly one of the fundamental, papers of what became the theory of implicit contracts. The second speaker will be Jean-Louis Beffa, who is currently honorary chairman of the board of the Saint-Gobain Corporation and was until recently also Chief Executive Officer; he is also the co-chairman and really the 'idea person' behind the Cournot Centre. The last speaker will be Bina Agarwal, who is Professor at the Institute of Economic Growth at the University of Delhi – and I *do* know what she is going to talk about, which is the new world division of labour in agriculture – a subject that has been lacking in our discussion so far.

Martin Baily Elhanan Helpman [see Chapter 3] said earlier that he did not give advice to other countries. In chatting with him later I said, 'Well you know I wrote a book about transforming the European economy, and while generally it got a pretty good reception, there were a few people who said why didn't I go back to America and stop worrying about the European economy' – to which Professor Helpman replied, 'Well, it serves you right, doesn't it!' I learnt two lessons from that: one is that he is not a man to go to for compassion and, two, that I would focus here on the *US* economy and how it is being affected by the division of labour.

The current situation in the US economy is clearly constrained by weak aggregate demand, as is much of the rest of the world. We got into this situation by a combination of factors. Part of it was that nobody believed that housing prices in the USA could go down. But, at perhaps the more fundamental level, it was that companies failed to put in place adequate risk management strategies, and regulators failed to insist on better risk management. Consequently, when house prices started to go down, the whole financial house of cards that had been built on stable house prices – or rising house prices – collapsed around it. That was not the only thing: there were a few people around the world, in Europe and elsewhere, who had invested in speculative assets as well, but the US was certainly hit the hardest.

For the most part, policymakers have done the right things to respond to this crisis. I say that while recognizing that a lot of mistakes were made along the way. It would probably stick in my throat to commend Henry Paulson, but overall this crisis has been surprisingly well managed; things have turned around, from a cyclical point of view, much more quickly than I had expected. The Treasury injected capital into the banks, the Administration and Congress passed a fiscal stimulus, and there was strong GDP growth in the third quarter of 2009. One reason the banks turned around was not necessarily anticipated: the big Wall Street banks became more profitable more quickly than anyone had realized, enabling them to offset some of the losses that they had experienced. That was both through their trading activities and because lending itself became much more profitable. They were taking lower risks and earning higher margins than they had done prior to the crisis.

That said, it is likely that this will be a slow recovery, and that, in particular, job growth will be a pressing question for several years to come. The United States will probably get back to something close to full employment – whether that is defined as 5 per cent or, as we used to think, 6 per cent, I am not sure. The United States has very little in the way of a social safety net. This means that people have to work in order to eat, and so they take the jobs that are available. Nevertheless, it will take a while before we get back to that full employment level. The jobs question over the longer run for the US is probably: What is the nature of the jobs over the course of the recovery? Are we going to get good jobs or are we going to get McDonald's jobs?

The recovery should be, in my view, a more balanced growth path, one with a lower US current account deficit and a correspondingly smaller current account surplus for the rest of the world. At least for the moment, US consumers are doing their part by slashing consumption. Given that about 14 trillion dollars' worth of wealth was lost – only some of which has come back – it is likely that US consumers will not spend at the same rapid rate going forward as they did in the early years of this century. In order for that balanced growth path to work, the rest of the world has to increase its domestic demand to make up for the fact that the US is no longer generating demand in the form of its trade deficit. I am not sure if that will work: China may change its stripes a little, but I do not think it will be a huge source of global net demand. To some extent the onus is on Europe to increase domestic demand, as well as on Japan.

The cyclical jobs issue is the background of a longer-term concern about macroeconomic growth and job growth. Job growth, even prior to this recession, was slow, much slower than it had been in the 1990s. In part, that was because labour force growth was slower. Female labour force participation has flattened out, and we are now getting the effects of the baby-boom generation: the influx of young people has slowed down, and the baby boomers are starting to retire. So there is a sense in which we do not need as much job growth going forward as we had, let's say, in the 1990s. Looking at 2000 to 2007, the job growth occurred mostly in construction, a fair amount of which has disappeared. Those were not great jobs – they were not well paid. Some were skilled trade jobs, but many were not. The jobs were filled mostly by immigrants from Latin America, some of whom have returned to Mexico or other countries, some of whom have remained in the United States. In the financial sector, which were well-paid jobs – in many cases too well paid – it seems unlikely that we will get back the same level of job growth that we had between 2000 and 2007. During the same period, professional services grew substantially and generally speaking were good jobs – engineering, business consulting, architecture – with the exception of service areas, such as the cleaning of buildings, and so on. Healthcare was a major source of job growth, and there was a substantial increase in state and local government jobs. The food and drink industry was also a big source of job growth, accounting for 1.4 million jobs, or 18 per cent of net job growth over the same period. So, the notion that we have created a lot of McDonald's kind of jobs is in fact correct. Over the period prior to the recession, manufacturing lost 3.4 million jobs, and has probably lost another 2 million since the recession. Most people in the US (but not necessarily most economists) point to international trade as one of the key sources of that decline in job growth. Even among economists there is an increasing view that international trade is costing jobs.

In the US labour market, international trade and the international division of labour have also affected the distribution of earnings and the distribution of income. Up until the 1970s or so, there was no real widening of income distribution, and at one point Richard Freeman of Harvard wrote a book called the *Over-educated American*, because the wage premium on college degrees had actually gone down. Right after he wrote the book, the college wage premium rose substantially. It is not clear that it is still rising, particularly for those with just a qualification – 'any degree'. If you go to Harvard or Yale, the premium does still seem to be rising, but it is less clear that a college degree in itself is still earning a rising premium. What has been true for the last ten years or so is the widening income distribution at the very top. Whether that involves CEOs, Roger Federer, or international lawyers, there is clearly a superstar salary phenomenon, and it is hard not to hold globalization responsible to some degree. I do not think it is just globalization: famous sportsmen and women would probably earn a lot of money even if nobody outside the United States had heard of them, but given that CEOs manage large global companies and that movie or rock stars have a global audience has surely enhanced the income of that superstar category. So, the international division of labour has accentuated the superstar phenomenon.

Let me turn away from this tiny minority of the population towards manufacturing. How has US employment and the distribution of income in that sector been affected by trade? The first point, discussed quite a bit in the previous contributions, is that international trade has changed the composition of manufacturing production. For example, there is very little apparel that is now made in the United States, similarly for leather goods, shoes, toys and so on. Most of that production has gone except for items that are protected by special tariffs. A lot of the labour-intensive goods have disappeared altogether. The other phenomenon is that the value chain is getting broken up and the pieces are being sent overseas. So there is no question that manufacturing in the US has been heavily affected by the global division of labour. Have US workers lost out as a result of that?

Because the United States runs a consistent trade deficit, there have been fewer jobs in manufacturing than if there had been a trade surplus or balanced trade. That probably accounts for a million, a million and a half jobs at the height – that was something Robert Lawrence and I looked at in a Brookings paper in 2004.[1] The trade deficit did not prevent the US economy from reaching full employment (which occurred in 2000, and again in 2007), but it did change the mix of employment. One mitigating factor is that not all the jobs lost in manufacturing were good jobs. The apparel jobs, for example, were not well paid; similarly, some of the jobs lost in the high-tech sector – the biggest loser of jobs over the period 2000–07 – were mostly lower-paying assembly jobs, fitting computers together and putting them into cases. So, to some extent, US manufacturing has been affected by trade, and there are probably fewer production workers as a result. Lawrence and I found, however, that the great bulk of the loss of jobs in manufacturing was associated with the shift in technology. You can say, 'we import steel, and we used not to import steel', but the big difference is that if you go into a steel mill today, you see half a dozen people watching computer screens rather than hundreds of people making steel. So it is more the technology and the automation that have changed the demand for production workers in the manufacturing sector. Nonetheless, those workers would clearly be better off if we had balanced trade rather than a trade deficit.

Is it possible for the manufacturing sector of the US economy to have balanced trade? A lot of people have concluded that the US can no longer manufacture anything. In fact, I have had a number of reporters asking me, 'Well, do we make anything? Do we export anything at all?' Actually the US does: it still has the largest manufacturing sector on a value-added basis. It is not the largest exporter, but is close behind – at least in normal times – Germany and China. That does not mean that we are going to be the largest exporter again anytime soon, but the technological capability and the ability to increase output is still substantial in the manufacturing sector. My own work, including that with Robert Lawrence, suggests that this sector is sensitive to the exchange rate. There are people who disagree with that, who estimate equations looking at the effect of the exchange rate on prices, and prices on the trade deficit. We short-circuited that and looked at the relationship between the exchange rate and the trade deficit, and it is very strong and clear: tradable goods in the US generally respond to exchange rate changes. US trade could be balanced at the right value of the dollar.

The exchange rate is not a policy variable, directly. The only thing I know of that can readily change the exchange rate is a shift in the saving–investment balance in the United States. The US is both a low-saving and a high-budget deficit economy, and consequently, it has a high capital inflow. So, the value of the dollar is heavily influenced by the volume of capital inflows and does not settle at a value that would give equilibrium in terms of trade. The only answer then is to match more closely domestic saving with domestic investment. That, however, would put us in a heavy dilemma right now, because there are a lot of policymakers who would like to increase jobs by spending more government money, either on infrastructure or by financing technology, clean technology, those kinds of things. I sympathize somewhat with that view: our infrastructure is in many respects lousy, and it would be a good idea to finance some investment in clean technologies and ways of reducing carbon emissions, and so on. But with all the other things going on, including the recession and healthcare, it is going to be difficult to find the money to finance such investments while at the same time reducing the gap between domestic saving and domestic investment. That is one of the big policy dilemmas we face right now.

Now, let's turn to the division of labour in the service sector. The US has a thriving service sector. My friend Alan Blinder – also a former student and co-author of Bob Solow and someone whom I admire and think is one of the most sensible economists around – wrote a much quoted article[2] that echoed Tom Friedman by saying, basically, that the world is flat and a very large fraction of service jobs are more or less 'up for grabs', and that this is going to be a huge revolution in the US economy. This has become a common view. On this issue, I disagree with Alan. In my work with the McKinsey Global Institute, we did a very comprehensive study of which jobs could be or were likely to be offshored – what was the potential? We came up with a much smaller number than the one that Alan Blinder found. Based on what has happened over the last few years, the smaller number seems to be closer to the mark.

My second point is that the phenomenon of offshoring, and particularly offshoring to India, seems to be way overstated. Tom Friedman comes back from India and dazzles everybody with descriptions of what is happening in Mumbai. According to US trade data, however, in 2006, service imports from India were 0.05 per cent of US GDP – a very small number. To be fair, this number has been growing at a rapid rate, but it started from a very low base. As of today, the dollar has declined and some of the jobs that were offshored are coming back. Recall another branch of economics that was in favour not long ago – the economics of 'agglomeration effects', the idea that there are advantages in having people work together. Anyone who has been in an academic job knows that – you 'talk to the people down the corridor'. A number of companies have brought teams back to the United States rather than spreading activities out. That is not to say that service sector offshoring will not continue; I think it will.

The one place I would love to see an increase in offshoring is in medical care, because the US healthcare industry could use a bit of competition from somewhere more efficient. If India turns out to be that place, or Thailand, I am all in favour, even if a few jobs are lost along the way.

Since a lot of my work, as Bob mentioned, has involved looking at productivity, I now want to turn to the relationship between productivity and employment. In my view, increasing productivity is a necessary component for generating more jobs. The two go together; they are complementary. Different periods of US history show that. Productivity growth was rapid after World War II, and so was employment growth; unemployment was low. In Europe, again after the War, the period of rapid productivity growth was one of very strong employment growth and very low unemployment. When productivity growth slowed down in the US and Europe, unemployment moved higher, and in Europe has remained higher. Productivity gets a bad name on the employment front because some productivity takes the form of restructuring older industries, which generally leads to job loss in those industries. Productivity in the US over the last couple of quarters has increased by something like 6 or 7 per cent – that is a restructuring of productivity. It is a different kind of cyclical effect than we used to get. Nowadays, when businesses are caught in a cyclical downturn, they send people out the door very quickly; that was not the case in earlier business cycles, but seems to be very much the case now.

Looking at productivity going forward, the US economy is already pretty lean; we have already done a lot of restructuring, if not before 2007, now, in the recession. So the potential for job growth should be associated with innovation, which creates new business opportunities, new output and new services. That is what we are really looking for in terms of job growth.

How can policy encourage job-creating innovation? I do not know a good answer to that question, but I will mention a couple of things that might go in the right direction. The first one is something you have all heard many times before. There have to be adequate skills available in the workforce. Innovation can generate the demand for jobs and create jobs, but if workers do not have the skills needed, those jobs will end up somewhere else. In terms of elite educational institutions, the United States is probably the strongest country in the world. At the secondary school level, however, the US education system is lousy, at least in a good part of the urban school system. It does not provide skilled training for kids who do not go on to college. Even in some of the best school districts, the education is totally geared to getting people into college, and the proportion of the population that graduates from four-year institutions is only about 20 per cent, so there is 80 per cent of the population that are not getting the kind of skills that they need to fill those jobs. Second, despite concerns about the budget deficit, there is an appropriate role for the government as a catalyst for innovation, and historically that has been done without spending huge amounts of money. So it is good policy to use government spending selectively, in small amounts, to serve as a catalyst to advance technology and consequently innovation.

Jean-Louis Beffa My presentation is based on my experience at the company level, in the world of industry over the last 30 years or so. Corporate strategy is a revealing indicator of the dynamics of the international division of labour. To understand why the actions of States and the reactions of the companies operating within their borders illustrate how nations adapt to changes, I will concentrate on the emblematic companies of a country. I define such companies as those that have their corporate headquarters in a given country and are therefore influenced by both the country's domestic corporate law and international shareholder expectations. I will take the company as my point of departure: (1) to show how its situation has been transformed, within its domain of activity, by international changes, notably the opening of markets; (2) to explain how the situation of different companies has been affected depending on their main activity, to determine whether the changes that have taken place in the economic environment have had a significant effect on their competitiveness or not; and (3) to examine how States react vis-à-vis companies, in other words, how does the environment that the State provides for companies change their strategic behaviour – and conversely, how does a company operating within a country make a contribution in return in terms of integration in international trade.

I will focus on industry, presenting the figures for foreign trade balances. They show that services, even when well developed in a country – such as financial services are in England – play a secondary role compared to industry. Transformations in industry have been largely responsible for structuring the international division of labour not only by the growth of countries, but also by the relations between them. That does not mean that services are not essential, particularly for creating employment within the borders of each country, but they do not play the most important role in the relations between countries, as expressed through international trade. Two remarks before I begin. Since the Eastern European countries and China have entered the 'free market economy', and since India has in some ways abandoned a fairly socialist system, the free market economy today is accepted by all the important countries of the planet. That is well established. I will not make any distinction between the levels of acceptance of the free market economy, even if different countries can be more or less protectionist. Second, in the same way, practically all the big countries today accept that the economic result of a company is the best way to evaluate its efficiency. Consequently, company managers seek to produce the highest possible profit – in any case a positive result – within a given time horizon.

Let us start by looking at how much the entry of new countries into the free-market economy of trade has led companies to rethink their division of labour. The first phenomenon is that for wages that were much lower, employees worked practically equally well. So the first question is: are the differences in productivity marginal compared to the differences in labour costs? The left-hand chart in Figure 7.1 shows the hourly wage in different countries. These figures show the same activities that Saint-Gobain exercises in these different countries. Developed countries are taken as the base

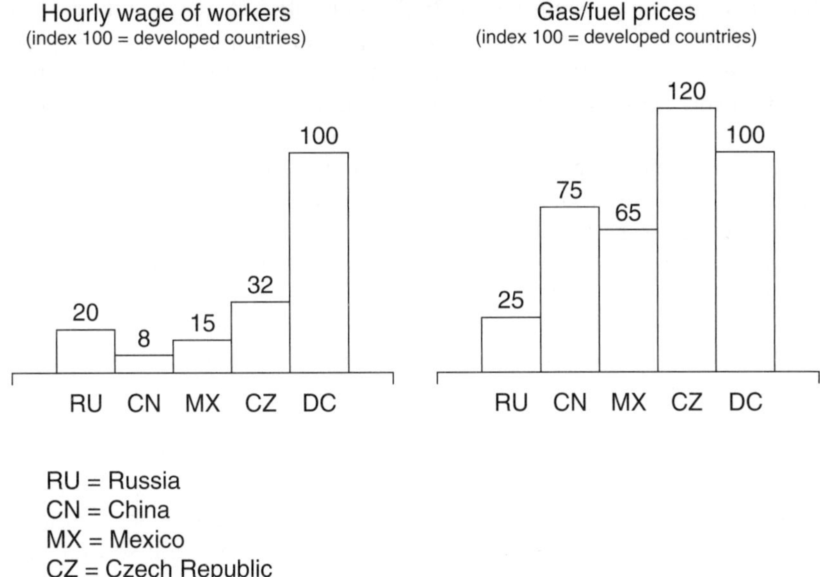

Figure 7.1 Hourly wage of workers and gas/fuel prices

index of 100. In comparison, China is at 8, Mexico 15, and much closer to home, the Czech Republic is still only at 32.

This obviously changes the whole calculation of cost price in a fundamental way. Given the tensions – which I believe will be lasting – on the energy market, it is interesting to look at energy prices. Here the differential is also very large. With a base index of 100 for the developed countries, the Czech Republic pays 120, China 75 – even more in some regions, as these are averages – Russia only 25, and the same is probably true for Algeria and Egypt. So differentials in energy prices, like differentials in labour costs, are also going to have a structural effect.

A third issue is the potential of highly qualified people. Looking at the proportion of university students around the world, the number of students in North America (12%) and Western Europe (10%) today is small compared to that in China (21%) or India (14%),[3] although the university systems in the two latter countries are not as efficient. We would get the same sort of figures for engineers.

From the point of view of companies, changes in the essential factors of production have been wrought by this opening up of the world economy, which is relatively recent. First, it has opened up new markets. Second, it has provided the possibility of setting up factories in new countries with different factors of production. Third, and above all, it has meant the appearance of new competitors, and that is an essential point that has dramatically changed the situation in a whole range of sectors. So those are the three consequences. I will not dwell on the opening up of markets or the localization of plants in new zones, but examine what has happened from the perspective of companies. One point that I rarely see treated in the economic literature, and yet which appears to lie at the heart of this issue, is the following: How does this change in the conditions of the factors of production affect a company's competitiveness?

Here, an important distinction must be made between local businesses and world businesses. A world business is one in which what it sells – whether a good or a service – could be produced by a competitor just about anywhere in the world. The reduction in transport costs, particularly from Asia to the United States and Europe, under certain conditions (the situation of infrastructures, especially ports, in emerging countries) has brought countries closer together. For world businesses – for example, the production of telephone exchanges, machines-tools, and so on – the conditions have been transformed. So, what has taken place? First, companies have relocated. In fact, they have adopted a dual strategy, exemplified by Japan and Germany. They keep their research centres and the firms in which they develop new products in their home country, and they complement that by setting up plants in low-cost countries – Eastern Europe in some cases, Asia in others, and so on. Innovation is the key factor for maintaining their competitive position. Consequently, the relationship between the science base of a State and its companies' innovative structures is crucial for world businesses. More generally, the institutions in which companies operate have a fundamental influence on whether they maintain their position vis-à-vis their competitors.

The way in which a State deals with the demands of its shareholders determines whether a company's strategy is well equipped for its domain of activity. Shareholder expectations are another crucial factor that influences a company's strategy. Some economic theory teaches that shareholders should all expect the same thing from a company. That is not true. The attitude of the company in terms of its 'reaction' to what the shareholders want, or indeed to what the country around it wants, differs greatly between countries. There is thus no uniform behaviour of companies, in the form of profit optimization for their shareholders, and so on. The way that directors act to meet the requirements of the shareholders – who, after all, decide their very existence – differs radically from one country to another. For a world business, the essential issues for a company are support for its innovative effort and its long-term and risk strategies, and, if necessary, deferred profitability. When a State provides this kind of support, most often the quid pro quo is that the company develops the maximum production and employment within the borders of that State. Consequently, there is a strong interrelation between the action of the company – supported by the State – vis-à-vis its world competitors, and what the company gives the State in return.

The third very important factor is the labour nexus. Will the staff support such a policy? Will they, as in Germany, be prepared to accept for some time low wages that remain competitive, to allow the maximum possible production to be maintained within the country, or will industrial relations be volatile? In the first case, in exchange for this policy of collaboration with personnel, managers do their best to avoid laying off staff to maintain the maximum number of jobs, and when there is reorganization, it is carried out in a particular way. In a world of flexible labour, on the other hand, there is a certain degree of freedom, but not the same level of cooperation in the attitude of the shareholders or trade unions (the difference between the trade unions of the US car industry and their German counterparts is a case in point).

The 'proximity' of a firm's business is another determining factor. Local business means that by the very nature of the business – for example, retail sales or distribution, like Saint-Gobain, of building materials – the competitors are similar: they have about the same wages and energy costs. The products coming from abroad are not going to disturb one's competitive position because of transportation costs. When Saint-Gobain saw all these changes at the international level, it considerably changed its portfolio of activities, through sales and acquisitions, to strengthen its percentage of local businesses. Why? A local business does not have to worry about competition from Asia, the exchange rate of the euro and the dollar, the rise in energy prices, and so on. Therefore, the conditions of its competitive position are not attacked by the fundamental movements that are the disruptions of globalization. The distinction between local and world businesses is also valid for services. In finance, for example, investment banking is a world business, while retail banking is local. The distinction exists in all sectors. Globalization gives local businesses new opportunities for setting up plants, and so they switch to a multiregional strategy to extend their activities. In our group over the last 20 years, we have grown from localization in 18 countries to localization in 54 countries, taking advantage, of course, of zones of high growth. For world businesses, the relation with the State is strengthened, because the two must support each other in order to work towards a common strategy. In local businesses, the leading multiregional company does not make any significant contribution to the foreign trade balance of its home country. This is striking for France; compared to Germany or others, most of the French industrial leaders are multiregional businesses. Lafarge, Air Liquide, Veolia, Carrefour, for instance, are very powerful world companies, but they do not contribute significantly to their home country. In contrast, Siemens, all the medium-sized German companies, the leaders in capital goods, or the big Japanese firms exporting from Japan, contribute a lot to their countries. So when a country has a lot of specializations, which are its greatest economic strengths embodied in the form of its biggest companies in local businesses, the State–company relationship is weakened.

Countries can also be divided into four main types, according to their foreign trade policy. Some, like the United States, France and the United Kingdom, follow a free-market or finance-led policy. Germany, Japan and China pursue a mercantilist policy. Then there is the energy rentier policy, adopted by Russia and Middle Eastern countries, and the more domestically oriented policy of Brazil and India.

The finance-led policy is inspired, roughly speaking, by the manual of the Organisation for Economic Co-operation and Development (OECD), in other words, not only the free circulation of goods, but also the completely free circulation of capital. One must allow companies to be disciplined by the action of their shareholders, hostile takeover bids must be facilitated, and so shareholder primacy is at the heart of this approach. Companies then optimize, and whatever happens to the country is not considered important, except in the United States where the market approach ends with the imperatives of homeland security. In England, that point is not deemed important, so there is no limit to the establishment of the free-market approach. France is a country that has changed its approach, and at one time became a free-market, finance-led country. This happened around 1984–86. I believe it was largely because we had a State deficit that needed financing, so we had to give a guarantee of 'good behaviour' to international investors. At that time, there was a rallying – largely led by a number of senior officials at the Ministry of Finance who thought it was the best way to reform France – in favour of a considerably more finance-led model. What are the main characteristics of this model? First, the priority given to shareholders, and consequently the short-termism that reflects their current behaviour. Second, acceptance of relocation and de-industrialization, and third, if there is a problem with the balance of payments, it is believed that the exchange rate will sort that out. There is no need to worry about structural phenomena, and so there is an indifference to trade deficits. The next three graphs (Figures 7.2 to 7.4) provide examples of countries with finance-led policies based on statistics from Saint-Gobain.

Three of the biggest industrialized countries in the world do not follow

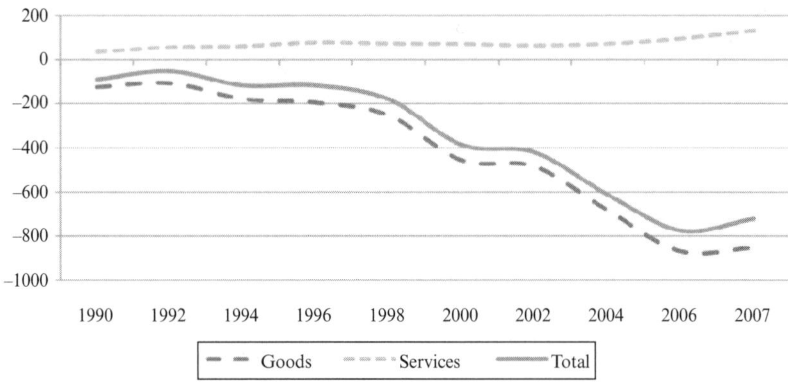

Source: Saint-Gobain (2008).

Figure 7.2 Foreign trade balance: United States

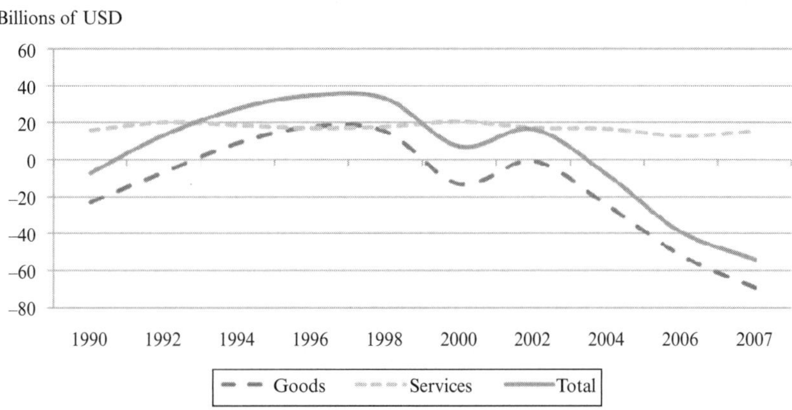

Source: Saint-Gobain (2008).

Figure 7.3 Foreign trade balance: France

a finance-led policy. These countries attach a high priority to achieving a trade surplus, in other words, producing more so that they can sell more to foreign countries than they buy from them. This involves a long-term strategy: long-term shareholdings are favoured; companies must be kept stable; shareholders must be prevented from exerting excessive influence over the management of companies, which must have a perspective of long-term continuity; and lastly, an innovative scientific policy must be promoted. The next set of graphs (Figures 7.5 to 7.7) shows the

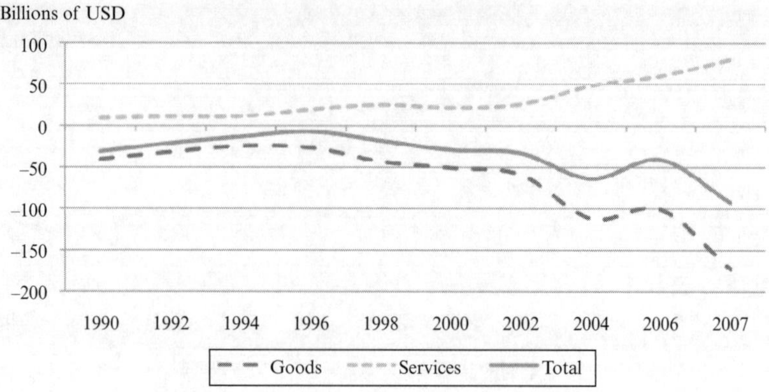

Source: Saint-Gobain (2008).

Figure 7.4 Foreign trade balance: United Kingdom

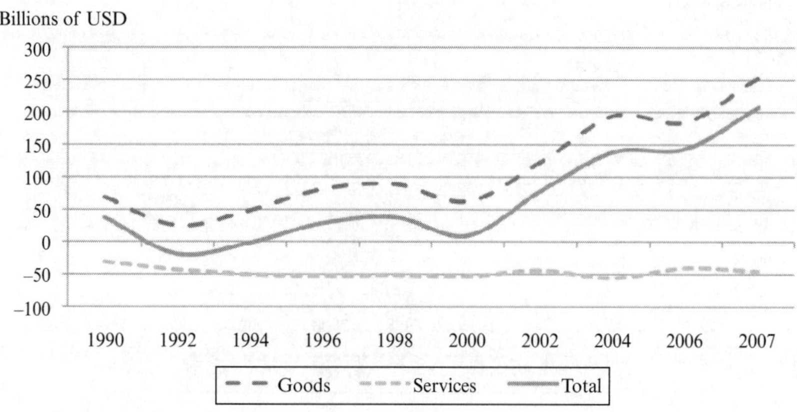

Source: Saint-Gobain (2008).

Figure 7.5 Foreign trade balance: Germany

consequences of this mercantilist strategy. China has led this policy. That major phenomenon, with everything that it represents in terms of objective advantages in production costs and now in upgrading technologies, has had huge repercussions.

The third type of policy is the energy rentier strategy, adopted by Russia and the Gulf States (there are similarities between them). They use the rent from raw materials not to develop the country's industry as a priority, but

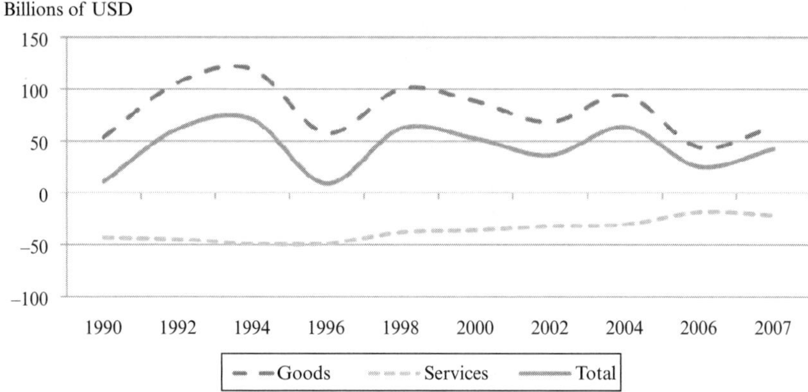

Source: Saint-Gobain (2008).

Figure 7.6 Foreign trade balance: Japan

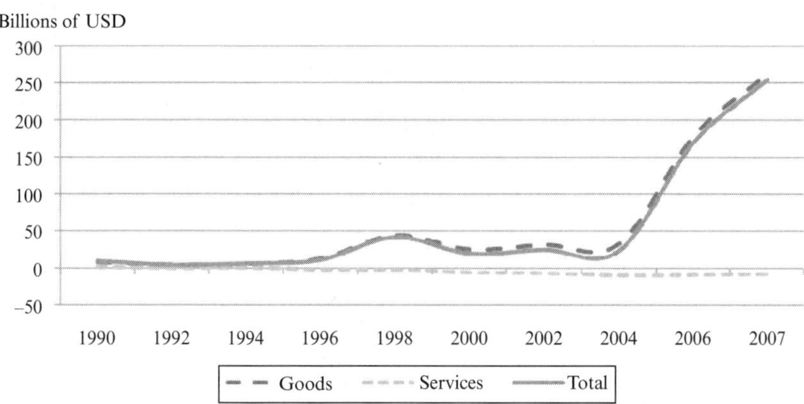

Source: Saint-Gobain (2008).

Figure 7.7 Foreign trade balance: China

to strengthen their political weight. The State strictly controls the rentier companies – in Russia, the companies that produce the rent – but it allows European companies, for example, to set up in the other sectors. Up until now, these countries have paid little attention to the conditions of industrial development other than that of the rentier companies. Figure 7.8 shows how this has affected the foreign trade balance in the Russian case.

The fourth and last type is the domestically oriented policy, characterized

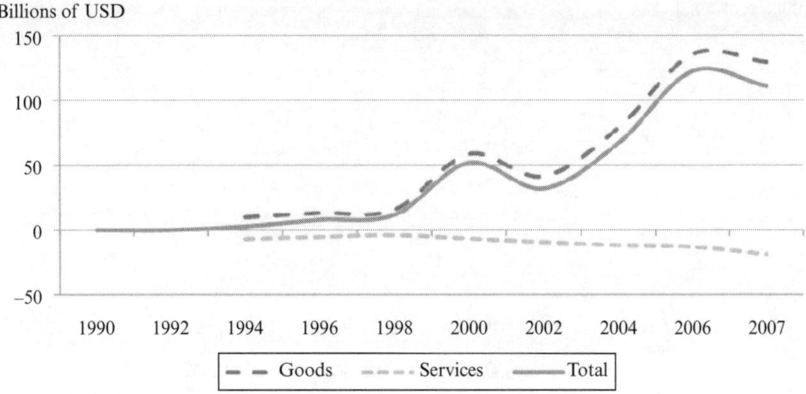

Source: Saint-Gobain (2008).

Figure 7.8 Foreign trade balance: Russia

by India and Brazil. These are large countries with a democratic political regime, where foreign trade and international integration are important but not a priority, which is reflected in both countries' willingness to accept a serious handicap in terms of infrastructure. In China, by comparison, the regime makes it possible to carry out compulsory sales of land rights in no time; motorways are still being built at top speed, and now the new energies are also being developed very fast. This is not the case in Brazil, and particularly in India where even today, there is hardly a motorway between Chennai and Bangalore, the essential zone. India is far behind China in the development of its ports. The next graphs (Figures 7.9 and 7.10) clearly illustrate the consequences of such a policy. Brazil has greatly developed its exports, but the figures are weak compared to China. India is in a slightly more difficult situation, despite its development of services.

The most important factor for understanding the international division of labour today is the institutional context, which dictates how the State treats its companies. This institutional context is a driving force behind the industrial specialization of countries, particularly between world businesses and local businesses. Those factors have gradually created a disequilibrium, notably between China and the United States, through the super-industrialization and current technological upgrading of one, and the acceptance of a very large trade deficit by the other, which, it appears – and I would like to know what the economists think – cannot be corrected simply by the exchange rate. Consequently, this raises an important problem for the future. As long as the United States refuses to adopt a policy of re-industrialization, I believe that serious tensions will persist,

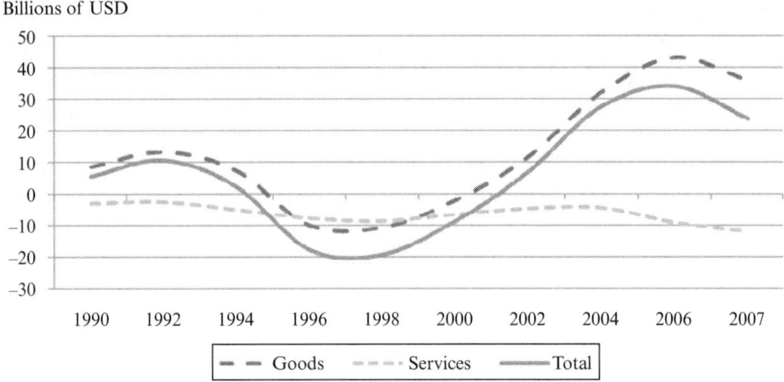

Source: Saint-Gobain (2008).

Figure 7.9 Foreign trade balance: Brazil

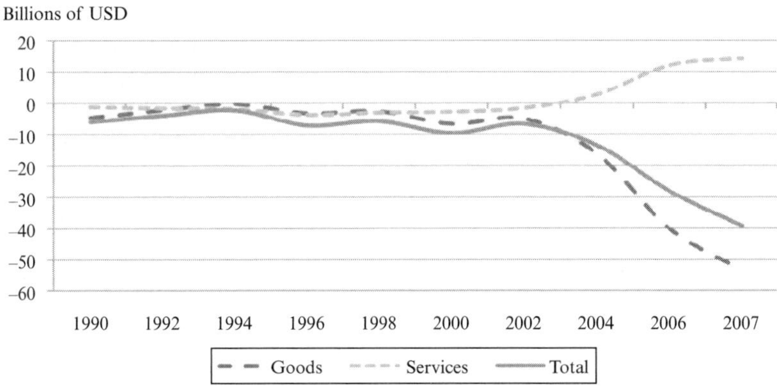

Source: Saint-Gobain (2008).

Figure 7.10 Foreign trade balance: India

with major economic repercussions for Americans not only in their standard of living vis-à-vis the rest of the world through the dollar exchange rate, but also for the traditional financing of the deficit through the role of the dollar as the only international currency of account. There will be a whole series of very serious problems, even in terms of employment in the US. It is clear that the main consequence of the recent crisis is the advantage ultimately accruing to the mercantilist countries, and above all, a weakening of the United States, despite having the most extraordinary system of innovation in the world. It continues to astound me that the United States is the most creative country, but it does not transform that into industrial production within its borders. If current trends are allowed to continue, I believe they will lead to major problems. The most important point is the behaviour of the State in terms of the context it creates, and the consequences that has on the long-term industrial structure of each country.

Bina Agarwal I think it would be fair to say that we are all obsessed with food, but every other day our newspapers take us to task for this because there is so much obesity in the world. I will nonetheless ask you to be even more focused on food since my presentation is on the subject: 'How will the world feed itself in a sustainable way?' I will begin by saying something about the existing situation, then examine the scenario under climate change, and lastly ask: how can nations adapt and innovate? This is a broad sweep of issues, and each of them could easily warrant a paper in itself.

Today, we are facing the most basic of crises – a crisis in the ability of the world to feed itself over the long term. This is a crisis both of agricultural production and its global distribution, under the looming shadow of climate change. In this context, the question of the international division of labour in agriculture is a critical subtext. Food security raises key questions about which nations or regions will produce the food needed by the many, and how surpluses will be distributed. Can nations adapt individually to the crisis, or do we need a new global order, a new set of international agreements, for this purpose? Indeed, the Food and Agriculture Organization of the United Nations (FAO), the International Fund for Agricultural Development (IFAD), and other international bodies are today debating exactly this question.

In 2007, we saw a dramatic rise in food prices globally. By the FAO's calculations, the food price index rose by nearly 40 per cent, compared to 9 per cent in 2006. Wheat prices almost quadrupled and maize prices almost tripled between 2000 and 2008. Rice prices also spiked. The worst effects of the price rise fell on food-importing countries and on net buyers of foodgrains within countries (in particular on the poor, and especially on women and children in poor households). According to an assessment by the United Nations Development Programme (UNDP), the price rise added about 105 million to the poor globally, with a large percentage being located in South Asia and sub-Saharan Africa. This crisis was over and above the quiet crisis of chronic hunger and malnutrition that large numbers continue to face. So, the question of food security has both immediacy and long-term importance.

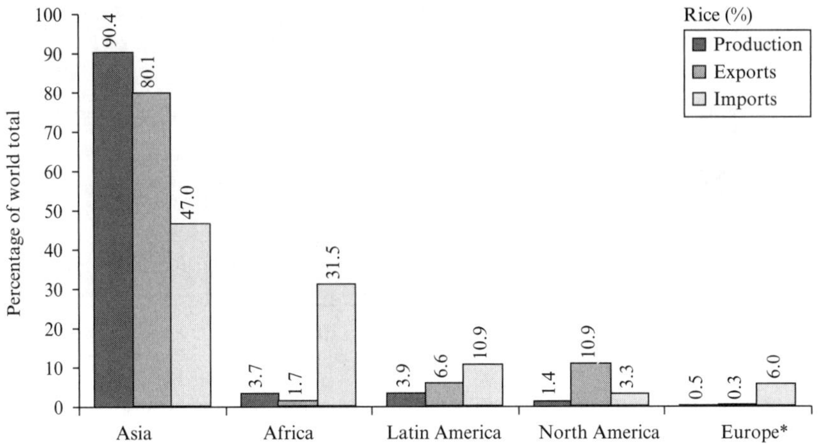

Note: * This includes the figures for Russia here and in subsequent graphs.

Source: Computed by author from FAO 2009 statistics (http:/faostat.fao.org).

Figure 7.11 Rice production, exports and imports (% of world total)

A vast proportion of the world depends mainly on foodgrains for its calories and protein, and the main staples – wheat, rice and maize – provide 92 per cent of the cereals consumed globally. Rice and wheat alone provide 80 per cent of cereals consumed and about 42 per cent of all food protein. Cereals (especially rice) also make up the major part of the diet of the poor. A focus on foodgrains thus appears to be the best way to illustrate the nature of the problem.

We might begin by asking: Which countries are producing foodgrains? Which are exporting and importing them? And who are the farmers? In 2008, Asian farmers produced 90 per cent of the world's rice and around 40 per cent of its wheat, as well as 42 per cent of total cereals. But much of what Asia produces it consumes. Grain exports come from only a few countries. Figure 7.11 shows that in 2008 over 80 per cent of rice exports came from Asia, but within Asia, exports came mainly from four countries: Thailand, Vietnam, India and Pakistan. Similarly, 85 per cent of wheat exports came from only four regions: North America, Russia, the European Union and Australia, while the importers were overwhelmingly the developing countries (Figure 7.12). Maize exports were even more concentrated: 81 per cent came from North America and Latin America (Figure 7.13) and within Latin America largely from Argentina and Brazil. Again, the importers were mainly developing countries. For cereals as

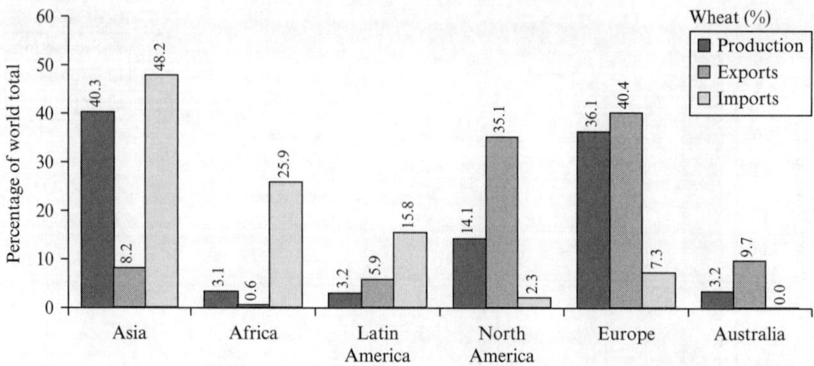

Source: Computed by author from FAO 2009 statistics (http:/faostat.fao.org).

Figure 7.12 Wheat production, exports and imports (% of world total)

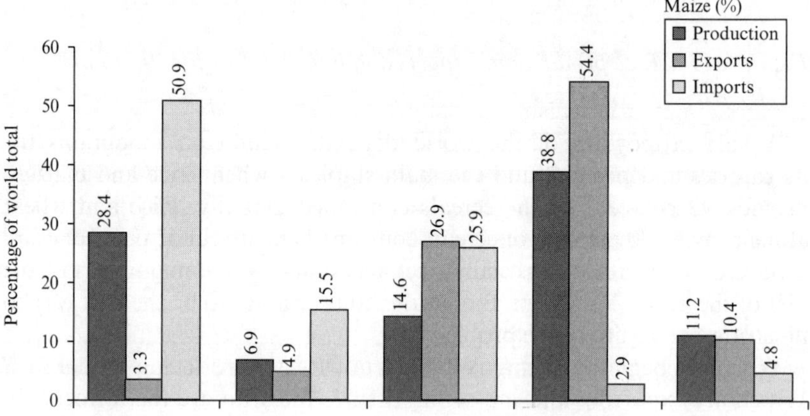

Source: Computed by author from FAO 2009 statistics (http:/faostat.fao.org).

Figure 7.13 Maize production, exports and imports (% of world total)

a whole, 65 per cent of exports came from North America and Europe (Figure 7.14).

This regional concentration of production and exports means that policies that are followed in these countries can have a major impact on global food availability and prices. For instance, it would matter a great deal if some of these countries shifted large areas from foodgrains to biofuels because of high energy costs; or if they cut their exports to deal with their

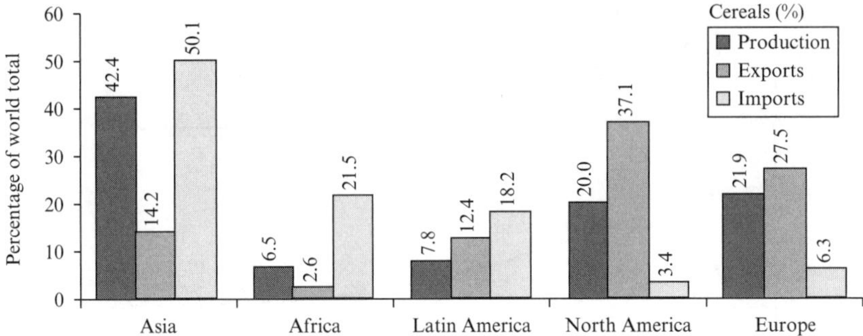

Source: Computed by author from FAO 2009 statistics (http:/faostat.fao.org).

Figure 7.14 Cereals production, exports and imports (% of world total)

own needs; or if they changed their diets from cereals to meat; or if they managed their agriculture inefficiently.

It was, in fact, precisely such factors that underlay the 2007 price rise. In 2007–08, for instance, almost a hundred million tonnes of cereals, or 4.8 per cent of all cereals produced, went into ethanol production. A large percentage of maize also went into ethanol rather than food and feed. US farmers, in particular, shifted large areas from soyabean and wheat to maize for biofuels; this was especially because of the subsidies given to them to grow energy crops. If the shift from food to biofuels persists, it could have a major adverse effect on world food security, especially in poor importing countries. Short-term responses by exporting countries in terms of restricting exports also worsened availability for importing countries. China, India and Latin America, for example, all imposed restrictions on foodgrain exports, varyingly. Added to this was speculation in commodity markets, panic buying by some countries, and hoarding for security reasons by millions of small consumers.

In addition, there have been long-term dietary shifts: as income levels rise, people move more towards meat and milk, which, in turn, increases the demand for grain to feed livestock. Most importantly, there has been an overall neglect of agriculture in developing countries in recent decades. Foodgrain production has not kept pace with needs because of production inefficiencies. In South Asia, wheat and rice yields are far below potential, and falling. This is the first reality to contend with in reviewing the current situation.

The second reality is the division of labour between sectors and genders, across and within countries. Agriculture accounts for a small and decreasing percentage of GDP and employment in most countries (see Figures

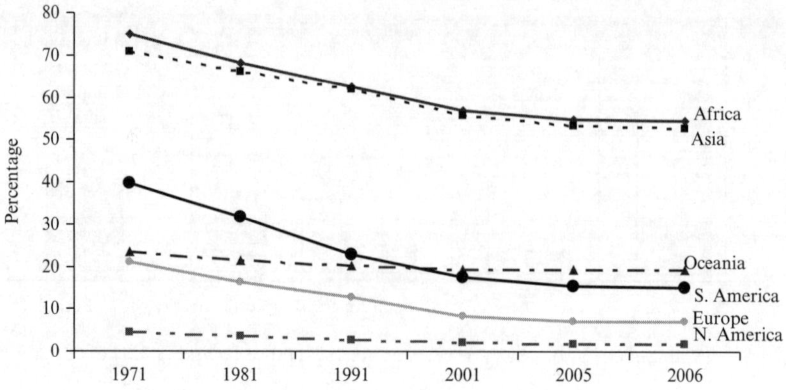

Source: Based on FAO 2009 Statistics (http://faostat.fao.org).

Figure 7.15 Total labour force in agriculture (%)

7.15 and 7.16). In Asia and Africa, however, agriculture still provides employment and livelihoods for the vast majority (see the top two lines of the graph in Figure 7.15), and in sub-Saharan Africa, it remains an important contributor to GDP. People in Asia and Africa also constitute a substantial part of the population of the developing world.

Nevertheless, the majority of farmers in these two regions – and to some extent also in parts of Latin America – are small and marginal, and many own minute parcels of land. In large parts of South Asia (such as India and Bangladesh), for instance, 80 per cent of farmers cultivate two hectares or less; this land is also often fragmented and unirrigated. Moreover, these small farmers are increasingly women. Figure 7.17 gives the percentage of women workers in the total agricultural labour force, in different regions of the world. There is an upward trend in all regions except Europe, and a substantial upward trend in Oceania.

Within these overall trends, there are intra-regional variations: for instance, overall in Asia, women constitute about 40 per cent of agricultural workers, but in some countries they constitute 50 per cent or more. In the two major rice-producing and exporting countries – Vietnam and Thailand – 47 to 49 per cent of agricultural workers, respectively, are women. Similarly, in sub-Saharan Africa, a large proportion of the main food producers are women. This fact, along with the noted continued dependence of a large proportion of the population of Asia and Africa on agriculture, highlights the second reality, namely that the farmers are, and are increasingly likely to be, small and female. They are thus likely to play an important role in global food security, both as consumers and as producers.

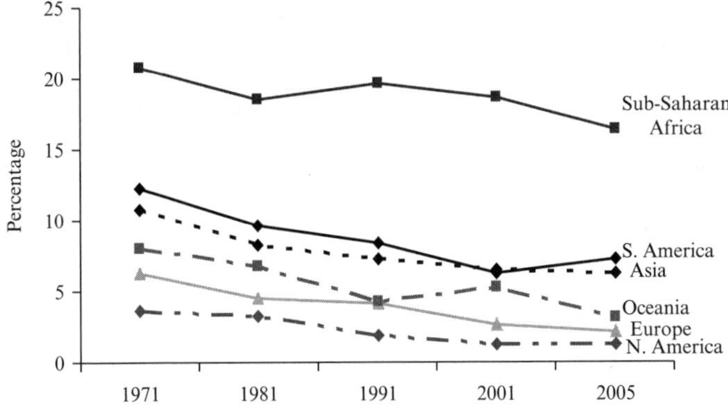

Source: Based on World Resources Institute Statistics (http://www.wri.org).

Figure 7.16 GDP from agriculture (%)

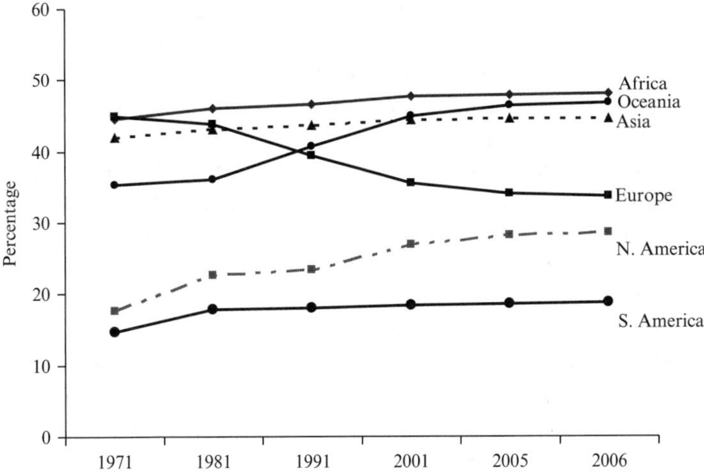

Source: Based on FAO 2009 Statistics (http://faostat.fao.org).

Figure 7.17 Females in total agricultural labour force (%)

There are, however, well-documented biases in the access that small farmers and especially women farmers have to agricultural land, technical information, credit, extension services, inputs, storage facilities and marketing options. Also, most of the systems that deliver new technology or information about improved practices are not geared to reach women

Table 7.1 Climate change effect on 2050 production relative to no climate change effect (% change)*

Region	Rice	Wheat	Maize
South Asia	−14.5	−48.8	−8.9
East Asia & Pacific	−11.3	1.8	8.9
Sub-Saharan Africa	−15.2	−35.8	−7.1
Latin America	−19.2	17.4	−4.0
World	−13.5	−27.4	−0.4

Notes: * This gives the additional per cent change in production in 2050 as a result of climate change (CC) relative to no climate change (NCC). For example, in South Asia rice production with NCC is predicted to increase by 49 mmt (million metric tons) (from 119.8 in 2000 to 168.9 in 2050), an increase of 41 per cent. With CC, however, production is predicted to be 24.5 mmt less, that is a decrease of 14.5 per cent from the NCC figure.

Source: Based on estimates by IFPRI (2009), op. cit.

farmers. Without steps to bridge these gender gaps, the growing proportion of women in farming will remain trapped in low-productivity agriculture. Equally, efforts to revive agriculture through infrastructure investment and other measures will not automatically reach them. Very few of the discussions on agriculture and the food crisis take this demographic shift into account. For reaching small farmers effectively, I believe we need a different institutional approach to agricultural production, one that allows for more collective institutional forms (as I will elaborate later).

These realities become even more significant when considering the potential effects of climate change. With climate change, it is expected that many water sources will dry up, rainfall will become more erratic, droughts and floods will stress agricultural systems, temperature increases will cause heat stress for crops, and so on. All this is likely to affect crop production negatively, as illustrated by the 2009 assessments of the International Food Policy Research Institute (IFPRI) in Washington DC, based on data from the Intergovernmental Panel on Climate Change (IPCC). Although assessments of the impact of climate change remain contentious, there is a degree of consensus about the direction of impact in relation to food production. As the next set of figures shows, the IFPRI predictions suggest dramatically adverse effects on food security (see Table 7.1 and Figures 7.18 to 7.20).

These figures are based on varying assumptions of temperature rise, precipitation, and so on. The prediction is that unless steps are taken to mitigate the effects, there will be a serious negative impact on the output of the most important cereals – rice, wheat and maize. The two regions to

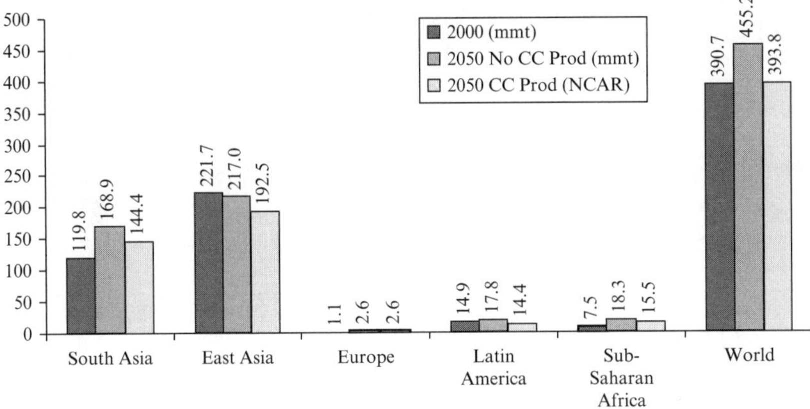

Note: mmt = million metric tons; No CC Prod = production with no climate change; CC Prod = production with climate change; NCAR = National Center for Atmospheric Research, USA.

Source: Based on estimates by IFPRI (2009), 'Climate change: impact on agriculture and costs of adaptation' (Washington, DC).

Figure 7.18 Climate change and rice production

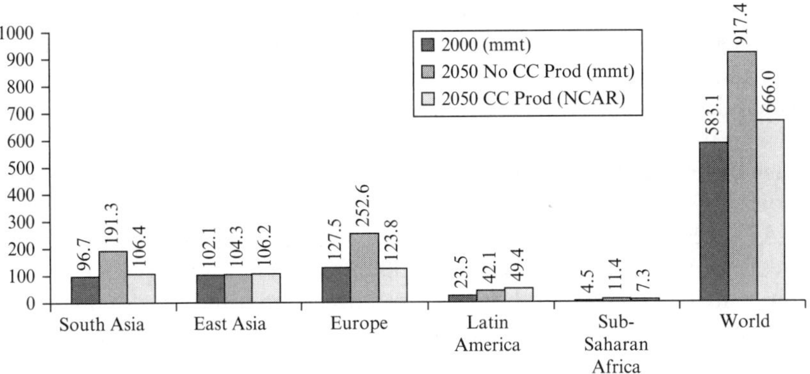

Note: mmt = million metric tons; No CC Prod = production with no climate change; CC Prod = production with climate change; NCAR = National Center for Atmospheric Research, USA.

Source: Based on estimates by IFPRI (2009), op. cit.

Figure 7.19 Climate change and wheat production

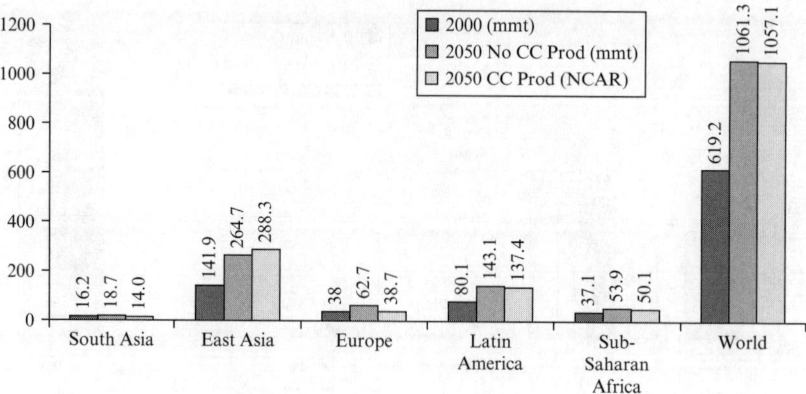

Note: mmt = million metric tons; No CC Prod = production with no climate change; CC Prod = production with climate change; NCAR = National Center for Atmospheric Research, USA.

Source: Based on estimates by IFPRI (2009), op. cit.

Figure 7.20 Climate change and maize production

be worst affected will be South Asia and sub-Saharan Africa. East Asia will have mixed effects, and the southern part of China will be somewhat differently affected from northern China. But for the world as a whole, there will be a gravely negative impact. The graphs provide comparisons between actual production in 2000 with predicted values for 2050 with no climate change and with climate change. Consider rice production: as can be seen from the last set of bars in Figure 7.18, world production for 2050 after climate change is almost the same as production in 2000 (namely, around 390 million metric tons).

As a result of the predicted adverse effect on cereal production, the predicted per capita daily calorie availability (according to IFPRI) will be lower in 2050 relative to the 2000 level, throughout the developing world (Figure 7.21). This could increase child malnutrition by 20 per cent relative to the no-climate-change scenario. Moreover, these effects are averages and do not reveal the disproportionately higher negative impact on the poor. In fact, even with the best of efforts to mitigate climate change, poor farmers, and especially women and children, are likely to be hard hit.

So what can nations do? What can people do? Even without climate change, we would need extraordinary efforts to meet food security demands for an estimated 9 billion people by 2050. Such efforts become even more imperative with climate change. To ensure long-term food

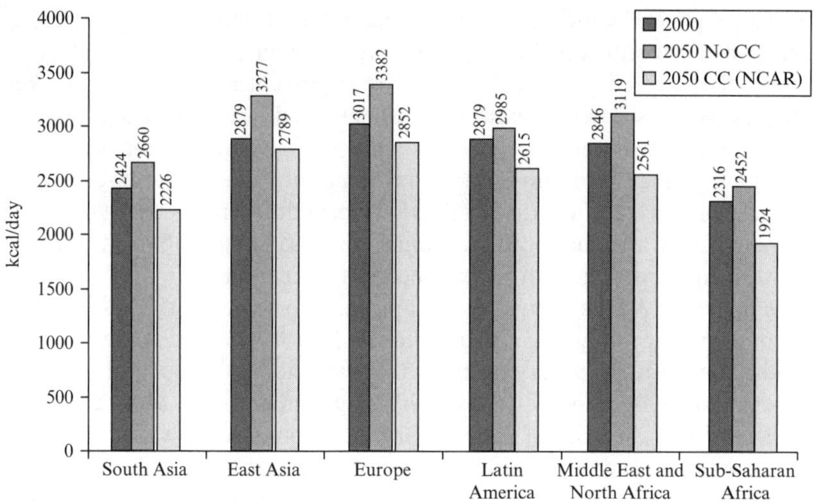

Note: No CC = without climate change; CC = with climate change; NCAR = National Center for Atmospheric Research, USA.

Source: Based on estimates by IFPRI (2009), op. cit.

Figure 7.21 Climate change and daily calories per capita

security, we need to increase production, stabilize food availability *and* improve distribution. All this also has implications for the international division of labour in agriculture in terms of food production and its distribution between developed and developing countries, and for the division of labour and resources within countries.

Improved global food security will require measures to be taken both nationally and internationally. Most efforts will need some form of cooperation and collective action within and across countries. There is a substantial consensus that in order to increase production, developing countries will need to invest more in rural infrastructure, especially on irrigation and roads. In a country like India today, for example, only 42 per cent of the net cultivated land is irrigated, which means that there is a huge potential for increasing irrigation, with significant payoffs in yields. Globally, we also need research and development (R&D), the promotion of more efficient agricultural practices, and measures to restore soil fertility and to conserve water, although different regions may need an emphasis on different measures. In addition, we need institutional innovations.

Let us first look at infrastructure. People often talk about this in aggregate terms, measuring the percentage of GDP spent on infrastructure development, of which rural infrastructure is a sub-category. There is rarely a discussion on the multiple ways by which rural infrastructure could be delivered. Such a discussion is important in order to make key choices. For instance, irrigation can be delivered in various ways, such as via large dams or tubewells, or through locally managed rainwater harvesting systems. Much investment has gone into the former two, but, in recent years, we can see the productivity benefits of rainwater harvesting systems, built and managed by communities in some semi-arid parts of western India, despite erratic and uncertain monsoons.

Similarly, R&D is needed for adapting crop varieties to existing conditions and for mitigating climate change. South Asia and Africa, in particular, need water-conserving crops that can withstand heat and resist the expected increase in pest attacks with rising temperatures. More emphasis is also needed on efficient farming practices to conserve water and soils. The use of fertilizer and pesticide, for instance, can be greatly reduced by fine tuning their application procedures and frequency. Such practices would be beneficial both environmentally and in terms of production efficiency.

A key question remains: are small farmers, especially women farmers, in a position to make localized investments in infrastructure or take advantage of new production practices or inputs? Can gender biases in access to land, inputs, credit, technology and other farm services be overcome? Small farmers face high risks and resource constraints and have no crop insurance. How can they tackle such constraints? I believe an important part of the answer lies in new institutional mechanisms, in particular more collective approaches to agricultural investment and farming. I know that the word 'collective' often sends off alarm bells and causes an outcry, 'but socialist collectivization had disastrous results'. That is not the route I am suggesting.

I am suggesting a very different, bottom-up, participative, small-group approach to forming 'collectivities' (as I term them). These would be in sharp contrast to the very large collective farms, and the top-down, coercive, non-participative approach to their formation, that characterized early socialist collectivization. There are a number of success stories that indicate that a bottom-up group approach can work. Indeed, group investment in irrigation goes back a long way historically in many countries. Even today, as noted, some regions in South Asia – where local communities have cooperated to build small irrigation systems – show high agricultural growth. There are also examples of a further leap in successful cooperation by farmers who have pooled their land and skills, or leased land jointly. These examples are of at least two types. The first relates to the transition economies and the second to India.

In many transition economies of Central Asia, Eastern Europe and Latin America, large-scale collectivization during the 1950s and 1970s was followed by de-collectivization in the 1980s and 1990s. This gave farmers the choice to revert to individual family farming. Many farm families, however, chose to create new group enterprises on the restituted land. In Romania, for example, by 1993, around 43 per cent of de-collectivized agricultural land had returned to cooperative forms of production, on a voluntary basis. In Kyrgyzstan, family cooperatives constituted 63.6 per cent of all farm enterprises in 1997. There are also examples of farmers in East Germany and Nicaragua regrouping by choice to take up small-scale cooperative farming after de-collectivization.

These cooperatives have proved to be more efficient than individual family farms. Recent studies show that in Kyrgyzstan, the total annual crop income was 1.8 times higher on family cooperatives than on individual family farms. In Romania, family cooperatives compared with individual farms had substantially higher crop yields of wheat, maize and sunflower. They also had consistently higher labour productivity and higher land productivity for farms up to 6.5 hectares. Similarly, in East Germany, the returns from inputs were much greater on family cooperatives than on individual farms. These collectivities variously provided more secure access to land and machinery, shared production risk (which is especially important in the absence of crop insurance), benefits from labour and skill pooling, economies of scale, and better access to credit and marketing services.

My second example comes from India. Here farmers in some regions are not only undertaking joint investment in irrigation, but women's groups in parts of South India are farming jointly for subsistence, in small groups constituted of eight to ten women. They lease land in groups or pool their own small plots. Here again, productivity per acre is found to be higher than under individual family cultivation. Nutrition and food security have improved, not only among the families of the women cooperating, but also at the community level: in over a hundred villages, women's groups have set up localized community food banks to help the poorest families obtain food at very low cost.

Both types of examples – those from the transition economies and those from India – demonstrate the potential of farmers voluntarily forming agricultural production collectivities. The Indian example is especially compelling, because it involves increased food security for the most vulnerable groups – women and children of poor, low-caste families.

You may ask – what about geographic reach? In the transition economies, especially in Romania and Kyrgyzstan, reconstituted family cooperatives already cover large areas, while in India there is considerable potential for geographically expanding existing efforts. Here there are 2.5 million rural self-help groups (SHGs), of which 2.3 million are constituted only of women. Each SHG contains about 10 to 15 women. At present they are organized mostly around credit sharing on a rotational basis, typically using the funds for individual family enterprises. Many SHGs, however, have the potential of undertaking joint farming ventures with State support and incentives. Similarly, in sub-Saharan Africa, where communal systems of land ownership are still widespread, I believe there is scope for exploring more collective forms of cultivation, rather than taking the route of individualized land titling. Few of these projects may succeed, however, without State financial support through credit, input access, and so on. The question is: will State support be forthcoming? Much will depend on whether existing policy blind spots around collective approaches to farming can be eliminated.

Alongside national efforts to energize agriculture, we also need collective action internationally, in both the short and the long term. In the short term, several steps could be taken. First, we need cooperation for building buffer food stocks. Figure 7.22 shows that world cereal stocks have been declining: in 2007 they were at the lowest level since the 1980s.

Building *regional* food stocks as buffers is also important, however, and this could work if production shocks are not shared across neighbouring

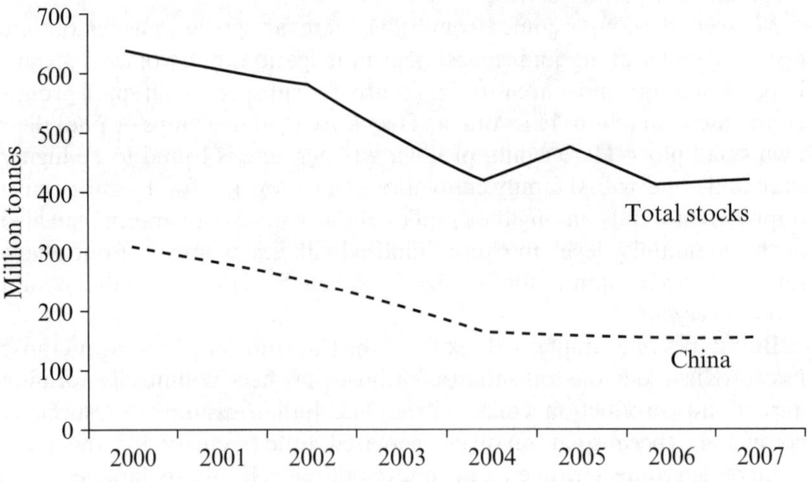

Source: von Braun, J. (2007), based on FAO data, 'The world food situation: new driving forces and required actions', IFPRI, Washington, DC.

Figure 7.22 World cereal stocks, 2000–07 (million tonnes)

,countries. International agreements for food security are another approach. There have already been some moves in that direction. In 2008, for example, the Food Board of the South Asian Association for Regional Cooperation (SAARC) met and agreed to build a regional cereal reserve, with each country in South Asia contributing a fixed amount of the targeted stock. India agreed to contribute 62 per cent and the other countries lesser amounts. Similarly, there is a South Asian Preferential Trade Agreement. African governments have also revitalized the African Union's programme to increase the region's budget allocation for agriculture. And the FAO very recently set up a new committee on food security. The key issue is to monitor these initiatives to see how they perform and sustain over time.

Second – and this is a standard point that economists tend to make – we need to remove price distortions. The US and European subsidies for energy crops for producing biofuels rather than food are a matter of major concern. It seems to me that unless the present rate of shift from food to fuel is stemmed, and more balance is attained between food needs and energy needs, food security will be severely undermined.

Third, we need food reserves in the short term for humanitarian food aid. As some have argued, this would also help vulnerable consumers feel more food secure, and thus reduce the tendency to hoard for security reasons during periods of volatile prices.

In the longer term, however, we must increase production. For this purpose, one of the most important global needs is R&D for producing crop strains that yield more while using less water and being more heat resistant. Today substantial R&D in agriculture is concentrated in a few countries, such as the USA, Brazil, China and India. There are also private global players, but their interest is in particular crops and not necessarily in all staples. We need more internationally focused institutions to play a bigger role, such as the CGIAR (Consultative Group on International Agricultural Research) institutions. This is necessary for focusing both on staple crops and on regions that will be especially affected by climate change. Take the example of wheat rust, which has been spreading globally and is causing alarm among wheat farmers. In 2005, the Borlaug Global Rust Institute was set up to deal with this. We similarly need more global bodies that will focus on staples and on vulnerable regions such as South Asia and sub-Saharan Africa. Success will involve not only developing new generic crop varieties, but also adapting such varieties for use in diverse local conditions.

There is also a need for an international commitment of funds for infrastructure development. To raise consumption enough to offset the negative effect of climate change on children, for instance, it is estimated that several billion US dollars' worth of investment in agricultural productivity will be needed. Clearly, all these estimates could rise if we want more sustained intervention, especially in R&D.

To conclude, long after the financial crisis has passed, the crisis of food security will persist. The world's ability to feed itself will remain a challenge, especially in the wake of climate change. Solutions will lie not only in new technologies and practices, but also in new institutional arrangements, nationally and globally. These arrangements will require local as well as global collective action. As part of the global architecture, we need global institutions for ensuring food security, perhaps even a new world order. But it should be an order in which the poor and women in low-income countries are seen not only as the main victims of the present crisis, but also as an important part of the solution.

Richard Cooper (Harvard University) [from the floor] My observation and question for Bina has to do with climate change. I do not know the source that you cited, which is a recent one, but I find the figures stunning and not quite believable. Let me say two things about it. First, the three things that we can all agree on that flow from climate change are (1) more carbon dioxide in the atmosphere – plants love carbon dioxide; (2) greater precipitation – plants love water; and (3) longer growing seasons in the temperate zones – the zones where frost is important. Now we human beings would have to have extraordinarily bad luck if in spite of those three pluses, speaking in general terms, the impact on food production – and I am speaking specifically about cereals – would be negative.

All of the additional water, for example, would have to go into the oceans. It could happen, but it needs an explanation. The second point is that the work of Robert Mendelsohn of Yale on Africa suggests that adaptation of farmers to climate change makes a huge difference to the ultimate impact of climate change – adaptation with *existing* technology. I suspect, but I do not know – that's the question – that the figures you presented assume that farmers just sit there for 50 years and take the tough climate change and do not adapt. That is a very strong assumption. None of this critical question is to undermine your positive suggestions at all; climate change redoubles the need for agricultural research to help in the adaptation. But I would suggest that with the kind of adaptation that we have seen in the last 50 years, the next 50 years will see a big increase in agricultural production, but not without human effort and organization.

Agarwal The specific calculations I have presented in the climate change table were undertaken by a team of experts at the International Food

Policy Research Institute (IFPRI) in Washington, DC, for their 2009 report on the impact of climate change on agriculture. IFPRI provides two estimates of climate change effects on crop production, with differing scenarios for temperature increases, precipitation, and so on. The illustrative estimates I have presented are those based on data from the US National Center for Atmospheric Research (NCAR), which uses IPCC information. These estimates do not take account of what is called 'carbon dioxide fertilization'. Nevertheless, estimates that take such fertilization into account still give adverse predictions on yields in developing countries for the major crops, although less so than the figures that do not take account of CO_2 fertilization. Moreover, the predicted impact of climate change on crops at the global level hides regional disparities. While the predictions for East Asia and Latin America are mixed, those for sub-Saharan Africa and South Asia are consistently negative. There may be disagreements between scholars on the exact extent of decline in cereal production, but there is consistency regarding which regions will be left worst off. South Asia and sub-Saharan Africa are also the two regions where, as noted, a large proportion of the population is still substantially dependent on agriculture. In addition, South Asia is heavily populated. The regional predictions therefore mean that a large percentage of the world's population is at risk.

The figures, however, are not doomsday predictions. They do not factor in what people will do. They say, given this possible scenario, we need to wake up and do something about it. We need to take steps to adapt and mitigate. On the question of adaptation, irrigation is a key factor. With climate change, we can, for instance, expect to get heat and water stress, as well as much more erratic rainfall. For irrigation, there are ways of adapting and possibly mitigating some of the consequences of climate change, through, for example, localized collective action, such as community cooperation for building rainwater harvesting systems and check dams. Many other steps can also be taken for protecting agriculture. Hopefully, in five years' time, these figures will look different, because we will have woken up, and farmers and governments will have moved in the right direction to mitigate or adapt to such predicted effects.

Baily Isn't it the case historically that productivity growth in agriculture is very rapid and that basically we are always up to our ears in food and cannot figure out what to do with it? So my question is: Does India have a food-shortage problem or a money-shortage problem? Does it invest too little in agriculture, or too much in agriculture? I thought there was a great deal of investment that was channelled into agriculture, with a very low rate of return. Wouldn't it be better to channel that investment into more productive places so that people had the money to *buy* the food as opposed to trying to increase the output of food?

Agarwal Today, India is facing both the prospect of food shortages and the inability of many to buy food because of poverty. Attention to agriculture and investment in agriculture were high in the early 1970s but fell greatly in the 1990s. In the 1970s, high-yielding varieties (HYV) of wheat and rice dramatically increased food production. Total foodgrain output trebled between 1950 and 1985, from 50 million tonnes to 150 million tonnes. With the success, however, of the green revolution technology – leading to large increases in crop yields – complacency set in. We assumed we were self-sufficient in food; foodgrain exports increased, even while agriculture was neglected. What we have therefore seen over the years is spurts in production, but low long-term growth rates. For the past several years in India, yields and production have been stagnating, while population has continued to rise, and rural poverty has remained high. At the very least, agricultural investment is essential in the short term, both to give people incomes to procure food and to increase production – indeed, many consume what they produce. Moreover, agriculture can perform much better with the right types of public and private investment and State support.

Many factors limit production, including the absence of further technical breakthroughs in foodcrop varieties, which could match the dramatic increases in wheat and rice yields in the initial green revolution period. Irrigation has also expanded much too slowly. So we have a two-fold problem: on the one hand, we have declining per capita availability of foodgrains, and on the other, we have highly unequal food distribution within the country because of low incomes, resulting in chronic hunger and undernourishment. People in some regions and communities are much more underfed than in others. Government investment in agriculture has also been limited. It is only recently that we have begun investing more in agriculture again, with the wake-up call given by the rise in food prices, some failed monsoons, and a recognition that agriculture is a damper to India's high growth story. In the eleventh five-year plan (2007–12), for instance, a notable percentage of the GDP has been allocated to rural infrastructure, of which a subset will be for agricultural infrastructure.

Solow Actually, I think the ratio of GDP is not the relevant number. I think that is a measure of the size of the effort relative to the national economy. What one would like to know, really, is what is the scarce factor? What is it that limits cereal production in India, and how much of an effort has been made, if one can be made, to lift that limit?

Agarwal I believe infrastructure investment as a ratio of GDP does have some relevance, but of course we also need to look at specific constraints and scarcities. Many factors limit cereal production in India: we reached the extensive margins of cultivable area a long time ago, and output increase is now dependent on yield increase. For this we need improvement in all the aspects I have mentioned, such as technological breakthroughs in crop varieties, expansion of irrigation, better rural roads, a shift to more skill-intensive farming techniques, and so on. As I mentioned earlier, agriculture received a lot of attention in India during the 1970s and 1980s, and the availability of HYVs for the major staples made a critical difference. Effort was also made to spread these varieties across the country. But HYVs depend on an assured water supply and intensive fertilizer use; they do not perform well under rain-fed conditions. Yet, even today, as noted, only 42 per cent of India's net cultivated area is under irrigation. We are also seeing the second-generation negative effects of the HYV package of practices, in terms of depletion of soil nutrients, drastic drops in groundwater levels because of the over-drawing of water through private tubewells, the pollution of water sources from chemical inputs, and so on. In the 1970s, hardly anyone was talking about the adverse effects of heavy fertilizer and pesticide use on our soils and waters. Today it is impossible to ignore these effects. We have neither invested enough in agriculture, nor in the right places.

Now we urgently need R&D in crop varieties that can perform well with limited water and withstand water and heat stress. We need more community cooperation for soil and water conservation. We need farmers to use more skilled practices that involve selective and timely use of production inputs. That means we also need higher literacy and more education among farmers. If more farmers are women, then the gender biases in access to information, inputs, credit, and so on, and low literacy among women could all prove to be constraints. Access to new information technology is again a case in point. Television often relays farm-related programmes, but in many villages the sole TV set is located in the village council office, and here the main audience of TV programmes is village men. There are many biases against women and poor farmers, and we need to find ways of overcoming such hurdles. These efforts need to dovetail with measures to reduce crop losses from poor storage facilities, and measures for providing adequate food to the most poor and needy.

Cooper [from the floor] Earlier, Jean-Louis Beffa used the term 'mercantilist' applied to China and to several other countries. He is a person of great practical experience, and I think it would be useful for us to know concretely how Saint-Gobain experiences Chinese mercantilism. The background of the question is that I do not think a rising trade surplus is direct *ipso facto* evidence of mercantilism. What is your experience of Chinese resistance to imports from elsewhere in the world or insistence on export performance from any plants you may have in China?

Beffa I use the word 'mercantilist' as an approximation of what characterizes the State strategies that have made my company reconsider its strategies. In the Chinese case, my annual visits for the last 29 years have helped me understand the policy moves. Economically, and perhaps also from a political long-term view, the Chinese want to produce everything on the planet in order to be the least dependent. The companies under SASAC (State Asset Supervision and Administration Commission), which controls the major state-owned companies of China, are a good example. For Saint-Gobain, which remains the world leader in pipes for water supply, the challenge came through the company Chiching. Chinese authorities have allowed that company (and my company) to completely restructure previously state-owned companies of China into one efficient group. It quickly integrated technology and is now selling products, especially to countries – for example in Africa – where it is part of China's strategic policy to sell water supply systems in exchange for long-term policies of buying raw materials and oil products. Is 'mercantilism' the appropriate term to qualify this? Another example: the Chinese have clearly discovered (and everybody knows) that the electric car will be crucial for curtailing pollution in the cities of China. They are big cities; transportation is necessary, and electric cars will be the solution. China controls a huge part of lithium, crucial for batteries. They have, in fact, just acted so that it is no longer possible to export lithium easily from China.

Cooper That is a very concrete example of the kind I was looking for. But I would like more such examples!

Beffa The will to be present in the aerospace or atomic industries are two other examples: I learnt from a recent visit that the Chinese government had just given SASAC 100 billion dollars, spread over an adequate period of time, to build a company that will be *the* competitor of Airbus and Boeing. The Chinese government has also given about the same amount of money to build a fully national nuclear plant with only Chinese technology.

Cooper Could it happen in France?

Beffa France used to be a mercantilist country between 1969 and 1974. I personally advocate France to go back to that policy. It is going to do very badly unless it emulates more strongly German policies, which in my view have also been clearly mercantilist.

Baily I do not want to get into a debate with Dick [Cooper] on this, because I know exactly his view, but maintaining an undervalued exchange rate is generally considered to be mercantilist.

Beffa I would like to make a comment about the exchange rate. I heard it very clearly stated by the general manager of the China Investment Corporation, 'We want to keep the renminbi pegged to the dollar, because we don't want to lose the value of that big amount of money we have sent to the United States. Let us buy some things that you don't want to sell to us because they are barred for military reasons'. This was quite aggressive. It is interesting to see how outspoken Chinese leaders are on that now; it is very different from the position they adopted in 2007. What can the United States practically do to make the Chinese change their minds? I read the document recently published by the Peterson Institute saying that it is in the interest of China to revalue the renminbi. None of the arguments in that document convinced me, and I certainly would not be convinced if I were Chinese.

Baily I did not propose that US policymakers should necessarily try to *do* anything to force the Chinese to change their exchange rate policy. Eventually the Chinese authorities will have to let the renminbi rise, but I do not want to get into that debate, so I am going to back off.

From the floor My question concerns demography. It has been underlined in each of your presentations, in different ways, but it would be interesting to have your viewpoints on the evolution of the demography. In asking this question, I have in mind the European framework, where today Germany has 1.4 active persons for 1 inactive, and in 40 years from now there will be 1 active person for 1 inactive. This is going to have dramatic impacts on labour costs, on innovation and therefore on the division of labour. So I have in mind the European framework, but it would be interesting to have the viewpoint of people from outside Europe.

Baily I wrote a book a few years ago, called *Transforming the European Economy*, and it did address exactly that concern about Europe – that demographic trends, combined with the social safety net and retirement pensions in place, were going to create specific long-term problems. There are a lot of economists in Germany and in the EU who address that issue. The only answer is to take steps towards improving labour force participation in Europe. I am not in favour of dismantling the European safety net, but there are ways to structure it so that it does not discourage labour force participation as much as it does now. You can provide more wage insurance, for example, and less unemployment insurance. Looking at Denmark, which has the 'flexicurity' system, they have a very high rate of employment and a very low rate of unemployment, much more so than Germany and France. So I think that even within Europe, there are examples of restructuring the social safety system so that it becomes more conducive to higher labour force participation. That does not eliminate the demographic problem, but it alleviates it quite a bit.

Beffa The demographic issue also concerns the role working mothers play, particularly in two of the most mercantilist countries. Japan and Germany have a birth-rate problem. The Japanese reaction in September 2009 was strong. How successful will the monthly stipend measures taken by the Japanese government be? Bills to help mothers to continue working could also be considered in Germany. On this issue, it can emulate French policy, and Japan as well. In China, I wonder whether the one-child policy will be somewhat abandoned, as they are starting to do in Shanghai. I think they have some flexibility there that they will use to their advantage. That, of course, does not change the attitude of the one-child generation and whether this generation, which is very different from the traditional family in China, will want to have as many children as the generations before them. But there is greater flexibility in China, because it was a government decision to influence significantly the birth rate. Now that the genie is out of the bottle, it is difficult to say what will happen! But it will be interesting to watch. In France, the birth rate is healthy enough, but the question of employment is persistent; it is above all a question of growth rate. We then return to the problem of the State to choose or to undergo policy such as developing industry. Another point is the need to change the retirement age in France.

Solow In addition to thinking about policies that might increase the participation rate, it is possible to be more serious about increasing productivity in Europe. It seems pretty clear to me that the progressive European economies have not fully exploited the possibility of improving productivity. It is too big a topic to begin to start now, but that would also help a lot.

From the floor My question concerns the distinction Jean-Louis Beffa made between finance-led and mercantilist policies. A *Fonds Stratégique d'Investissement*[4] was recently created in France, is that a positive development, moving towards more of a mercantilist policy?

Beffa Its effects are very marginal compared to the needs that should be implemented if one really wants to reverse the trend. To go against the drift, I also believe from my experience on the board of Siemens, that the presence of unions on the board of directors is very important. In France, we are underestimating the impact such a measure would have. Such union participation has a positive impact, at least for a mercantilist system, whether one likes it or not. But it does mean making the unions completely ready to make sacrifices and really be part of a mercantilist policy. In Germany, the agreement to make that kind of policy is not government-driven; it is driven by the unions and the management of the big and medium-sized companies – it is a national pact. The interactions that have brought about the changes in the structure of the size and power of different businesses in a country happen over the very long term, and you do not alter it simply by changing the exchange rate.

Baily I agree with that. The German auto industry makes a strong contrast to the US industry.

Solow The desirability of a policy depends both on its effectiveness and on the possibility of doing it in the first place. One of the advantages of dealing with the exchange rate is that you do not deal with it directly, as Martin pointed out, not today; so you could try operating on savings rates and things of that sort.

From the floor We have a productivity rate that has oscillated between 3 and 6 per cent in the most auspicious periods of recent history, and yet the required rate of return on capital imposed by the finance-led regime is somewhere around 15 per cent. How can the two be reconciled? I have experienced this in consulting missions carried out for groups like Pechiney, in which executives are obliged, by the top management, to ensure that these rates of return are respected, failing which they are simply replaced – which gives you some idea of the level of stress in these large groups. So that is a question rather for Mr Beffa.

Beffa The 15 per cent rate of return is impossible, except in very particular sectors. The top management may want that level of profitability, but they cannot obtain it. They can start firing everybody in the company, but that makes no sense.

From the floor I would like to thank Martin Baily for his very lucid analysis of the current situation in the United States, and I must apologize for being disagreeable, but I would like to return to the question of the exchange rate. What might happen if the Chinese and the Russians started demanding that oil and gas be bought and sold in euros? In parallel, everybody knows that the Chinese currently hold the biggest share of reserves of US Treasury bonds, and that with the current interest rate of the dollar, they are making huge losses. So what would happen if the Chinese simply decided to exchange these Treasury bonds for euros?

Baily On the exchange rate issue, I will respond watching Dick [Cooper] over my shoulder here. Oil is already priced in dollars and euros; the dollar is simply the unit of account, so setting the price in dollars is not so significant. The question is then what happens if the euro becomes more of a reserve currency and the US dollar less of a reserve currency? There would have to be a change in exchange rate, primarily I think the dollar–euro exchange rate. I am not sure that is something Europeans would like to see at the present time. The euro is currently at around 1.46, so a rise in the euro would not put European industry in a strong competitive position. In terms of the Chinese and the Russians dumping their dollars, well, we are in a sort of co-dependent relationship. The Chinese want to maintain the value of the dollar against the renminbi, partly because they have a lot of dollars and they do not want to devalue them, and partly because they want to keep exporting, not just to the US but everywhere. In other words, if the Chinese dumped all their dollars, the renminbi would rise and that would affect their own competitiveness. The US needs them to keep buying dollars at least for a while longer, and they need to keep holding them in order to protect the competitiveness of their industries, so it is a co-dependency. And co-dependencies are not very healthy relationships. Eventually it would be good to get away from that relationship, but I do not think it is going to end any time soon.

From the floor I have a question for Mr Baily. Everything that we know at present about the long-term prospects of the world economy shows that the United States has a huge responsibility in maintaining a number of important equilibriums, particularly with regard to what I could call, to simplify, reducing its spending or increasing its savings. I would like to hear your point of view on the capacity of the United States to assume such responsibilities from a long-term perspective.

Baily Professor Solow should answer this question also! It is very difficult in the United States to raise taxes, and we have a lot of things that we need to spend money on, so it is very hard to deal with the deficit, which has become very large as a result of this crisis, and may continue to be large because of the costs of an ageing population. That is a significant challenge, and I am unsure about our ability to face up to it. But at the same time, I think that it is possible to do. We are not that heavily taxed a nation, so if we institute a carbon tax or a gasoline tax or even a value-added tax, I think it would be possible to deal with the deficit. I will let Bob respond to the other parts of that question.

Solow I think that is the right answer, although it is not a very satisfactory one. As Martin knows, he and I have for *years* been in favour of trying to reduce the budget deficit of the United States, not just the leap that it took during the current crisis. That is very hard to do. It looks a little scarier now than it really is, because once the US and the world economy begin to recover, there will be some automatic improvement in the fiscal situation. Once again, there is a co-dependency here. For the past decade or so, the US consumer has been the 'buyer of last resort' for the whole world economy. That is coming to an end, or has already come to an end, and we can no longer go along under General De Gaulle's principle that France should have a budget surplus and everybody else in the world should have balanced trade. There will have to be a bigger dependence on domestic expenditure in Germany, in Europe generally, and in China. I think Martin was right about the Chinese: we are in a boat that is rocking, which is not exactly what the Chinese government wants at this moment. I think slowly, slowly, and with much 'double-talk', it will be possible for the US to move in the right direction. Whether we will get there in finite time, I am not so certain.

NOTES

1. Baily, M.N. and R.Z. Lawrence (2004), 'What happened to the great U.S. job machine? The role of trade and electronics offshoring', *Brookings Papers on Economic Activity*, **2**.
2. Blinder, Alan (2006), 'Off-shoring, the next industrial revolution', *Foreign Affairs*, March/April.
3. Figures taken from Hewlett, S.A., C. Buck Luce, L.J. Servon, L. Sherbin, P. Shiller, E. Sosnovich and K. Sumberg (2008), 'The Athena factor: reversing the brain drain in science, engineering, and technology', *Harvard Business Review Research Report*, No. 10094, June.
4. Strategic Investment Fund.

Index

absorptive capacity 11
additionality effects 82
African countries 7, 8, 9, 33, 108, 125–6, 179
ageing population (USA) 189
agglomeration effects 154
agriculture
  China 101, 104, 111, 114, 116, 119
  collective approach 176–8, 181, 183
  food security 166–83
  gender and 123, 125, 127, 130, 134
  India 5, 101, 103–4, 108, 111, 114–15, 116, 117, 119, 176–7
aid policies 108, 179
anti-dumping duties 108, 115, 117
Asia 1, 6, 7–8, 17, 23–5, 158, 167, 179
  see also individual countries
'Asian Tigers' 6
assortative mating 136, 137
autarky 70

balance of payments 160
balanced growth path 150–51
banking sector 150, 159
bilateral FDI 38–50
bilateral instruments 39–44, 50, 51
bilateral investment treaties (BITs) 39–43, 44, 50, 51
biofuels 168, 169, 179
birth rate 102–3, 107, 134, 186
Brazil 35, 118, 160, 163–5, 167, 179
budget deficit (USA) 155, 165, 188–9

capital 14, 21, 160
  account liberalization 32, 40–41, 45
  accumulation 8, 131, 135
  FDI and 3, 32, 34, 40, 50
  labour and 111–13, 116–17
  stock 79, 81–3, 88–91, 93–5, 100–101
  see also human capital; physical capital; social capital
cereals 166–9, 172–4, 178–80, 182–3
children
  care of 125, 127–31, 134–5, 142–3
  family structure and 123, 141
  working 135
  see also birth rate; infant mortality
China 6, 8, 151, 189
  agriculture 101, 104, 111, 114, 116, 119
  birth rate 102, 103, 107
  emigration 112–14
  exchange rate 164, 185, 188
  future 117–19
  imports 108, 116, 117
  integration of labour 5, 101–19
  mercantilism 160, 162, 163, 183–5
  openness 107–10
civic engagement 15, 22
climate change 166, 172–5, 176, 180–81
closed economy 69–71
co-dependency 188, 189
collective approach 176–8, 181, 183
communication 85, 94, 95, 109
  see also information and communication technology (ICT); telecommunications
companies
  labour market frictions 4, 56–71
  strategy, State and 5, 155–66
  see also multinational enterprises
comparative advantage 1–2, 87, 88
  China/India 111, 118
  gender and 122, 127–31, 133
  ICT 87, 88
  labour market frictions 4, 56–71
competition 11, 57, 59, 118, 132
  FDI 33, 40, 50
  gender attitudes 123, 139–40
competitive advantage 1–2, 78
competitiveness 156, 158, 159
  in ICT 4, 75–8, 79–82, 87, 94–6

consumption 4, 134, 136–7, 150
convergence 3–4, 6, 7–8, 117, 122
corruption 15, 16, 22, 77
cost advantages 47
cost curves 1
cost reduction 61, 158
costs
of exporting 58, 59–60, 61
labour 45–6, 77, 81–2, 91, 93, 100, 156–7, 185
transport 80, 158, 159
credit 14, 178
currency convertibility 108
current account deficit/surplus 151–2

decentralized decision-making 78
deindustrialization 1, 160
demand 61, 169, 174
China/India 116, 117
gender and 131–3, 134–5, 138
ICT 75–6, 79–81, 87, 90, 94, 96
USA 150, 151, 153, 155
demographic dividend 3, 103
demographic transition 3–4, 134–8, 185
Denmark 82, 88–9, 186
development
economic 15–18, 21–2, 27, 32, 123, 125, 127, 141–2
financial 3, 14, 57
industrial 108, 135
infrastructure 118, 153, 172, 175–6, 179–80, 183
institutional 41, 51
knowledge and 9–13
technological 2, 3, 8, 16, 76–7
discrimination 21
gender 39, 45, 47–9, 51, 123–7, 141
divergence (GDP per capita) 7–8
division of labour
adaptation to change 5, 149–89
between countries 2–3, 6–27
company view (frictions) 4, 56–71
concept (trends) 1–2
FDI as indicator 3, 32–52
integration into international (China and India) 5, 101–19
role of ICTs 4, 75–96, 100
sexual 3–4, 122–43
divorce 137, 138, 140, 142
domestic work/labour 3–4, 122–5, 127–32, 134, 135–6, 141
domestically oriented policy 160, 163–4
double taxation treaties 39, 41–4, 50–51

Eastern Europe 35, 101, 118, 156, 158, 177
economic development *see* development
economic growth *see* growth
economies of scale 57, 135, 177
education 22, 155
capabilities 10, 12, 14–16
China/India 107, 113–14, 116, 118–19
gender and 39, 44–9, 51, 132, 134–5, 138–9
emigration 111, 112–14, 118–19
employment 186
in agriculture 169–71
characteristics 5, 102–7
evolution of (China/India) 5, 101–19
full (USA) 150, 152
USA 45, 150, 151, 152–3, 154–5
women *see* women (in labour market)
see also labour; work
endowment
differences (FDI) 36–8, 50
factor 1, 36, 56, 111
skill 36, 139
energy prices 110–11, 117, 157, 188
energy rentier policy 160, 162–3
engagement 15, 22, 110–11, 117
England 134, 141, 156, 160
entry costs 59
equality, gender 124–7
Europe 109, 117, 127, 149–51, 154–5, 157, 179
Eastern 35, 101, 118, 156, 158, 177
GDP per capita 7, 17
openness 22–5
European Union 7, 84, 115, 188–9
demographic trends 185–6
employment and productivity 154–5
food sector 167, 169–71
labour market 60, 67, 185, 186
sexual division of labour 124–5, 134
exchange 2, 135, 136

exchange rate 4, 5, 81–2, 90, 187
  China 164, 185, 188
  corporate strategy and 159–60
  USA 153, 164–5, 185, 188
export market shares 79–81, 90, 95–6
exports
  China 108–9, 110, 118, 119
  food 56, 167–9, 170, 182
  India 108–9, 118, 119
  knowledge-intensive 4, 75–96, 100
  labour market frictions 56–61, 67, 69–70
  manufactures 58–9
  productivity and 59–61, 69–70
  USA 153

factor analysis 16, 22
factor endowment 1, 36, 56, 111
factories/factory system 114, 116, 158
factors of production 61, 110, 112, 132, 157–8
family 64, 107
  in agriculture 123, 177–8
  production 123, 127
  sexual division of labour 123, 127–8, 129, 134, 135–6, 138, 139, 140–41
  structure 123, 141
fertility 122, 125, 134–5, 137–8, 142
fertilizers 107, 114, 176, 183
finance capability 14
finance-led policy 160–61, 162, 187
financial development 3, 14, 57
financial institutions 57, 150, 159
financial markets 32, 110–11
'flexicurity' system (Denmark) 186
food aid 179
food prices 166, 168–9, 179, 182
food security 166–83
foraging societies 129–31
foreign aid 108, 179
foreign direct investment 8–9, 15, 18, 70
  bilateral 38–50
  China 101–2, 107–10
  global nature of 3, 32–52
  in ICT 77, 96
  India 101–2, 107–10, 118–19
  openness to 18–19, 20, 21, 26
foreign investors 40, 41, 47, 49, 50, 51
foreign trade balance 156, 159–65
France 58–9, 67, 160–61, 189
  mercantilism 184–5, 186, 187
free market economy 156–8, 160–61, 162
free trade 8
free-entry equilibrium 59–60
frontier effects 2, 4
full employment (USA) 150, 152

gas prices 157, 188
gender
  competition and 123, 139–40
  discrimination 39, 45, 47–9, 51, 123–7, 141
  task segregation 127–31
  wages and 3, 123, 127, 131–3, 135
  see also men (in labour market); women; women (in labour market)
General Agreement on Trade in Services 95
general equilibrium models 36, 65
general purpose technologies (GPTs) 78, 81, 94, 95
Germany 118, 153, 158, 177, 185, 189
  ICTs 82, 87–9
  mercantilism 160, 162, 185, 186, 187
  sexual division of labour 133–4, 138
globalization 152, 159
  FDI and 3, 32–52
goods 80, 160
  public 8, 9, 136–7
  trade in (determinants) 76, 77–8
governance 14, 15–16, 18–19, 21–2, 51
government spending 153, 155, 184
gravity-type models 37–9, 44–5, 47, 77
growth
  balanced (USA) 150–51
  China/India 101
  GDP 6–8, 18, 19, 79
  ICT and 4, 75, 76
  knowledge and 8, 9–13
  power and property rights 140–43
  sexual division of labour and 3–4, 122–43
growth rates 4, 182, 186
Gulf States 113, 162

home market effect 76, 80–81
honesty 14, 15

host country 36–7, 39–41, 43, 45–8
  poverty 32, 51–2
hostile takeover bids 160
house prices (USA) 150
household
  income 4, 123
  multi-agent 140–41
  public goods 136–7
  work 3–4, 122–5, 127–32, 134–6, 141
human capital 32
  gender and 3–4, 122–3, 128–9, 134–5, 138–40, 142
hunter-gatherer societies 129–31

imperfect competition 57
imports 4, 77, 79
  anti-dumping duties 108, 115, 117
  China 108, 116, 117
  food 56, 166, 167–9
  India 108
  tariffs 60, 101, 108, 152
  USA 154
income
  distribution (USA) 152
  household 4, 123
  women's 125–7, 135, 141–3
  see also wages
India 6
  agriculture 5, 101, 103–4, 108, 111, 114–17, 119, 176–8
  birth rate 102, 103, 107
  domestically oriented policy 160, 163–5
  emigration 112–14
  future 117–19
  imports 108
  integration of labour 5, 101–19
  openness 107–10
industrial development 108, 135, 163–4
industrial relations 119, 159, 187
industrial sector, State and 5, 156
industrialization 5, 123, 125, 160–61, 164
inequality 26
  gender 49, 143
  labour market friction and 4, 56, 58, 60, 67–71
  wage 60, 67, 69–70, 132
infant mortality 134, 142
inflation 39, 41–2, 114
information and communications technology (ICT) 10
  India 5
  information technology 118, 119, 132, 133, 183
  infrastructure 14, 16, 22
  role (export of knowledge-intensive services) 4, 75–6, 78–9, 81–96, 100
infrastructure 77, 158
  development 118, 153, 172, 175–6, 179–80, 183
  ICT 14, 16, 22
  investment 14, 153–4, 164
  rural 175–6, 179, 182–3
input–output analysis 80, 81, 84–7
inputs, intermediate 57, 75, 96
institutional development 41, 51
integration
  of labour (China/India) 5, 101–19
  market 114–17
intellectual property rights 15, 22, 51
interdependence, trade and 63–7
intermediate goods 80
intermediate inputs 57, 75, 96
internal migration 106–7, 111, 118
international division of labour
  changing 2–3, 6–27
  integration of China/India 5, 101–19
International Monetary Fund 8, 108
intersectoral linkages (role of ICTs) 4, 75–6, 78–96, 100
investment 3, 79
  agricultural 176, 177, 180, 181–3
  bilateral treaties 39–43, 44, 50, 51
  capability 11, 14
  infrastructure 14, 153–4, 164
  -savings balance (USA) 153–4
  see also foreign direct investment
investors 3, 160
  foreign 40–41, 47, 49, 50, 51
irrigation 175, 176, 177, 181–3
ISO standards 13–14, 16, 22
'iso-work' phenomenon 124, 125

Japan 2, 6, 8, 58, 117, 135, 151, 158
  ICTs 82, 87–9
  mercantilism 160, 163, 186
job growth (USA) 150, 151, 154, 155
job losses 5, 154, 155
joint ventures 116

know-how 32, 50
knowledge 8, 20–21, 26
  creation 9, 15
  development and 9–13
  gaps (in FDI) 32–52
knowledge-intensive services and manufactures (export) 4, 75–96, 100
Korea 8, 11, 35, 110, 118
  ICTs 82, 87–9

labour
  costs 45, 46, 77, 81–2, 91, 93, 100, 156–7, 185
  domestic 3, 122–5, 127–32, 134–6, 141
  industrial relations 159, 187
  mental/physical 132
  productivity 78–80, 82, 116–17
  rights 39, 44–9, 50–51
  skilled 112
  supply 101, 124–5, 128, 131, 132
  unskilled 5, 101, 111, 114, 116–18
  see also wages; workforce
labour market 3, 45, 157
  China/India 5, 102–7, 110–12, 114–17
  EU 60, 67, 125, 134–5, 185, 186
  frictions (impact) 4, 56–71
  search and matching 58, 61–3, 65, 67–9
  USA 122, 150, 151–2, 154, 155
  see also men (in labour market); women (in labour market)
land 107, 111, 114–15, 141, 164, 178
legal institutions 57
licensing 15
Lisbon Agenda 67
living standards (USA) 165
local businesses 158, 159–60, 164
localization 158, 159

manufactures 56, 58–9
  knowledge-intensive 4, 75–96, 100
manufacturing
  China 104–5, 110, 116–17, 118–19
  India 104, 105, 118, 119
  knowledge-intensive 87–92, 94–6
  USA 119, 152–3
marginalist equilibrium analysis 1
marital status 135, 136–7, 140–41
  see also divorce; marriage
marital surplus 136–7
market 1, 3, 8, 10, 11, 13–14, 37
  emerging 32, 34, 118, 157–8
  financial 32, 110–11
  free (economy) 156–8, 160–61, 162
  host country *see* host country
  integration 114–17
  protectionism 108, 117–18, 156
  work, gender and 13, 122–5, 127–9, 131–3, 135–7
  see also labour market
marriage 122, 123, 127–9, 140–41
  demographic transitions 134, 135–8
  see also divorce; family; fertility
materials 86, 159
  raw 117, 162, 184
matriarchal society 140
men (in labour market)
  equality 124–7
  gender task segregation 127–31
  human capital 138–40
  power and property rights 140–43
  wages (relative) 131–3
mercantilism 165
  China 160, 162, 163, 183–5
  France 184–5, 186, 187
  Germany 160, 162, 185, 186, 187
  Japan 160, 163, 186
Middle East 127, 160, 175
migration 15
  China/India 111, 112–14
  internal 106–7, 111
military modernization (China) 118
monopolistic competition 57, 59
Monterrey Consensus 32, 35, 51
mortality rates 134, 142
multinational enterprises (MNEs) 3, 32, 36, 37, 44, 46–7, 50–51
multiregional company/strategy 159–60

natural resources 19, 20, 50, 111
  see also raw materials
networks 4, 12
'new growth theories' 15, 20
new trade theory models 78
'non-economic' aspects (development) 13

non-exporters 58–9, 60, 67, 70
nuclear family 129

OECD 39, 43, 77, 80, 82–3, 107, 113, 138, 160
offshoring 57, 80, 154
oil prices 110–11, 117, 188
one-child policy (China) 186
OPEC 16
open economy 69–71
openness 14
  to business 21, 22, 24
  of China/India 107–10
  to FDI 18–19, 20, 21, 26
  to ideas 21, 22, 23
  to people 21, 22, 25, 26, 27
  to trade 9, 18–19, 20–21, 26, 39
output 63, 105, 119, 153
  food 172, 182–3
  –input analysis (ICT) 80, 81, 84–7
  productivity 59–61, 68, 155
  sexual division of labour and 127, 130
outsourcing 57, 109, 118, 119, 134

patents 13, 14, 16, 22, 79
patriarchal society 140, 142
pensions 185–6
'perfect knowledge' 10
personality traits, marriage and 136–7
physical capital/labour 132
political systems 14, 15, 18–19, 20
pollution 183, 184
population
  ageing (USA) 189
  employment and (China/India) 101, 102–7, 112–13, 119
  gender roles and 134, 140
post-industrial societies 123
poverty 2
  in host countries 32, 52
  India 105, 182
power 5, 140–43
pre-industrial societies 129
pregnancy 134
price elasticity of demand 90
price elasticity of supply 84
prices
  China/India 110–11, 117
  energy 157, 158
  food 166, 168–9, 179, 182
  house (USA) 150
  ICT and 4, 81, 82, 95
production
  capability 11, 13–14
  factors of 61, 110, 112, 132, 157–8
  function 59–60, 68
  technology 129–30, 131, 133
productive units 1
productivity 8, 186, 187
  employment and 5, 154–5
  exports and 59–61, 69–70
  gap (men/women) 128
  ICT and 4, 76, 79, 80, 82, 95
  labour 56, 78–80, 82, 116–17
  specialization and 1, 2, 20
  total factor 59, 65–6, 78, 116–17
profit/profitability 59–61, 69, 158–9
property rights 14, 16, 123, 140–43
  intellectual 15, 22, 51
protectionism 108, 117, 118, 156
public goods 8, 9, 136–7

rate of return 187–8
raw materials 117, 162, 184
  see also natural resources
real wage 64, 114, 117
regional trade agreements 41, 42
relative wages 3, 131–3
reproductive role (of women) 128–31
research and development 14
  agriculture 175, 176, 179–80, 183
  capabilities 13, 14
  expenditure 13, 22, 89
  ICTs 78, 81, 82, 88–91, 100
resources 37, 58, 129, 130
  access to 10–11, 12
  allocation 4, 140–41
  natural 20, 50, 111
  property rights 140–43
retirement pensions 185–6
returns to scale 63
risk
  aversion 139, 140
  management (USA) 150
  -neutral workers 63, 64, 67, 69
  strategies 158–9
Russia 118, 160, 162–4, 167, 188

Saint-Gobain 149, 156, 159, 183–4
savings 153–4, 188
science base (of State) 158
science-relevance matrix 76
scientific invention/knowledge 13, 79
scientific publications 14, 22
search and matching frictions (labour market) 61–3
sector-specific skills 128, 129
self-help groups 178
services 154, 156, 159
  knowledge-intensive 4, 75–96, 100
  trade in (determinants) 76, 77–8
sexual division of labour 3–4, 122–43
shareholders 160, 161
  expectations 156, 158
Singapore 8, 35, 38, 110
skills 36, 139, 141
  capabilities 12, 14–15
  sector-specific 128, 129
  skilled labour 112, 155
  unskilled labour 5, 101, 111, 114, 116–18
  wages and 47, 132–3
social capability 12, 13–14, 16, 21, 27
social capital 12–13
social norms 129, 135
social safety system (Europe) 185–6
socialization 123, 139, 140
special economic zones (India) 118
specialization 3, 5, 111–12, 160, 164
  gender and 122, 127–30, 135–6, 137, 141
  ICT sector 4, 75, 79, 81, 89–90, 96
  productivity and 1, 2, 20
State (role/behaviour) 5, 155–66
state-owned enterprises 105–6, 115
structural change 3
structural functionalism 129
subsistence communities 129–31
sunk costs 40, 58
supply 13, 84, 134
  curves 1
  labour 101, 124–5, 128, 131, 132

Taiwan 8, 38, 58, 110, 115, 118
tariffs 60, 101, 108, 152
tasks 1
  segregation (gender) 127–31, 133, 135, 136
taxation 3, 48, 189
  double (treaties) 39, 41–4, 50, 51
  evasion 43
technological capability 11–12, 13–14, 16, 21, 26–7, 56, 153
technological change, employment and 5, 149–89
technological dynamism 78
technology 11, 153
  access to 3, 32, 50
  agriculture and 180, 182, 183, 184
  diffusion 4, 8, 75, 76, 112
  -gap approach 76, 78
  gender and 3, 121, 131–3, 134–5
  general purpose 78, 81, 94, 95
  transfer 15, 50, 111
  see also information and communications technology (ICT)
telecommunications 21, 77, 81, 83, 85
terms of trade 111, 117, 153
threat point (marital bargaining) 140–41
tolerance 14, 15
total factor productivity 59, 65–6, 78, 116–17
town-and-village enterprises 115–16
trade 1–2, 5, 15
  balance, foreign 156, 159–61, 162–5
  barriers 4, 77, 108
  China/India (policies) 107–11, 119
  comparative advantage 4, 56–71
  deficit 152–3, 160, 164
  effect on inequality 4, 56–71
  free market economy 156–8
  in goods (determinants) 76, 77–8
  interdependence and 63–7
  liberalization 60–61, 119
  openness to 9, 18–19, 20–21, 26, 9
  in services (determinants) 76, 77–8
  surplus 152–3, 161, 164, 184
  terms of 111, 117, 153
trade unions 119, 159, 187
trademarks 22
transition economies, agriculture in 176–8
transport costs 80, 158, 159
Treaty of Amsterdam 67
trust 13, 14, 15, 22

uncertainty 40, 41, 59
UNCTAD 33, 35, 40, 43, 44
underemployment (India) 104
unemployment
  China/India 104, 116
  Europe 154–5
  insurance 116, 186
  labour market frictions and 4, 58, 61–3, 65, 66–7, 69–71
  USA 154–5
unilateral policies (FDI) 39, 44–9, 50–51
United Kingdom 82, 87, 160, 162
United Nations 32, 48, 108, 110, 166
unskilled work/labour 5, 101, 111, 114, 116, 117, 118
urbanization
  China 101, 105, 106
  India 105, 106, 114–15
USA 7, 8
  budget deficit 155, 165, 188–9
  economy/policies 149–55, 188
  exchange rate 153, 164, 165, 185, 188
  foreign trade policy 160–61, 164–6
  labour market 122, 150–52, 154, 155
  manufacturing sector 119, 152–3
  sexual division of labour 122, 127–8

value chain 152
voting rights 142

wages 57, 159, 186
  China 5, 101, 106, 112, 114–17
  FDI and 45, 46, 47, 48
  gender and 3, 123, 127–8, 131–3, 135, 138
  hourly (comparison) 156–7
  ICT sector 81, 82
  India 5, 101, 104, 112, 114–16
  inequality 60, 67, 69–70, 132
  integration and 5, 101, 114
  labour market frictions 4, 60, 63–5, 67–71
  real 64, 114, 117
  relative 3, 131–3
  USA 151–2
Washington Consensus 3, 8, 9, 26
wealth 6, 123, 130, 137, 150–51
welfare 66–7, 143
women
  income 125–7, 135, 141–3
  power/property rights 140–43
women (in labour market)
  agriculture 170, 171–2, 177, 178, 183
  China 103, 106
  equality 124–7
  gender task segregation 127–31
  human capital 138–40
  India 103, 106–7
  USA 151
  wages 3, 123, 127–8, 131–3, 135, 138
  work 122, 123, 124–31, 134–8, 186
  working mothers 186
work
  domestic 123, 124–5, 127, 132, 135–6
  men's 122, 123, 124–31
  women's 122, 123, 124–31, 134–8, 186
  see also employment; labour
workforce 47, 69
  female 122–3, 124–31, 134–8, 143, 186
  see also labour; labour market; skills; wages
World Bank 8, 44, 109, 113, 141
world businesses 158–60, 164
World Trade Organization 58–9, 77, 95, 108, 117, 160, 161–4
'World Value Survey' 15